THE PATHLESS LAND

TIM HANNIGAN is originally from the far west of Cornwall. After leaving school he worked as a chef for several years. He escaped the catering industry via a degree in journalism and a move to Indonesia, where he taught English and worked as a journalist and guidebook writer. He is the author of several narrative history books, including *A Brief History of Indonesia* and the award-winning *Raffles and the British Invasion of Java*, as well as the critically acclaimed *The Travel Writing Tribe*, and, most recently, *The Granite Kingdom*. He's also an academic, with a research specialism in contemporary travel literature. He lives with his family in the west of Ireland and he teaches writing and literature at the Atlantic Technological University in Sligo.

ALSO BY TIM HANNIGAN

The Granite Kingdom

The Travel Writing Tribe

A Brief History of Indonesia

Raffles and the British Invasion of Java

Murder in the Hindu Kush

THE PATHLESS LAND

Finding a Way Across Ireland

Tim Hannigan

HEAD of ZEUS

An Apollo Book

First published in the UK in 2026 by Head of Zeus Ltd,
part of Bloomsbury Publishing Plc

9 7 5 3 1 2 4 6 8

A catalogue record for this book is available from the British Library.

ISBN (HB): 9781035908455; ISBN (XTPB): 9781035908448
ISBN (ePub): 9781035908462

Cover Illustration by Matt Johnson
Cover Design by Gemma Gorton
Maps by Jamie Whyte
Printed and bound in Great Britain
by Clays Ltd, Elcograf S.p.A.

MIX
Paper | Supporting responsible forestry
FSC® C018072
www.fsc.org

Bloomsbury Publishing Plc
50 Bedford Square, London, WC1B 3DP, UK
Bloomsbury Publishing Ireland Limited,
29 Earlsfort Terrace, Dublin 2, D02 AY28, Ireland

HEAD OF ZEUS LTD
5–8 Hardwick Street
London, EC1R 4RG

To find out more about our authors and books
visit www.headofzeus.com
For product safety related questions contact productsafety@bloomsbury.com

PART III

From the Plough to the Stars

9. Partitions: Knockbridge to Newcastle 269
10. The Bull and the Field 295
11. A Sense of an Ending: Newcastle to Burr Point 307

Notes 322
Picture Credits 339
Acknowledgements 340
Index 342

List of Maps

Ireland viii–ix
Dunmore Head to Portumna 19
Portumna to Dundalk 113
Dundalk to Burr Point 267

DONEGA
SLIGO
LEI
MAYO
ROSCOMMON
REPUBLIC
GALWAY
CLARE
TIPP
LIMERICK
KERRY
CORK
ATLANTIC OCEAN
DUNMORE HEAD

BELFAST
BURR POINT
TYRONE
FERMANAGH
MONAGHAN
ARMAGH
DOWN
CAVAN
LOUTH
WESTMEATH
MEATH
DUBLIN
DUBLIN
KILDARE
OFFALY
LAOIS
IRELAND
WICKLOW
CARLOW
KILKENNY
WEXFORD
WATERFORD
Irish Sea
N

Introduction: No Entry

We saw them coming from a long way off: a white pickup truck jolting along the rising track from the road.

The Burren, on a day of running cloud-shadow. Cara and I had left the car at the roadside a few kilometres to the south, walked up a narrow valley between whalebacks of grey stone, then ranged across the high ground until we hit the head of the track. It would bring us back off the hill. We'd stopped halfway down to drink the dregs of our tea, eat the remnants of our packed lunch. And that's when we saw the pickup, passing through the gateway where the track met the road and beginning its slow ascent. And we could be sure that whoever was in the cab had seen us too.

'What do you want to do?' Cara asked.

I looked back up the track the way we'd come, left and right across the silvery hillsides. 'Not much we can do, is there?'

So we packed up the flask and hastily gathered the orange peel and walked on with the pickup truck coming up the track towards us. Ahead lay the Burren's easternmost ridges, with the low country beyond running flat as water towards Gort. But the day had already been punctured. The air was leaking out of it as the pickup truck approached.

We stepped in off the track as the truck rattled to a halt. The window came down. Two men, wedged into the cab: the passenger an older man, his face the colour of washed limestone; the driver middle-aged, dark curls, weather-blushed cheeks.

'Are ye hillwalkers?' the driver said, friendly enough.

As always in these moments, I edged back, kept my mouth shut, left Cara to do the talking. 'We were just headed down to the road,' she said, with a tone of merry innocence, sketching the line of our earlier route loosely with her hand.

The response came slow. 'Ah, right…' Then, after a measured pause: 'Just so ye know – this is all private land.'

Cara stuck with the same tone. 'Oh, is it? Oh, sorry now, we didn't know…'

He raised a hand from the steering wheel to dismiss the gravity of the trespass. 'Ah, you're alright; it's just so ye know. We've cattle on the land so we've to keep people off.'

'Sorry now; we'll know again, so…'

But he changed tack and asked, smiling, but with just a little too much quizzical force, 'Where are ye from?' Cara gave a vague location, across the county boundary to the north, and a little dance ensued as he pressed for a detail, a family name, a parish, a townland – only because he wanted to know, wanted to place us – and she resisted.

The older man was eyeing me from across the cab through all this. Suddenly, he raised a grey finger and said, with the same slightly too forceful smile, 'Do I know you? Would you have been a hurler?'

But Cara replied for me. 'You wouldn't know him. He's from Cornwall.' And I grinned stupidly.

We left them with a promise not to come this way again. They rumbled on towards the high ground and we went on down the hill. Where the ground levelled out there were a few cross-bred beef cattle. They ambled off mildly at our approach. We clambered over the gate, into the road. Affixed to the bars was a huge red and white sign, making its single point three times over in different formulations:

PRIVATE PROPERTY

TRESPASSERS WILL BE PROSECUTED

NO HILL WALKERS

'Don't say it,' said Cara.

But I couldn't help myself. Beyond the gate, beyond the red-and-white sign, there were thousands of rough acres with a few bow-backed blackthorns gathered in clumps.

'In other countries, there'd be open access to all of this,' I said, pointing to the long sweep of the hillside, the arc of country we had crossed earlier in the day, the other ridges across the road. 'All of it.'

* * *

I am from a tiny hamlet of granite cottages and barns, facing the Atlantic Ocean in the far west of Cornwall. Cara, my partner, is from an old walled town with a ruined Dominican priory, just off the M6 motorway in Co. Galway in the Republic of Ireland. The first time she brought me there we arrived in the dusk. As she drove us through the matrix of roundabouts and bypasses spanning the gap between the motorway and the town I saw a strange thing: people – mostly older women as far as I could make out, and mostly in pairs, all wearing baggy hi-vis vests and all striding ferociously along the verges.

'What are those people doing?' I asked, as we swung through another roundabout.

'They're walking,' said Cara over the steering wheel.

But that didn't explain anything. I couldn't remember ever seeing people walking along the side of the Penzance bypass – and certainly no fluorescent legions doing so for exercise or pleasure. What I should have asked was *why*: why are all those people walking around the ring-road? I found out soon enough: *there was nowhere else to walk.*

In any Welsh or English town of similar size – a small place, where the first fields appear among the housing estates within fifteen minutes' walk of the centre – there would have been public footpaths striking off in all directions, marked by yellow arrows on council-installed fingerposts. Those closest to the town would be well trampled by evening dog walkers and morning joggers. But within a kilometre or two the heavy foot traffic would fall away. Equipped with a 1:25,000 Ordnance Survey map, you could easily plot your own unique journey – a loop or a linear trajectory towards the next town or the one beyond that, with grass and beaten earth beneath your boot heels the greater part of the way.

I'd gleaned a first inkling that these paths might be unusual in an international context in my late twenties when I guided groups of American hikers around Cornwall during the summer months. Taking them along a field path sometimes prompted a puzzled query – 'Is this *public land*?' – and an equally puzzled response from my side: 'No, of course not; there isn't really any public land here.'

'And you're just allowed to *walk* across it?'

But I had, like most people, taken for granted the vast network of countryside rights of way that span Wales and England – until I came to Ireland, where there was nothing remotely comparable.

* * *

After a few years tacking back and forth across the Celtic Sea, Cara and I settled down in Co. Galway. Cara got a permanent job teaching in a country school; I gradually shifted from precarious freelance travel guidebook writing to marginally less precarious short-term academic contracts, and then, eventually, a full-time university post. We had a little girl with curly blonde hair and blue eyes. We gave her an Irish name paired with a Cornish name: Róise Senara. We lived for a while in a house just off the crooked market square in Cara's hometown, and then we moved to another town a little further east. At the end of our street there is a tarmacked loop 'walk' a kilometre long around a patch of rough grassland at the edge of a lake. Across the water fields rise steeply, hedged with heavy trees, and further off there are pine-darkened slopes with wind turbines on the high ridges. But there is no way to reach them across country on foot.

Walking over the land has been an essential part of my life since early childhood. My grandmother had two standard loops from our Cornish homeplace: 'the stepping stones', down across the fields to a boggy stretch of the coast spanned by the eponymous stones, and back around; and 'over Garden Mine', across the heathery hill that rose above our hamlet, crowned with the ruined engine house of a tin mine. I accompanied her on these as soon as I could cope with the three-and-a-half-kilometre distance. My parents took me on longer, interconnecting walks that gradually triangulated the entire surrounding landscape. And a few years later I took to striking off on my own, on the coast path, across the moors or along the field paths. Walking this way wasn't a deliberate pastime; it wasn't something I needed to write down when I listed my hobbies. It seemed to me, growing up, an inevitable and essential aspect of existence within a place. Later, as an adult, whenever I spent an extended period in an unfamiliar part of England – Cheltenham for university in my mid-twenties; a later spell in Milton Keynes for work; a few years in and out of Leicester for further study – one of the first things I did was to buy a local map. On winter weekends or summer evenings I'd begin to trace the nearest of the map's dotted green lines into the surrounding countryside, steadily extending my personal network with each foray, stitching my own temporary centre into the fabric of the land – and assuming, like so many others, that I'd be able to do exactly the same thing if ever I moved to another country. But I couldn't do that in Ireland. I had to learn to make do.

There were, as it turned out, some alternatives to striding along the verges of the ring-road: state-owned forestry land with permissive access on the yellow trackways; the small national parks; a scattering of well-publicised 'loop walks' from sprawling car parks in popular tourist areas and a few lesser-known permissive circuits where landowners had signed up to a voluntary 'walks scheme'. (There were also some long-distance waymarked 'ways'; but when you looked up the details these often turned out to follow minor roads for much of their length.) Then there were the upland areas – the Burren, Connemara, the mountains of Kerry and Mayo and Donegal – where the unfenced expanses seemed to invite wandering. And indeed, once away from the roads you were usually safe enough. But the signs prominently affixed to the gates and the men in pickup trucks met on the trackways made it clear that you had no *right* to walk there.

In fact, there is almost no statutory right of access to the countryside *anywhere* in Ireland.[1] As the journalist Fintan O'Toole has pointed out, not even the stony ascent of Croagh Patrick, the holy mountain in Co. Mayo, is a proper right of way. This is perhaps the best-known and most venerated footpath in Ireland, but 'neither pilgrims nor any other visitor has any right to walk that punishing path [...] In principle, the climb could be stopped and the path blocked.'[2] If you've ever been for an off-road walk in Ireland, you almost certainly did so entirely at the whim of the landowner – either that, or you were trespassing. And the Irish authorities seem generally to side with the principle of absolute and exclusive private ownership. There have been numerous cases of a landowner suddenly closing a long-established path giving access to a popular beach or mountain or running along a stretch of coastline walked daily for decades by local people.[3] And if anyone asks the local council to intervene or attempts to take the matter to court, things seldom work out well for the walkers. In 2003, a landowner in Co. Wicklow blocked a track in Glencree Valley that had been used by hillwalkers for decades – and was shown as a road on maps dating back to the eighteenth century. Two members of a local hiking group attempted to prove in court that the route was a public right of way. The case went in favour of the landowner; the walkers appealed and lost, and the Supreme Court refused to hear a further appeal. They were landed with huge legal costs.[4]

* * *

The fact that you almost always have to *drive* if you want to go for an off-road walk in Ireland, even if you live in the countryside, generated a strange disorientation for me as a new resident. The walking I did came in discrete fragments. I would set out in the car as if by boat across a trackless green ocean until I reached the far shore – a layby at the foot of a hill or a gravel patch at the edge of the wood. And the walk that followed was always bounded, as if on an island. If you went far enough in any direction, you'd invariably run up against the unfordable green tide of the cultivated country. The forests at Monivea and Woodlawn were islands. The promontory at Tawin was an island. And the Burren itself was a tightly clustered archipelago. There were no connecting causeways – besides those made of tarmac. All this left the point of departure itself unanchored and adrift in my mental geography. It took me an inordinately long time to work out whether Cara's hometown was to the north or south of the motorway and to understand which of its radial roads ran east and which ran west.

But gradually I got used to the idea that if I wanted a quick walk beginning at my own front door, then it would have to be entirely on tarmac. I got used to the red-and-white 'no trespassing' signs in field gateways – far more of them than you'd find in even the most hostile corners of rural England. And I came to accept that should I ever stray from the road there was a chance that a figure would appear – from behind a hedge, from a nearby bungalow or in a pickup truck – usually friendly enough, even apologetic, but firmly insistent: *private land*. I was happy in Ireland, found a natural affinity with the landscapes of its western seaboard – so much closer in form and atmosphere to the west of Cornwall than any expanse of Leicestershire sheep pasture. But there was always that one thing that stopped me feeling entirely at home here: the inability properly to walk the land, to pace myself into a sense of place. In the 1980s, the Swiss travel writer Nicolas Bouvier had written that 'In Ireland I always felt a sense of incompleteness'. There was, he thought, 'Something blank, a hole somewhere, like an octave with a missing note, a chessboard where the castles had been taken away.'[5] Bouvier had been unable to put his finger on the nature of the absence. But for myself, I knew exactly what was missing: the footpaths.

From time to time, the frustration would bubble over. Cara had to put up with me endlessly pointing out that in Wales, England, Scotland or Scandinavia there would be a statutory right to wander freely on *that* mountain, *this* bog, *those* hills. And I'd latch on to quotations about the quasi-sacred status of footpaths and stories about access struggles in other places. In the 1870s, the American naturalist John Burroughs wrote (with the limited access rights of his own country in mind) that a nation

> that has no footpaths, no community of ownership in the land which they imply, that warns off the walker as a trespasser, that knows no way but the highway, the carriage-way, that forgets the stile, the footbridge, that even ignores the rights of the pedestrian in the public road, providing no escape for him but in the ditch or up the bank, is in a fair way to a far more serious degeneracy.[6]

Reading that, I found myself first nodding enthusiastically, and then ashamed at the hyperbole. Was it really such an outrageous aberration that the countryside was so inaccessible here? Or was this just one of those small differences – like having to pay upfront for your tap water in one place, your refuse collection in another – that you eventually stop noticing and end up mistaking for a universal norm? Relatively few of the people around me in Ireland seemed concerned by it. And when I tried to explain the different arrangements for countryside access in other European countries, I'd often be met with the same baffled response – sometimes even from people who professed to be keen walkers themselves: 'But you can't just *walk* on other people's land – lads would be getting sued the whole time, for a start…'

* * *

As I was trying to come to terms with all of this in Ireland, I began to notice a peculiar discourse about countryside access emerging in neighbouring Britain. For many foreign visitors – not least those from Ireland – Wales and England appear remarkably welcoming to walkers. But in a run of books and newspaper comment pieces, certain writers made the claim that access to the countryside there – specifically in England (Scotland has different access arrangements and for some reason Wales is often erased in these narratives) – was especially iniquitous. One campaigning newspaper columnist declared that he felt 'unbearably trapped' by the supposed lack of public access to the English countryside,[7] while the champions of a new 'right to roam' campaign routinely insisted that '92 per cent of England' was off limits to the public[8] – a highly contestable and thoroughly misleading claim.*

Looking on from the other side of the Irish Sea, all this seemed like a sort of inverse English exceptionalism. If England – the indubitable centre of the universe for so many of its residents – couldn't be the *best* in the world in a particular category, then it simply had to be the *worst*! And there was something else: the emerging body of polemical writing about countryside access in England sometimes seems to be less concerned with the practicalities of setting out for a walk than with *who owns what*. If the residents of England are excluded from the land to an unparalleled degree, the argument seems to go, it is because huge swathes of it are still controlled by mansion-dwelling earls, dukes and billionaire tycoons, ensconced among their pheasant woods and deer parks as they have been for centuries, grown fatter than ever on agricultural subsidies. They are the ones supposedly keeping the common folk off the land. Again, from a viewpoint a

* Designated 'access land', on which there is a statutory right of open access, covers about 8 per cent of England (and a significantly higher proportion of Wales – which may be one reason Wales is so often erased in this discourse). This is the basis of the 'no access to 92 per cent' claim. But there are also open access arrangements in places other than designated access land, including coastal margins, most publicly owned woodland and some parts of the Crown estate – as well as urban parks. And the '92 per cent' takes no account of the existence of the vast network of public footpaths in Wales and England, running across the very land said to be 'off limits'.

short way to the west in postcolonial, twenty-first-century Ireland there seemed to be something badly awry here. In Ireland, many of the equivalent aristocrats – the landed denizens of the Protestant Anglo-Irish Ascendancy – were dispossessed by the land reforms of the late nineteenth and early twentieth centuries. Those who resisted the reforms into the 1920s sometimes had their grand houses burnt to the ground to encourage their departure. Their estates were broken up, and the land was equitably redistributed among the erstwhile tenants in what looked – on paper, at least – like a textbook decolonial process. And yet it was Wales and England that ended up with robust and quietly radical countryside access legislation while Ireland ended up with 'no entry' signs on the field gates. There was a mystery to be unravelled here.

Whenever I went back across the water, I felt anything but 'unbearably trapped'. When I looked out from a piece of high ground there – from the windy hilltop of Bartinney near the westernmost tip of Cornwall, say – I saw endless possibilities. From Bartinney I looked out on a sprawling patchwork of 'access land' – the open 'mountain, moor, heath or down', amounting to around 8 per cent of England and 20 per cent of Wales,[9] on which, since the passing of the 2000 Countryside and Rights of Way Act, you have been free to wander at will – with the farmland between spanned by countless public footpaths, many of them first formally recorded and protected under the 1949 National Parks and Access to the Countryside Act.

The comparisons made by 'right to roam' campaigners in England to back their calls for change often seemed to be with countries where the dominant landscape was radically different from that of England – wilderness-heavy Scandinavia and Scotland; thickly forested Central Europe. And they seldom seemed to dig down into the specific practicalities of access in the bits of those countries that best bear comparison with the bulk of the Welsh and English – and, indeed, Irish – countryside. The celebrated *Allemansrätten* which allows supposedly total access to the Norwegian countryside, for example, does *not* apply to agricultural land and explicitly excludes the *innmark*, the 'infield', enclosed farmland of the sort that makes up most of Ireland, Wales and England – unless it is covered with snow.[10] Where there is no specific exclusion, there are still caveats and exclusions when farmland is in active use for agriculture – as it often is. In Sweden, for example, any 'cultivated land' is off limits.[11] And none of these places – not even Scotland – has an extensive infrastructure of public access to predominantly agricultural and overwhelmingly privately owned countryside comparable to that of Wales and England. The '92 per cent of England' (and around 80 per cent of Wales by the same calculation) to which there is allegedly 'no public access' is crisscrossed by the largest public footpath network in Europe. There are some 190,000 kilometres of footpaths in England and 33,000 kilometres in Wales,[12] all of them formally recorded and legally protected.

'Roaming' at will across farmland might be a nice idea in theory. But in practice, navigating across country in a maze of thorn hedges, sheep fences and barbed wire can be as challenging as finding your way through a jungle. But footpaths across such country come with the stiles and footbridges that John Burroughs mentioned, and with small gateways designed for walkers rather than tractors. Little wonder that Keep Ireland Open, the tiny voluntary organisation that campaigns for better access to the Irish countryside, includes on its website a gallery of images from England – photos of stiles, yellow arrows, well-trodden paths across fields. One of the captions states 'We can aspire to this'.[13]

* * *

The current set of rights that allow access to the landscapes of Wales and England is the product of a long-fought battle and a gradual accumulation of legislation over the twentieth century. But the footpaths themselves are often much, much older. They had their origins not as facilities for outdoor leisure, but as simple routes for those whose only means of transport was their own feet – the poorest people, the people with the least power, the people compelled to walk. There have *always* been footpaths, running through the fields to places of worship, markets, water sources, woodlands and homesteads, trodden into the fabric of the countryside by the long passage of feet. These paths had customary status: the right to pass along them was enshrined merely by the repeated act of walking. When a path was no longer used, the right of way dissipated.

Was it really possible that Ireland had never had a comparable path network of its own? Could it really be true – as one or two people suggested to me – that it had been the oppressing Anglo-Irish landlords who'd forbidden access to these landscapes? (And if that was true, then why on earth hadn't things been put right a century after the more intransigent of those landlords saw their big houses go up in flames?)

In her classic study, *The English Path*, the poet and literary scholar Kim Taplin notes that footpaths have often been 'too slight, too humble and too local to attract the historian'.[14] Taplin's own focus was on the representation of public paths in poetry and prose. In her trawl through a vast body of literature, she kept an eye out not only for overt mention of the word 'path' itself, but also for such phrases as 'through the fields' and 'through the corn', which, she wrote, imply 'neither vandalism nor poetic licence but the existence of a public right of way'.[15] She turned up dozens of such references in the eighteenth- and nineteenth-century literature of England. I found myself wondering if the same would be true of books about Ireland from the same era – and even a cursory search suggested that it was. In nineteenth-century novels set in rural Ireland, characters wander along paths through fields and woods as often as do their contemporaries in English fiction. The 1894 novel *The Real Charlotte*, cowritten by Edith Somerville and Violet Florence Martin, features much strolling along paths in Co. Galway, including one 'trodden round the rocks' and leading to a holy well and a thorn tree hung with votive rags.[16] The narrator of Sydney Owenson's *The Wild Irish Girl* walks the final twenty miles of his journey to a remote estate in Co. Sligo along paths sometimes shady, sometimes 'steep and trackless'.[17] Sheridan Le Fanu's 1863 gothic mystery, *The House by the Church-Yard*, mentions both footpaths and stiles along the banks of the River Liffey.[18] And *Knocknagow, or The Homes of Tipperary* – a novel entirely concerned with the iniquities of landownership and tenancy regimes in the mid-nineteenth century by the prominent Irish Republican Brotherhood member Charles Kickham – mentions various journeys along field paths and includes a nice description of a stile with 'two or three long stone slabs fixed [...] as steps' in an embankment at the edge of a field.[19]

Out of all of this an idea began to form – impelling long hours hunched over the map of Ireland, and spurring nonsequential Google searches in idle moments. But then, before the idea ever had time to crystallise, came the COVID-19 pandemic.

* * *

For five weeks in the spring of 2020 all residents of the Republic of Ireland were forbidden to travel further than two kilometres from their homes. On the first evening of the lockdown I laid the local map across my desk, marked my location, and drew a circle with a two-kilometre radius. All the places that I usually went to walk were off limits. The Burren was impossibly distant. The coast was a good twenty kilometres off. Even the woods where I regularly went for a leg-stretch at the end of a working day were out of bounds. I feared at first that I'd be marching around the ring-road with everyone else for as long as the lockdown lasted. But in the end, I found ways through. I ducked into little patches of woodland, chanced it across the odd field and fought through the blackthorns along abandoned laneways. At long last I was going through the process I would have begun during my earliest days in a new location elsewhere: walking my way into a sense of place. By the time lockdown ended, I felt a new sense of connection with the local landscape – though without footpaths it had been a hard-won affinity.

At the same time, I began to read more deeply about the history of the Irish countryside. I also spent a great deal of time staring at old maps in online archives, especially the GeoHive website, provided by Ordnance Survey Ireland (now renamed Tailte

Éireann). It included three old Ordnance Survey series, going back almost two centuries and covering the whole of Ireland. You could layer them over the modern satellite image, with little slide rules to adjust the transparency. It made for a dynamic palimpsest. A brief sweep of the mouse could bring the 'Historic Map 6 inch Colour' into focus, then push it back so the roads and housing estates of twenty-first-century Co. Galway leapt back into view. You could see what had been where in different decades, what had changed and what had remained fixed.

The most recent of the sheets – which GeoHive called '6 inch Cassini' – dated from the 1930s and 1940s. The next layer down – 'Historic Map 25 inch' – was from the 1880s. And the oldest was the product of one of the most ambitious cartographical exercises of the nineteenth century: the original six-inch survey of Ireland conducted in the 1820s and 1830s. These were maps made at a much larger scale than those commercially available for Ireland today. Just within the range of my two-kilometre circle, they were packed with fascinating detail. I was so distracted by the wealth of now-vanished placenames and archaeological sites that it took me a long time to spot another feature on the old maps. The most recent sheet – the '6 inch Cassini' from the early twentieth century – was marked all over with double dotted lines. They struck off from road junctions towards distant buildings and ran between the radial roads. And when you zoomed in you could see that the map tagged each with the same set of initials: 'F. P.'

It took me a few moments to work it out: F. P. – *Footpath!*

There was a whole network of them, running across the same land that was now so firmly off limits: diagonals striking clean across fields or bending in along the hedge lines; sensible shortcuts between parallel roads and least-resistance cross-country routes. I zoomed out, swept east across the surface of Ireland, then zoomed in again at random. I had landed somewhere in Westmeath – and yes! They were there too: footpaths through the Irish fields, the same sort of footpaths that still exist in Wales and England; hundreds of kilometres of them, plainly marked on an eighty-year-old map.

That evening, I went out into the countryside at the edge of town – trespassing, with a screenshot of the old map on my mobile phone. The field boundaries here had remained unchanged since the map was made, and there was a heady anticipation as I scurried along the line of the drystone wall. The evening was hot, the sunlight coming low as if through a dirty window. According to the map, the line of the old path intersected with the wall just up ahead – but what were the chances?

But it was there, just as I'd hoped! I've never been so thrilled by a piece of rustic stonework: a single cross-stone, built into the wall at thigh-height, the most rudimentary of stiles, allowing you to step, rather than scramble, into the next field. I traced the line southwards, and further on, at the edge of a strip of woodland, I found another ghost stile, more elaborate this time: three cross-stones, set at a rising diagonal to carry a pedestrian daintily up and over and into the next field, exactly where the old map said it should be. I went home giddy in the warm gloaming.

It wasn't that Ireland had *never* had paths, then; it had *lost* them – and lost them relatively late, *after* the colonial landlords had been removed from the scene. The idea – the idea that had been nothing more than a faint itch before the lockdown – was beginning to take on a proper form: the form of a line on a map.

* * *

In the late 1960s the writer John Hillaby set out to walk across Britain from Land's End to John O'Groats 'with the intention of avoiding *all* roads', of keeping 'to cross-country tracks and footpaths all the way'. The book he wrote about the walk, *Journey Through Britain*, is a sprightly narrative, full of humour and deftly disbursed historical knowledge. Reading *Journey Through Britain* today, it's clear just how much things have improved for walkers in Britain in the last fifty years. At the time of Hillaby's journey, the long process of legally enshrining countryside access was still at an early stage. His plan to avoid tarmac altogether 'turned out to be practically impossible for notwithstanding what's been written about the ancient by-ways, many of them are now hopelessly overgrown; others have been enclosed, ploughed up, or deliberately obstructed in one way or another'.[20] He often found himself 'squeezed into the little capillaries of transport'. John Hillaby's walk across Britain in the 1960s seemed to involve many of the same challenges you'd encounter trying to walk across Ireland in the twenty-first century. And so there it was: the idea.

I laid out the map of Ireland. For his route across Britain, Hillaby had chosen the standard start and end points: the top and the bottom. In Ireland, that would be Mizen Head to Malin Head, the southernmost and northernmost extremities. But when I sketched a line across the map between those two points it seemed strangely equivocal. It cleaved to the west – the part of Ireland where I felt most comfortable, most at home, and the part with the greatest expanses of unfenced upland. Significantly, with the gentlest of nudges from the right, the line could be made to steer clear of the most potent of all marks on the Irish map – the border between the Republic of Ireland and Northern Ireland. But the idea I had in mind didn't involve sticking to the peripheries. And in any case, Hillaby's route hadn't actually been from top to bottom, but simply between the two most distant points. The northernmost point of mainland Britain is Dunnet Head, ten miles from John O'Groats, and Land's End isn't the most southerly point (that would be the Lizard), but the most *westerly*.

I had to turn to Google to identify the westernmost Irish equivalent: Dunmore Head, looking out to the Blasket Islands from the tip of the Dingle Peninsula in Kerry. And its easternmost counterpart? Burr Point on the Ards Peninsula, the long limb that bends at the knee beyond Belfast to enclose the waters of Strangford Lough. *This* line ran right through the middle of Ireland – and, in its final stages, right across the border. As the crow flies, it was a little over 425 kilometres. Google Maps claimed you could walk it in 110 hours. But Google Maps kept you on the 'capillaries of transport' and made no allowances for sleep or lunch breaks. I reckoned that on the ground the journey would be longer by a couple of hundred kilometres – and by very many hours.

I looked more closely at the map, looked at the topography, began to sketch the rudiments of an itinerary. The first stage would follow the mountain spine of Dingle, where there was wide open space – physically challenging, but a navigationally easy start. Then came a daunting expanse of low-lying farming country running all the way to Limerick. From there, a natural guiding line ran northeast: the Shannon, bulging into Lough Derg with the forestry lands of Slieve Aughty on the west bank then wriggling through the bogs of the Midlands. After that came the deep countryside of the northeast, and then the border. It would be difficult, but that was the point.

My plan wasn't deliberately to trespass or to boldly try for a straight bearing across country (I knew well from trying to follow unused and overgrown footpaths in Cornwall that that would be a frustrating and often impossible task). I wanted to find the ways through, to see what was possible. The last long-distance walk I'd done had been a meandering journey through Cornwall. Planning that, I'd simply sketched a rough trajectory on a large-scale map, confident that there would be enough paths on the ground to realise it without too much road walking. What would happen if I tried something similar in Ireland?

The journey would, I knew, bring challenges beyond the purely practical. I'd never particularly enjoyed trespassing – anywhere in the world. But walking onto forbidden farmland in Ireland always made me particularly uneasy. There was a reason I stepped back, let Cara do the talking on the occasions when we ran into a landowner on our hikes in the Burren or Connemara. I might determinedly call myself 'Cornish' in Britain, but here in Ireland my tongue was plainly branded with a different word.

So much of Ireland's unhappy colonial history was tied up with issues of land – who lived on it, who controlled it, who owned it. And the iniquities here – from the earliest sixteenth-century plantations and the outrages of the Cromwellian Settlement, to the nineteenth-century evictions and the notorious 'Quarter-Acre Clause' of the famine era – went beyond almost anything that had ever happened in England. I wanted to learn more about that history as I walked, to try and work out how it might connect to the contemporary lack of public access, the abundance of 'no trespassing' signs, the distinctive Irish attitudes to landownership. But a shout of 'Get off my land!' in Ireland has uniquely fraught contexts, and the idea of trespassing here with an identifiably 'English' accent roused a horrible postcolonial anxiety. And somewhere deep within this anxiety was a complicated personal question. It was one which I had never been asked, not even as an immigrant in Ireland. In my comfortable white British complacency, I'd never really even considered it: 'Where are you *really* from?'

The absence 'like an octave with a note missing', the absence that had kept me from feeling entirely at home in Ireland, was the barrier to walking across its countryside. But if I could find a way through a pathless land, then maybe I could also walk myself into a sense of belonging.

PART ONE

The Law of the Land

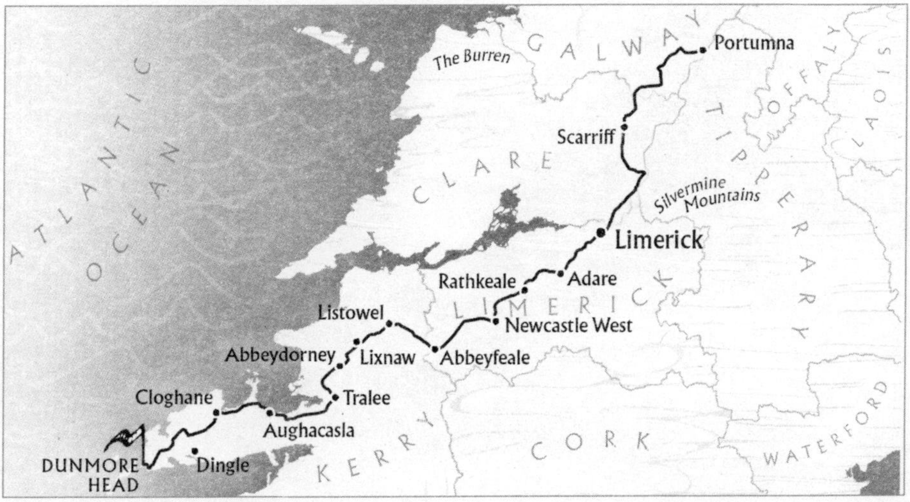

1

The Pack-Donkey's Way: Dunmore Head to Tralee

Where does a journey begin?

This, certainly, is the spot you marked on the map many months ago, hovered over on Google Maps in idle moments at your desk: *Dún Mór*, Dunmore Head, the southwesternmost extremity of mainland Ireland. But now you're here, it feels arbitrary, faintly ridiculous.

You left the house in Co. Galway yesterday lunchtime, and fragments of travel have already accumulated in your notebook and in your memory. The first view of the mountains from a high point on the Limerick–Tralee road, far off to the south under a greyish sky. A bus driver spilling an anti-immigrant monologue to the only other passenger, heedless of the immigrant with the backpack and the trekking pole sitting quietly a few seats further back (though you don't suppose *you're* the kind of immigrant he had in mind). Two choughs strutting and cackling over the cropped grass by the narrow gullet of Dingle Harbour in the evening light, taken for a good omen. Fish and chips and a night in a hostel in Dingle Town, a hubbub of American accents. Then an early minibus to the Blasket visitor centre, shuttered at this hour – as close as you could get by public transport. You've walked four kilometres already; your shirt is already wet with sweat at the shoulders and your pack feels heavier than it should. But you're here now, at the start – or are you?

Dunmore Head slopes away to an equivocal terminus, the sandstone strata flaked like pastry among the sea pinks. How far down should you clamber to be able to say that you began at the beginning? To the tideline? Or beyond? Hop the slippery boulders and surging gulleys to the outcrop marked on the map as *Carraig na Sasanach*, 'The English Rock'? Or do you need to go further still? Two kilometres offshore *An Blascaod Mór* rises, the Great Blasket Island, three white cottages like bleached teeth on the slope above its beach. And then further west again the smaller islands of Inishvickillane and Inishnabro show blueish under pearly cloud. Ireland begins – or ends – here with an uncertain ellipsis.

A red yacht tilts northwards through the channel; a fulmar banks along the foreshore on stubby wings and a bone-white gannet passes low to the south. The air is greasy and still, promising great heat. You've gone far enough; this will do; turn around: start walking.

* * *

Half an hour later, beyond the roadside straggle of houses and the labyrinth of steep and stony fields at Coumeenoole, I paused at a pull-in on the main coast road. From here the full formation of the Blasket Archipelago was clear, stretching twelve kilometres into the Atlantic. Dunmore Head looked even less like a proper starting point.

An Englishwoman was setting up a stall from the boot of her car, polished pebbles inscribed with ogham, the early Irish alphabet. Her first potential customers of the day had just arrived: a tour bus full of Americans, Germans, Australians.

'You're welcome to take a look!' she called cheerily as they emerged squinting from the bus. 'I can explain what they meant to the ancient Celts!'

None of the visitors bought a stone. But the day was new, and she didn't seem to mind. When the tour bus had driven on, she chatted without the sales patter. She was from Yorkshire, she said, descended from Vikings – 'But I'm a hippie,' as if that ameliorated the ancestry and explained her presence here. Then, after a pause: 'Where are you from?' She placed the quizzical emphasis on 'you' that English-accented people in Ireland so often seem to use when they ask me the question – and which I fear I deploy myself when I ask the same of them.

'Cornwall,' I said, hearing the resistance to any assumed commonality in my own voice. 'But I live in Co. Galway.'

'Do you miss England?'

I muttered pedantically about Cornwall not being England for a moment, then caught myself and softened. 'I miss the footpaths,' I said.

But there were footpaths here on the Dingle Peninsula – certainly not as many as you'd find on any similar slice of coastal land in Wales or England, but more than I'd encounter anywhere else this side of the border with Northern Ireland. In the coming days, my own route would intersect with two waymarked trails: the Cosán na Naomh (known as 'the Saint's Road' in English, though *cosán* is more usually translated as 'path'), which runs for eighteen kilometres from the strand at Ventry to the foot of Mount Brandon; and the Dingle Way, a 162-kilometre loop connecting Tralee to Dingle Town. Neither route is entirely off-road, but they give a walker moving across the peninsula some sustained escapes from the tarmac.

Two hundred metres on along the road, a green trackway angled inland to a fence crossed by a metal stile – part of the Dingle Way. I followed it briefly, then struck steeply up the flank of Mount Eagle. There was no official trail on this mountainside; but halfway up, sweating and gasping under the weight of my pack, I came to a galvanised gate set in a low drystone wall. A friendly request was marked in black paint across the top bar: 'PLEASE CLOSE THE GATE'. It felt like a positive welcome to a walker, and it drew me on, up the steepening ridge. And then, where the mountainside opened, a band of bare earth materialised at my feet – an unofficial path, marked on no map. I stepped onto it and let it guide me, left and right, through the sharp stones to the western summit.

* * *

The great Swiss-French architect Charles-Édouard Jeanneret, better known as Le Corbusier, had a problem with donkeys. The human, Le Corbusier believed, instinctively walks in straight lines, 'because he has a goal and knows where he is going; he has made up his mind to reach some particular place and he goes straight to it'. The pack-donkey, in contrast, 'meanders along, meditates a little in his scatter-brained and distracted fashion, he zigzags in order to avoid the larger stones, or to ease the climb, or to gain a little more shade; he takes the line of least resistance'.[1] The idea came to Le Corbusier in Paris in the autumn of 1924. Looking out at the motor traffic which clogged the Champs Elysée, he was struck by an awful revelation. The cities of twentieth-century Europe, he decided, were doomed by a fatal design flaw, baked in during prehistory. And it was all the fault of the donkeys.

As the first inhabitants moved across the primeval landscapes of Europe, Le Corbusier believed, their precise trajectories were determined by the lumbering passage of the donkeys that carried their belongings. Every bump and hollow, every stream and mire, was an obstacle which demanded a kink in the journey, and in this way 'were born roads and tracks'. The first hut clusters sprang up alongside these meandering tracks and grew into villages which in turn grew into towns and cities with the irrational itineraries of long-dead donkeys fossilised in their streetscapes. 'The Pack-Donkey's Way', wrote Le Corbusier, 'is responsible for the plan of every continental city; including Paris, unfortunately.'[2] Europeans, he thought, needed to look to 'the rectilinear cities of America' for inspiration if they were to escape their own hopeless urban tangles which 'use up our bodies' and 'thwart our souls'.[3]

'The Pack-Donkey's Way' is a compelling idea, but it's complete nonsense. The first modern humans moved into Europe from the Middle East around 50,000 years ago, and the earliest archaeological traces of human settlement in Paris date back to the Mesolithic, some 10,000 years ago. But the first donkeys only arrived in Europe in the second millennium BCE. Their forebears had been domesticated in East Africa around 7,000 years ago[4] – well before horses but long after cattle, sheep and goats. It may have been desertification and the gradual advance of the Sahara across what had once been fertile land that prompted a need for hardy pack animals, capable of long journeys in tough conditions. Domestic donkeys spread north to Egypt and east into Mesopotamia, and eventually the international trade routes of the Bronze Age brought them to Europe. The Romans bred giant donkeys, 155 centimetres at the shoulder, the size of a modern racehorse.[5] They brought the species to Britain, from where they almost certainly first reached Ireland – surprisingly late, given the later ubiquity of the Irish donkey. The earliest archival reference to donkeys in Ireland dates from the twelfth century.[6] And as donkeys moved across these new territories, they did so on meandering paths and trackways first created not by their own kind, but by *people*, moving on foot.

Even without the ahistoricism, this is what is so obviously awry in Le Corbusier's characterisation of the 'happy-go-lucky heedlessness' of 'the Pack-Donkey's Way' with its scatter-brained meditations, its shade-seeking detours and its stone-avoiding sidesteps: it is entirely *human*. Never mind the donkeys; this is exactly how *we* move, instinctively, across the landscape. And this is why we feel so ill at ease in the orderly grid of a planned city where every trajectory is direct, every base unit of a pedestrian journey the same length.

Plotting my own route through the Dingle Peninsula I *did* know where I was going. I took a hypothetical diagonal from Dunmore Head to the centre of Tralee as my guide, a straight line fifty-six kilometres long. Then I scoured the map for paths of least resistance along its length: the open mountains and bogs where I might pass unhindered; the unsurfaced tracks where walkers might be tolerated; the stretches of the Cosán na Naomh and the Dingle Way that fitted my own purpose; and, where there was no other option, the quietest country roads. It was the same approach I'd take to route-planning all the way to Burr Point. And when I later retraced the ground reality of this first section on the map, accounted for all the jinks and kinks and totted up the total, it came to eighty-one kilometres – which seemed like pretty good going in the circumstances.

* * *

There was a trig point at 516 metres, the very summit of the mountain. Dingle Town showed to the east beyond a gridwork of fields. Further off to the south, across an expanse of smooth grey sea, the histrionic flourish of Valentia Island's terminal cliffs rose darkly. Beyond them, the awful fang of Skellig Michael punctured the horizon. And to the northeast lay all the country I had yet to cross: the long bending ridge from Rahinnane to Lateevemore and the level country below, patched with forestry and specked with white houses; the sickle of pale sand at Murreagh; and the thousand-metre hulk of the Mount Brandon massif. I'd started out with a notion of reaching the summit this evening, camping somewhere on the eastern slopes. But now it seemed impossibly distant.

Another, broader path ran downhill east from the trig point. This was obviously the route that most people used to reach the summit. The hillsides around it were tightly clad with heather, but regular use had kept the path itself clear. It didn't run entirely straight. It bent left, for no obvious reason, then right again. But it would require tremendous perversity of any walker descending eastwards from the trig point to step away from it. The grass grew green at the path's edges, then in a stripe of stunted yellow in the middle where footfall was heaviest. You'd be able to see it from a great distance on a clear day.

This is the remarkable thing about footpaths: they are humanmade infrastructure, as plainly marked upon the landscape as walls and monuments; yet they are not *built*. Ancillary structures – stiles, gates, bridges – may come into being along their length; but paths themselves are made only by the act of walking – and *maintained* only by the act of walking. People walk along paths only because they exist, and they exist only if people walk along them – a perfect feedback loop of legacy and renewal. The very first people to arrive in a new landscape – to reach an uninhabited island, say – will need to make their own way through the scrub and undergrowth from the beachhead. And when they decide they've gone far enough, they'll return the same way. If others arrive at the same beach in the weeks and months that follow, they will surely notice the bent branches and broken stems and travel the same way. And a thousand years later the paved track from the harbour to the village might well preserve some of the arbitrary twists and turns of that very first journey. Paths can come into being incredibly quickly and with minimal input – look at the 'desire lines' cutting the corners between the paved walkways of city parks;* look at the strip of

* These days, the term 'desire line' is much used to discuss informal paths – and from there adopted as a lyrical metaphor. But this use is very recent. The term seems to originate with traffic planners in the 1940s to mean 'a straight line between a point of origin and a point of destination for a trip or group of trips without regard to the actual routes traveled via existing streets' (see 'Hearings Before a Subcommittee of the Committee on Public Works, United States Senate', 1949, p.63). The 'desire line' of my own journey, then, was the direct diagonal from Dunmore Head to Tralee, and onwards to Burr Point.

slightly darker grass running across your own lawn to the washing line. But they can last forever.

For path researcher Jack Cornish, footpaths 'are the oldest part of our collective heritage still in use for their original purpose'.[7] But there is a difficulty when it comes to establishing just *how* old. The editors of *The Oxford Companion to Archaeology* note that roads and tracks, let alone simple footpaths, 'are one of the more difficult subjects for archaeology to document', for they leave 'no recoverable traces'.[8]

The 'Ridgeway', the path that runs along the chalk downs of southern England from a point near Avebury in Wiltshire to the Goring Gap on the River Thames in Berkshire, is often claimed to be 'Europe's oldest road', in use for 'at least 5,000 years'.[9] This may, in fact, be wishful thinking, for there is little archaeological evidence for continuous use of the Ridgeway or other similar high-ground routes before the medieval period.[10] It is only where people actually *built* their routes across the countryside that prehistoric provenances can be confirmed. The 'Sweet Track' – a raised plank walkway supported on crossed posts stretching for 1,800 metres across the soggy Somerset Levels in the English West Country – has been dated precisely through dendrochronology to the winter of 3807–3806 BCE, which really does make it Europe's oldest known path.[11] A similar, albeit later, plank walkway has been found in Ireland at Curraghmore near Clonmacnoise in Offaly. It dates from around 1500 BCE.[12] More recently, in 148 BCE, Irish builders created another rather more substantial wooden route in the Corlea Bog in Co. Longford, this time wide enough to carry wheeled transport. Some three hundred large oak trees were felled to construct the kilometre-long Corlea *togher*, or bog road, with the hewn sleepers laid atop twin birchwood logs like an inverted railway.[13]

But other ghostly, undatable threads surely stretch back for thousands upon thousands of years beyond these identifiable Iron Age and Neolithic beginnings. Those very first modern humans, moving into Europe fifty millennia ahead of the donkeys, were *not* entering an entirely untrodden landscape. There had been Neanderthals there ahead of them for hundreds of thousands of years, and they probably followed some of *their* pathways on their journeys north and west. The famous lines of the Spanish poet Antonio Machado – 'Traveller, there is no path / The path is made by walking. / By walking you make a path' – are only half right. Paths *are* made by walking. And by walking you *remake* the path. But the path is usually already there ahead of you.

But not always. After a kilometre, the path that I was following on Mount Eagle – which may have existed since the first settlers arrived in Dingle, or which may have been cut into an unmarked hillside by someone on a quad bike a couple of winters back – turned sharply west. So, with tremendous perversity, I struck off into the tussocks, making my own way towards a little cottage at a low pass on the Ventry–Dunquin road below. This was ankle-turning ground, with boggy voids between the clumps of purple moor grass. I kept the cottage in view, yet my line was anything but straight. I was drawn too far left by the contours, turned sharply to the right to correct myself, then found myself on the wrong side of a gorse-covered bank. When I looked back up the hillside, I could see my wandering trajectory marked in the bent brambles and broken grass stems. If another walker were to seek a similar route off Mount Eagle in the days that followed, they would probably stumble on the traces of my own descent and turn instinctively to follow them, assured that they had to lead *somewhere*. If someone else came along after *them*, they would find the way a little clearer. And if perhaps a dozen others over the summer months took the same alternative direction off the hill, by the time the vegetation died back in autumn there would be a distinct new path on the hillside – a path that might last for as long as there are humans walking over the Dingle landscape. But if no one came after me, within a few weeks there would be nothing to show that anyone had ever passed this way.

At the bottom of the hill, I clambered out across a stone-and-earth bank onto the road beside the cottage. There was a fake cromlech in the garden and a 'for sale' sign by the gate. While I was straightening myself and picking the burrs from my shorts, a blue car pulled up and a thin woman with long brown hair got out. I nodded, but she didn't acknowledge me. She stalked across to the 'for sale' sign and peered past the cromlech to the small, red-framed windows. It looked like she was considering a possibility. When she'd driven on, I unfolded the map. I'd like to say that I noticed it right then on a day in late May with the clouds clearing and Dingle Bay turning from grey to blue. But I didn't. It was only much later that I connected my passage across Mount Eagle to Le Corbusier and his mythical pack-donkeys. And it is only now – *right* now, at the moment of writing, after I've drafted everything above – that I notice the words on the map, italicised in a tiny font, a placename marking the very hillside on which I inscribed a potential path. I have to call Cara to confirm that it means what I think it means, and then I have to give her a very convoluted explanation for my laughter: *Casán na nAsal* – 'the Donkey's Path'.

* * *

Over a wobbly gate tied to an old pallet, and on to a yellow track beneath the Rahinnane ridge in the midday heat. There was no red-and-white 'no entry' sign here; but I felt the first queasy unease of the trespasser, and it deepened where the track ended and I had to clamber across a fence into a small block of forestry humming with midges, and then on across another gate into a field. But there was no one around, and another track brought me out to a strip of worn tarmac almost straight enough to please Le Corbusier. A few roadside bungalows. Two dogs with dusty coats – a border collie and a miniature old English sheepdog – panting after me along the lane. In the hedges: fuchsias, foxgloves, common vetch, herb robert – the familiar wildflowers of home.

It was a couple of years since my last long-distance walk – 450 meandering kilometres across Cornwall – and I'd had little time to prepare myself for this journey with training hikes and exercise regimes. The ascent of Mount Eagle had been a lung-bursting struggle. I'd told myself that you can always walk your way to fitness, building on the distances already covered with a rest day here and there. It had always worked for me in the past. But I hadn't factored in the road walking. It only took a couple of kilometres on tarmac to raise the first blister under the ball of my right foot and an ominous ache in my heels. The idea of crossing Mount Brandon today had been absurdly ambitious. I'd walked – what? Fifteen? Twenty kilometres? This did not bode well if I was really going to walk right across Ireland. At Gallarus I shambled gratefully into a roadside campsite.

'You can tuck in behind the hedge there,' said the owner; 'give you a bit of shelter from the rain.'

I raised an eyebrow and glanced up at the clear blue sky, paling to white at its seaward edge.

He grinned. 'Never stays the same for long.'

When I'd pitched the tent behind the sheltering laurel, popped the blister and showered off the sweat of the morning, I hobbled up the road to the little Gallarus Oratory, facing towards the falling sun on its daisy-starred terrace. The four corbelled walls angled inwards to a crowning ridge. A tiny window pierced the eastern gable and a low doorway opened to the west. It had the look of a thing turned out – a sandcastle or a blancmange. A few pennywort spears rose from the stonework like candles.

Seamus Heaney came here in the summer of 1966, a long way from home, stepped through the doorway into the 'core of old dark' and sensed a vanished community at prayer.[14] But there's no record of this as a place of communal worship – nor even as a cell for a single hermit. Some suggest that it was a shelter for pilgrims heading for Mount Brandon, and – rather fancifully – that its name might mean something like 'the foreigners' house' for the strangers who came here to climb the mountain. With no mortar or wood used in its construction, it is almost as difficult to date as a footpath. Provenances ranging from the fifth to the twelfth centuries have been proposed.[15]

There were two American couples posing for photographs outside when I arrived, a pair of easterners and a pair of southerners – 'Where y'all from?' – on a different kind of pilgrimage.

When they'd gone on their way, I sat for a while against the drystone wall that ringed the oratory. Sheep calls drifted from the hills and a faint smell of cut grass carried on the rising southwesterly breeze. There was a simple three-step stile built into the wall immediately behind the oratory – three projecting tongues of stone rising on a forty-five-degree angle to allow easy passage to the east. This, for me, was instantly more compelling than the oratory itself; a palpable connection with the communities of the past through an act less obscure than worship. I placed my aching feet onto the first tongue, then the second and the third – like how many others before me? But there was no longer a clear footway trodden into the private field beyond; just some thistles, a scruffy hem of bracken and a few cross-bred beef cattle further up the hillside.

* * *

When were the very first paths trodden into Irish soil by human feet? The conventional version of the story has it that people turned up late in Ireland – very late, by European standards. At the height of the Last Glacial Period, the whole place was icebound and uninhabitable. And then, as the glaciers retreated, the land-bridge to Britain quickly submerged, long before the tides overran Doggerland and cut the larger island off from the continental mainland. This early isolation stifled the postglacial recolonisation of Ireland by flora and fauna and is the reason that even today it has markedly lower species diversity than either mainland Europe or Britain. The legendary lack of snakes is just the start of it. As one scholar puts it, 'Ireland is characterised more by what is *not* than what *is* present.'[16] Until recently, it was assumed that a similar belatedness and paucity characterised Irish human prehistory too. The earliest known settlement is at Mount Sandel on the River Bann, close to Coleraine in Northern Ireland. Only twenty kilometres separate Ireland from Scotland here, so it seems an obvious place to find evidence of early arrivals. The Mount Sandel site dates from the Mesolithic, the 'Middle Stone Age', around 8000 BCE – fully 4,000 years after the earliest known postglacial settlements of southern Britain.[17] The people of Mount Sandel lived in dome-shaped huts made of bent branches covered with hide. They ate salmon and eels and wild boar meat. And as they gradually extended their hunting and gathering grounds southward, they moved into virgin forest, trampling new pathways through the undergrowth – or so the long-established story has it. But when it comes to our understanding of prehistory, the tiniest of objects can change the narrative entirely.

In 2016, two researchers, Marion Dowd and Ruth Carden, were reviewing finds from early twentieth-century archaeological digs which had been stored in cardboard boxes in the National Museum of Ireland's natural history division for almost a hundred years. Among several dozen bear bones in the boxes was a patella – a yellowish lump a little bigger than a golf ball. It was scored with five obvious parallel blade-marks. The original Edwardian archaeologists had noticed this and had mentioned in their report 'a knee-cap of a large bear' clearly showing 'the incisions of a knife, which was probably used to divide the tendons'. But neither they nor the modern researchers had any idea how old the bone was.

Marion Dowd suggested sending it for radiocarbon dating. The results came as a shock: the bear had lived, died and been butchered by someone with a sharp flint blade sometime between 12,810 and 12,590 years ago – two and a half millennia before the earliest traces of a settlement at Mount Sandel.[18]

The abrupt extension of confirmed human presence in Ireland is striking enough, but the discovery has further implications. It was previously believed that the Mount Sandel pioneers had arrived in an island thickly covered with trees, and thus, in a small way, began the relentless process of its deforestation. But whoever sliced at the knee joint of the bear in the eleventh millennium BCE had lived in an Ireland *before* trees. The Last Glacial Period reached its maximum extent 20,000 years ago. Ireland was largely free of permanent ice cover by around 15,000 years ago. But for many centuries to come, the place was dominated by tussocky tundra with just a few patches of scrub in the sheltered valleys.[19] This, and not some sylvan Eden, was the landscape the bear-butcher knew. The other arresting significance is the location of the bear bone's original discovery. It was found far from any obvious Irish Sea crossing points, in a cave near Ennis in Co. Clare. By 12,500 years ago, then, people had already moved on foot across the entire breadth of Ireland.

We don't know if a permanent human presence endured between the bear-butcher and the Mount Sandel settlers. You might expect there to be abundant evidence if it did. But these early populations would have been tiny and mobile, and they possessed little that would last in the archaeological record. Thinking now of my own journey across Ireland, I can identify no enduring physical traces: footprints and a few flattened patches marking the presence of a small tent; a dozen discreet latrine holes dug and backfilled in woods and bogs; a stone dislodged here and there on a hillside. And I had metals and plastics about me that a Palaeolithic traveller lacked. I don't think I dropped a tent peg or a sardine tin anywhere; but even if I had, what are the chances of it falling into soil poorly oxygenated enough for it to survive the centuries? And what are the chances of someone *finding* it 12,500 years from now? The Co. Clare bear bone was cut at the start of a period known as the Younger Dryas – a 1,200-year climatic spasm when the general postglacial warming faltered and the weather turned abruptly colder. Life would have been extremely challenging at the height of the Younger Dryas, and it's possible that humans retreated from Ireland for a time once more. But the cold snap had been over for around 1,700 years by the time the first traces of the Mount Sandel settlement show up. If there were hunter-gatherers moving across Irish landscapes *before* the Younger Dryas, then why wouldn't they have also been present during the milder centuries that followed?

When thinking about prehistory, it's hard to resist a telescoping effect: a single boat from Scotland arrives at the mouth of the River Bann and the settlers leap out and clear a site for a village; a lone hunter-gatherer traverses Ireland east to west and catches a bear at the end of the journey. But a single human lifespan – the true limit of our personal conception of time – is minuscule against the scale of prehistory. Chances are that the people of Mesolithic Mount Sandel and Palaeolithic Co. Clare believed that they and their people had been *here* forever – or at best had only a hazy, heavily mythologised conception of ancestral arrival. The paths that *they* used to move across the landscape may have belonged to their own prehistory. So here's a notion, detached from the strict business of museum catalogues and radiocarbon dating, but not impossible: a pathway first trodden into a bare landscape in the Palaeolithic – as a way between the shellfish grounds of the foreshore and the bilberry patches of the hills, perhaps – *could* have endured. It would have been kept clear by human feet as the birch and hazel scrub thickened around it and the oaks and Scots pines rose. It would have served as a hunting trail through the woods for a while; then, as the trees were cleared away, it became a route to the winter grazing grounds. It may still be there today: a track running down from a stony plateau to an aluminium gate on a quiet road, fixed with a 'no trespassing' sign.

* * *

Grey at first light, the red flowers of the fuchsias hanging heavy in the hedges. A clutch of eighth-century beehive huts beside a road like huge fungal vents grown out of the hillside among the white bungalows and abandoned farm cottages, and a green apron of land running back to the blank waters of Smerwick Harbour. It was a Saturday morning, before seven o'clock, and there was no one else about. But at Kilmalkedar a hare limped away up the track ahead of me, showing the pale underfur of its overpowered hind legs. To the right, among a clutch of other monastic ruins, the roofless twelfth-century church of St Malkedar stood in a weedy graveyard. By the uneven cobbled path, an ogham stone – not of the sort carved for tourists. It was slender, tall as a grown man, probably dating from the turn of the seventh century. The lines chiselled into its edge recorded the name of one Máel-Inbher, son of Broccán. They looked like knife-marks on a Palaeolithic bear bone.

I was on the Cosán na Naomh here, the 'Saint's Road' running towards Mount Brandon. I'd followed sections of it yesterday too – a path at the edge of the fields near the Gallarus Oratory and a beautiful green lane between high banks, curving along the northern flank of the Lateevemore ridge. Waymarked trails with purported historical origins often turn out to be decidedly spurious. There is another 'Saints' Way' in Cornwall, claimed as a medieval pilgrimage route. But though it follows the general trajectory of medieval cross-peninsula traffic, it has been stitched together from modern footpaths and lanes. But the surviving off-road sections of the Cosán na Naomh do seem to be authentically ancient. It may once have been the southernmost of three major mountain pilgrimage routes on Ireland's western seaboard.[20] The northernmost, at Slieve League in Donegal, has similarly fallen out of use and only the route to the summit of Croagh Patrick in Mayo still sees regular pilgrim traffic today.

The earliest record of Mount Brandon as a place of pilgrimage dates from the mid-sixteenth century.[21] But connected sites strung along the Cosán na Naomh from Ventry to the mountain – ogham stones, beehive huts, monastic sites, oratories – all seem to date roughly to the second half of the first millennium CE. This suggests that the route was already in use by that stage. Pilgrims began their journey at Ventry – perhaps having arrived by boat from outside the peninsula. They then made their way northeast along the Cosán na Naomh – which seems to have remained a simple earthen path throughout its history.[22] At the end of the journey, they offered prayers at the 952-metre crown of the mountain. It is unclear when or why the tradition ended (though such practices came under pressure from the colonial authorities around the turn of the eighteenth century). The earliest Ordnance Survey map of Dingle, published in the 1840s, records the 'Saint's Road' name (in English, rather than Irish). But the route is already fragmented, suggesting that its purpose was remembered at the time of the survey, but that it was no longer regularly used for pilgrimage. An attempted revival by the Bishop of Kerry in June 1868 drew a huge crowd, but failed to reignite an annual tradition.[23]

In its heyday, the pilgrimage was probably dedicated to St Brendan the Navigator, the sixth-century abbot who – according to an account written many centuries later – took to the North Atlantic in a leather boat, camped out on the back of a whale and, so some of his modern devotees like to think, reached North America before any other European. There is an oratory just west of the church at Kilmalkedar, very similar in design to that at Gallarus, which is named for St Brendan today. But this association may have developed long after the first pilgrims climbed the mountain. Mount Brandon may, in fact, be named for the hero of an earlier voyage narrative, Bran.[24] And the main date on which pilgrims historically ascended the mountain seems to have been the last Sunday of July – the same day on which huge crowds still climb Croagh Patrick. The influential twentieth-century folklore scholar Máire MacNeill argued that this date was based on the pagan festival of Lughnasa, celebrated to mark the start of the harvest, and that summer pilgrimages to the summits of Irish mountains are a barely Christianised continuation of a much older tradition. And if the pilgrimage is ancient, then so, surely, is the Cosán na Naomh itself. The route that I followed up the hill behind Kilmalkedar, across a couple of reedy sheep fields and on to the rough ground, was the same as that marked as 'Saint's Road' on the 1846 OS map. But the field boundaries around it had shifted. Old walls had vanished, new ones had appeared. And all the way behind, past Gallarus and back along the green lane under Lateevemore, fields had changed, bogs been drained, plantations sprung up, dwelling places reconfigured. The fabric of the countryside had been woven and rewoven, over and over. But one thread had remained constant for a thousand years and more: a path intended for those moving across the land on foot.

* * *

The campsite-owner was right: the weather had changed. At the top of the rise, Mount Brandon reared into view. But it was not the same benign peak I had seen in the distance yesterday. The entire massif lay ahead like the carcass of a lion, a roiling froth of cloud skimming the sharpest point of its shoulder. There was rain in the air and seventy-kilometre-per-hour winds forecast for late morning. This was no day for a mountain pilgrimage, and at the bottom of the hill I turned away southwards, onto the Dingle road, then uphill into a narrowing glen past bungalows with crab pots and children's playthings in the gardens.

Beyond the last of the houses, a man in a green raincoat was coaxing a geriatric Jack Russell through its morning walk. He stood in the middle of the lane, looking back patiently as it waddled stiffly after him.

'You're a mighty man to be out in this weather!' He nodded at my backpack and the rain gear I'd put on at the bottom of the hill.

'I'm not so sure about that,' I said, halting alongside him and leaning heavily on my trekking pole. My feet were already throbbing from the last three kilometres on tarmac. The Jack Russell shuffled up and stood panting between us. I said that I'd planned to climb Brandon but had thought better of it.

He nodded. 'Ah, you're right; it's not the day for it. You've to respect a mountain like that.' He'd been up there on a bad day himself, he said, had heard other walkers, suddenly disorientated, calling in panic in the blanketing cloud. But the lower route I'd chosen across the 397-metre Mullach Bhéal pass was a good one, he said – 'Navigable, like' – with a view from the top to the lakes in the further valley.

The tarmac gave way to a broad ride between blocks of Sitka spruce. The rain turned suddenly ferocious here, and I ducked beneath sheltering branches. I shucked off my pack, settled myself on the carpet of fallen needles and took out my little saucepan and camping stove. I boiled water for coffee then heated a sachet of instant pasta for a mid-morning snack. I had a dried Spanish sausage from the Lidl in Dingle Town, and I cut a few slices with my penknife to add to the pasta. As I did so I felt a sudden surge of happiness, a pleasure in the little domestic tasks of a long journey on foot: the heating of coffee on a rainy mountainside, the washing of socks in the sink of a campsite shower-block, the unzipping of the first-aid kit to deal with a blister – the discrete sufficiency of it all. For as long as it took me to eat the pasta, the huge and uncertain distance between this place and Burr Point felt like a promise.

Beyond the last of the spruces: half-grown lambs, magpies and a wet wind from the west. The trail snaked back and forth towards the pass. Unlike the Cosán na Naomh, this was a built pathway, the switchbacks walled up with stone, the surface roughly cobbled. An information board back at the roadhead had said that this was once a major route across the Brandon massif for local communities, the Slí an Éisc, 'the Fish Way', used to carry fish and other produce in and out of the western peninsula. The inevitable humiliation of the recreational walker: a hardy mountain hike revealed as an everyday route for grocery shopping. But these days most people went by road across the Conor Pass, four kilometres further east, and there was no one else on the Slí an Éisc this morning. The pass itself was a cleft between black cliffs. The rain came flying sideways here and behind me Mount Eagle and the other western hills swam away into the murk. Below the pass, the wind dropped, and a rough track ran downhill. The country here had that peculiar scruffiness that sheep bring to a mountain – the reeds and the sagging fences, the widely scattered droppings. At the bottom of the slope, among stony traces of older settlements, was a farm – a ruined cottage, a low concrete house, rusty sheds and sheep pens. The place looked abandoned, but as I came closer, I saw two men, tinkering with a car. They raised their hands in unbothered greeting as I passed.

Below the Mullach Bhéal pass on what was once a major route in and out of the western Dingle Peninsula

Coming over the pass, and then all the way down the long valley beyond the ramshackle farm, I allowed myself a promise of a bowl of hot soup, a slice of brown bread, maybe a glass of Guinness. But when I reached sea level at Cloghane the pub was closed. There was a smell of low-tide seaweed and the village street was empty but for one old man with an impressively pristine set of new teeth. He caught at my elbow as I passed and asked eagerly if I was going to the mountain, as if I might run him an errand on the way.

'I'm coming down,' I said, sorry to disappoint. 'And not from Brandon; it didn't seem like the day for it. I came across Mullach Bhéal.'

'Mullach Bhéal,' he said, vaguely, slightly sadly. 'I know it, I know it…'

Onwards into a sodden afternoon, across the greasy mud of a little estuary with razorshells splintering under my boots, through a field of excitable red cattle and on to the great expanse of beach at the inner edge of Brandon Bay. I'd been on tarmac since the foot of the pass, and my feet were throbbing. A reminder here of the other defining aspect of a long-distance walk, less pleasurable than making coffee under dripping conifers: hours and hours, entire days even, underscored by constant low-level pain. As I went on along the strand I thought about the different surfaces I'd walked on so far. Unyielding, unvarying tarmac was always – *always* – the worst. A stony track demanded sharp focus; but the constant tiny variations, the fact that no footfall was ever quite the same as the one that preceded it, staved off blisters – and prompted a constant firing of the synapses. But the most pleasurable surface of all was a path made only by the passage of feet across a field in a season when the soil still held a little moisture. Sand could go either way: too soft, and your feet bog exhaustingly with every step. But the sand here was nicely compact, with just a slight cushioning give.

The tideline was strewn with thousands upon thousands of dead spider crabs. They'd been torn from their breeding grounds in the bay and flung ashore during a recent northerly gale. A sweetish smell rose from their decaying carcasses. I came off the beach just before Lough Gill and picked my way east along a wet road. My rain gear had worked as far as Cloghane, but now I could feel the wet wicking up my arms and across my shoulders. At Castlegregory I went into a pub pungent with aftershave and noisy with weekend drinkers watching the rugby, and sat sheepishly in a corner eating lasagne and chips while the rainwater pooled on the tiles around my feet.

Marshland, flag irises, little egrets paper-white in the wet green, and three hares streaking away across a reedy field. The rain cleared with the evening and the tide slipped inland along a network of tiny creeks. Fourteen hours and thirty-eight kilometres from Gallarus, I hobbled into a campsite by the beach off the main road in Aughacasla. I could hear a small groundswell shushing onto the sand all through the night.

* * *

The waves were still shushing onto the sand in the morning, and a thin mizzle was falling. It was twenty-six kilometres to Tralee. Cold cloud smoked along the line of the mountains to the south, and the shore to the east was dotted with figures in bright rain jackets. A hooded crow picked at a dead dogfish by water's edge. I was on the Dingle Way now, and where it turned off the beach near Camp a local woman clutching a small white dog was chatting to a retired couple from Yorkshire. They were standing across the path and, instead of stepping aside, they simply made space for me in their conversation.

'They were just telling me that they're touring Ireland – in a van!'

'Our daughter gave us three weeks off from the grandparenting duties, so we just took off!' said the man. He had smooth cheeks and iron-grey stubble.

'And what about you?' the woman with the dog turned to me. 'You've a bit of an accent – just a little bit.'

They asked where I was going, and I was suddenly bashful, embarrassed by the planned extent of my journey, the hubris of it.

'Tralee,' I said. It was true anyway. I'd need to break off at the end of today's walk, go back to work for the week and pick up the thread again next Friday.

The dog woman nodded. 'It's a nice walk to Tralee. And you always meet lovely people when you're walking – the same interests.'

I felt a sharp sting in the tendons of my left knee as I climbed the steep lane to Camp, but it came to nothing, and a little while later I reached a long stretch of off-road trail following the muddy route of the old Tralee and Dingle Light Railway, closed in 1953. The mountains rose sharply to the right and I could hear the weekend traffic on the main road below. But the trail itself was a tunnel of wet foliage, nettles, ferns and montbretia at ankle level, rising to fuchsias and blackthorn at head height with an overcanopy of slightly sickly ash. At Killelton, the ruin of a tenth-century church stood in a clearing, an ivy-strangled holly tree alongside, hung with blue and white clooties. The blotched white lichen on the damp stonework, the muted birdsong and the faint scent of decay prompted an unexpected transportation: suddenly I was twenty years and 13,000 kilometres away, at a ruined forest temple beside a mountain road in Java. There would be more of these strange moments of transportation later in the journey, random flashes of other places, other lifetimes in the middle of an Irish bog or on a quiet country road. I could never make sense of them, never ascribe to them a significance or a meaning.

Where the Dingle Way turned uphill, away from the line of the old railway, I started to meet other walkers coming down in the opposite direction, a few hours out of Tralee on the first day of their hike. Thirtysomething American couples; a lone woman with earphones and a determined forward gaze; a posse of older Irishwomen, gossiping merrily as they went; and a young American man accompanied by an older woman all in pink, with pink trekking poles to match.

'How are you?' she asked with a tone that implied she really did want to know as I stepped wearily aside to let her past.

'Grand.'

'Grand! That's a good answer!'

But there was nothing grand about the state of my feet by this stage. The distance to Tralee – in view below now, a pale smudge on the far bank of the River Lee – seemed to grow the further I went, until at last the trail ended by a paddock with two shivering horses.

For a walker emerging from mountains in stormy weather, a

way ahead leading to low green country should bring a sense of relief, of the worst being over. But it didn't seem that way here. Of the eighty-one kilometres I'd walked from Dunmore Head, forty – just shy of half – had been on roads. On any long-distance walk elsewhere in Europe – and especially in Wales or England – that would be a terrible ratio. But here in Ireland it was probably the best I could hope for.

By the time I reached the bridge over the Lee at Blennerville, my feet felt like pulp inside my wet boots. I limped along the pavement. Traffic snarled past and a cold wind blew from the sea. It was election season, and the faces of candidates for county council and European Parliament seats grinned or glowered from every lamppost. Many belonged to newly registered parties with words like 'National' and 'Freedom' in their names, slogans demanding 'Ireland for the Irish' and talk of 'Our land'.

2

Forgive Us Our Trespasses: Tralee to Limerick

On a cold bright Saturday afternoon in early February 2013, a small crowd gathered beside the derelict station building at Abbeyfeale in the far southwest of Co. Limerick. There were maybe 150 people, mostly older folks, men and women, active retirees; woolly hats and brightly coloured raincoats, lots of hi-vis vests. It was fifty years to the day since the last passenger train had stopped here, en route between Limerick and Tralee. But the people gathered at the old station were less concerned with the past than with the future of the line. They were all supporters of the 'Great Southern Trail'.

In the decades since the railway had closed to traffic a few sections had been demolished to make way for new roads; the old rails had been torn up and the embankments had grown in thick with brambles and thorns. But the whole thing – a strip of land, fifteen metres across and a hundred kilometres long – remained the property of Córas Iompair Éireann (CIÉ), the state-owned enterprise that organises public transport in Ireland. In 1988, Shannon Development, an agency tasked with economic development in the region, commissioned a report on the possibility of turning it into a public trail. The original idea was that the trail would be less for cyclists than for 'the horse rider and the long distance walker for whom bridle paths and footpaths are non-existent'.[1] There was immediate opposition to the idea from some adjoining landowners and other residents, and in 1991 Shannon Development abandoned the project. But it was taken up by the dedicated local volunteers of the Great Southern Trail Action Group. They worked throughout the 1990s to turn the original proposal into an actuality, campaigning for official support and funding and doing much of the initial work of clearing the overgrown track, repairing bridges and erecting homemade signage. Since the early 2000s, Limerick County Council had got properly onboard and put €1.5 million into clearing, resurfacing and signposting a thirty-eight-kilometre stretch from Rathkeale to Abbeyfeale.[2] In the months before February 2013, they'd added another three kilometres to the total, bringing the trail right up to the Kerry border near Duagh. The Great Southern Trail campaigners hoped that Kerry County Council would soon follow suit and open up the next ten kilometres of the line to Listowel – and then maybe all the way to Tralee.

The people gathered at Abbeyfeale Station that Saturday afternoon were there to walk the new section, three weeks ahead of its official opening by the Minister for Transport, Tourism and Sport. And those with welly boots and tear-proof clothing planned to continue for another two kilometres along the undeveloped track into Kerry. Refreshments would be laid on in the pub at Duagh at the end of the walk, and transport back to Abbeyfeale had been arranged.

Before they began, the chair of the Great Southern Trail Action Group, Liam O'Mahony, spoke to the walkers. He had been part of the campaign from the very start, and before that among those calling for the preservation of the railway itself. He'd grown up close to the line in Barnagh. For an only child in an isolated rural home, the railway had been an object of fascination and connection. He learnt to count by totting up the passing goods trucks, and to tell the time by marking the regular passage of the trains. Even with the rails gone, he believed that the line should remain a shared community asset. The Limerick section, he told the walkers, was now complete, thanks be to God. 'But the trail is unfinished until the Kerry half is done,' he said. 'It's like someone with two lungs – one is operating, and the other is idle at present.' When O'Mahony had finished speaking, they all set off west, into the low slant of the winter sun.

It was a good afternoon for walking, dry and still, with views down across the valley of the River Feale. But while the walkers were gathering at Abbeyfeale, another group had mustered three kilometres to the west. Most were of a similar generation – people well over fifty. But there were far fewer women in this second group, and far fewer hi-vis vests. They were Kerry farmers with holdings along the route of the old railway. They had got wind of the organised walk, and they had no intention of allowing the participants to cross the county border. Over the years since the railway closed to trains, some had taken to using it as an access track for outlying fields; others wintered cattle there or used it as a place to stack silage bales; still others had simply left it to go wild. But all considered it their own, and now that there was talk of turning the thing into a public hiking trail, they planned to claim the land from CIÉ through the principle of 'adverse possession' – popularly known as 'squatters' rights'.* They certainly didn't want members of the public walking along it. Where the new surface on the Limerick side ended, they had erected a blockade of old pallets and affixed to it a red-and-white sign: 'PRIVATE PROPERTY – NO TRESPASSING'.

* * *

I first heard about the 2013 confrontation – which ended when attending gardaí declined to remove the obstruction and the walkers had to retreat to Abbeyfeale – from Michael Guerin, a retired town councillor from Listowel. A round-faced man in his late seventies with thick white hair, he had been involved in the Great Southern Trail campaign for years, and had also done his best to fight the blocking of long-established paths along the River Feale by landowners – though with little success. He was a keen amateur videographer and he loved documenting both wildlife and local community events on film. He'd been there that day in February 2013 with his video camera, and he pointed me to the YouTube link.

I met Michael at the 2025 annual general meeting in Dublin of Keep Ireland Open, the campaign group which – with minimal funds and a tiny membership – has spent thirty years quietly lobbying for better access to the Irish countryside. Their website states it plainly: 'In Ireland you have no legal right to step onto private land, including commonages, no matter how remote.' What they seek is 'a network of well-marked and maintained public rights of way to allow short walks to reach open ground and provide access to our rivers, lakes and seashores', and a 'freedom to roam

* Adverse possession is the legal principle through which it is possible to claim ownership of another's property simply through long occupation. The process is full of legal niceties: you must demonstrate that you have been in full effective *possession* of the property; simply treating a piece of land as if you had a right of way across it, for example, would not be enough. And you need to demonstrate that you *intended* to claim possession from the outset. In Ireland, the property must have been occupied for at least twelve years before an adverse possession claim can be made; and where the original legal owner is the state – as in the case of the Limerick–Tralee Railway – that extends to thirty years.

over rough grazing land – that is about 7% of our total land area'.[3] This is a model very similar to that provided by the Countryside and Rights of Way Act 2000 in Wales and England.

It was Michael's first time at the meeting. He'd been paying his annual twenty-euro membership for a while, receiving the sporadic email newsletters. But after his own years of local campaigning around Listowel, he 'wanted to see what it was all about' at a national level. So he had caught the train up from Tralee.

'My family wonder what I'm doing,' he said, 'heading off at my age!'

I had the feeling that he was a little disappointed: a dozen people scattered around a high-windowed meeting room, most of them of his own generation. 'If the young people aren't interested, what hope have we?' he said.

It was my second time at the Keep Ireland Open AGM. The previous year I'd come up by train from Galway on a bitterly cold Saturday in early March. Like Michael, I'd been curious. The meeting was in Tailors' Hall, a fine old building of weathered red brick on a backstreet in the Liberties. It had once been the headquarters of the Dublin Tailors' Guild and there was a list of guild-masters going all the way back to 1464 on the wall. Tailors' Hall had hosted the 'Back Lane Parliament' of the eighteenth century which sought an end to anti-Catholic discrimination, and it was later a meeting place for the United Irishmen. A portrait of Wolfe Tone in profile hung above the fireplace.

There were maybe twenty-five people present, spread thinly along the rows of red-upholstered chairs; mostly older folks, a definite whiff of the South Dublin middle classes, a few faintly English accents. The chairperson was the former Labour TD Robert Dowds, and he introduced the guest speaker, a retired county council footpaths officer from Shropshire. She was shocked by the access arrangements in Ireland, she said, coming, as she did, 'from a country with a right of way system where you can walk almost anywhere'. She explained how the processes of legislation and registration worked in Wales and England, how well-protected in law a right of way there was. As a council paths officer, she had overseen the 'Definitive Map', the legal record of public rights of way in her county. There were, she said, around 5,500 kilometres of public footpaths in Shropshire alone. A low gasp rose from the room at this, then subsided into a trail of tutting. In fact, she continued, in parts of Shropshire there were *far too many paths* – a mess of duplicated and unused routes that badly needed rationalising. More astonished gasps and head-shakes here. She was a landowner herself, she said, kept a smallholding with horses. There was a public footpath across her own fields. It simply wasn't a problem.

During the coffee break, I sidled up to her and asked what she thought of the current 'right to roam' campaign in England. She grimaced and glanced around conspiratorially, as if what she was about to say was embarrassing in these circumstances – which it was, I suppose. 'We have enough already,' she muttered; 'really, *we have enough*.'

A Fine Gael TD took the moment to explain her commitment to a walking route along the Liffey Valley and a young Sinn Féin council candidate from Wicklow told a story about finding an old dog-walking route across a field near his home abruptly blocked one morning. They were both in campaign mode for national and local elections later in the year, and they vanished immediately after the coffee. In the afternoon, Robert Dowds ran through the latest campaign updates, stories of blocked paths at Wicklow Head and Enniskerry and Bray (Co. Wicklow seemed to be the frontline of access conflicts). He talked of lobbying political parties for manifesto pledges, spoke of the value of letters to newspapers, struck a generally upbeat note. But as he was speaking, an Englishwoman called Judy – whom I'd met at lunchtime and who had been involved in a long campaign over a blocked coastal walk in Waterford – leant across and whispered to me.

'We won't win, you know,' she said. 'I've been involved in all this for years, and we'll never win.'

* * *

The morning had a familiar feel: the flatness in the light before the sun; the little cringe at the feel of factor-fifty sunblock on the line of my shirt collar; the promise of heavy sweat to come; and a faint smell of bad drains on the street outside the hotel. It was early starts during motorbike trips in Indonesia two decades ago I was thinking of – that strange interference from past journeys again. But I wasn't in Java or Nusa Tenggara now; I was back in Tralee, a week later and in better weather, hoping to make it all the way to Limerick along the line of the old railway over the long weekend.

After the 2013 standoff, CIÉ had asserted their ownership of the railway beyond the Kerry border – and later passed that ownership to Kerry County Council. Eventually, in 2022, another ten kilometres of what had become the 'Rathkeale–Listowel Greenway' opened for walkers and cyclists. The council also managed to open a separate greenway, starting at the other end of the line and taking in the first couple of kilometres of the old railway out of Tralee, then turning off on the short former branch line to Fenit at the mouth of the River Lee. This also opened in 2022 – and was immediately blocked to users overnight with a set of locked gates, presumably by a disgruntled adjoining landowner.[4] The greater part of the line between Tralee and Listowel remained undeveloped.

On this bright June morning, the first stretch of the greenway was busy with cyclists, dog walkers, women striding along with earbuds in. It cut a clean line through the Tralee suburbs – the sort of line that would have pleased Le Corbusier. The tarmac had a glossy, newish look but the banks on either side were thick with nettles, bindweed, buddleia. Car part shops; older housing estates with knobbly walls and mossy roof tiles; a couple with ladders and paint pots in a narrow front garden, starting in on a weekend project; and beyond the houses, the long bank of the Dingle mountains, a few scraps of cloud still snagged on the ridges. Gradually, the town fell away, and where the surfaced route to Fenit bent to the left, a new aluminium gate stood across the old Listowel line. Affixed to it was a sign: a stick figure inside a barred red circle and the words 'NO ENTRY'.

Here it was, then: my first knowing trespass. If I continued, I'd do so aware that someone had explicitly forbidden it – whether it was the council worried about health and safety or a farmer hoping to make an adverse possession claim. I stood there in the sunshine, pondering. All the way across the Dingle Peninsula I'd avoided this. Even where I'd cut across a field or ducked through a small plantation there had been no such sign and I hadn't *known* that the landowner would mind. I didn't *want* to trespass, didn't want my walk to be an act of performatively confrontational machismo. I wanted to slip through the cracks, find the places where access *was* permitted – or at very least not expressly forbidden. I wanted to cross the countryside on a determined route *without* confrontation, without my passage causing outrage, without it producing any conundrum of conflicting rights. That was the way movement along a public footpath should be, after all.

But I was overthinking things, it seemed, for as I stood there worrying, a woman in fluorescent leggings passed me with a friendly nod. She had two dogs – a border collie and a golden retriever. She ignored the no entry sign, slipped through the little gap at the end of the gate and vanished among the dock leaves and celandines. An unofficial path! A desire line kept open by local custom! I gave it a minute, then followed gratefully. The path was well worn, though it only lasted a kilometre, halting at an impenetrable thorn thicket. But this was a good start. I could see the dog walker in the distance, following a pale track out to a busy road.

This was the pattern for the morning. The line of the old railway ran close to the road. I'd pick my way along the verge, flinching at the traffic, then every so often I'd spot a promising gateway or clear embankment and try to get onto the track. But the undergrowth was usually impassable. At one point I managed a few hundred metres, wading through thick grass. But then I came to a 'no entry' sign and a set of very firmly wired fence panels and had to retreat. A little later I tried again and made it through a blockade of cut branches to emerge in a narrow field where a rusty signal pole was all that marked the line of the vanished rails. But on the approach to Abbeydorney the line was ever more fragmented. As in many parts of rural Ireland, the road frontage here had been carved up for building plots and in places houses seemed to have been built right up against the track – the fifteen-metre-wide strip of state-owned land absorbed into a tightly mown private garden. I gave up and stuck to the road.

A hot wind and an empty blue sky over heavy farming country; low hills away to the south and a sense of everything slowing towards a midday halt. In the shop at Abbeydorney, an old man in dirty wellies was collecting six hot dinners from the deli counter: slabs of greyish beef and gloopy mash in plastic trays. It was silage time. There were huge tractors on the roads, and all the corvids of the country were in uproar. Columns of crows spiralled and spilled over the land like the ash of giant bonfires.

* * *

It was three o'clock and my feet were throbbing as I approached Lixnaw. At the edge of the village, in the townland of Ballinageragh, a walled-off pathway – 'kindly donated' by a local family, according to a plaque – led between a paddock and a bungalow to a holy well in a whitewashed concrete courtyard. There was a concrete altar, and a concrete statue of the Archangel Michael, gently slaying a devil with an expression of profound regret. The archangel's skin was milky white; the devil had been newly painted brown. The well itself lay down a flight of steps, covered with a hinged blue lid. I lifted it and dipped my fingers in the cool, clear water beneath. The surrounding concrete seemed like an attempt to contain the well, as if it were something dangerously unstable. A framed notice proclaimed 'very strong healing energies coming from the ground', effective for 'cancer, motor neurons [sic], autism, cerebral palsy, cystic fibrosis, MS, ME, and all ailments of the immune system'. There were laminated cards explaining the correct way of 'doing the rounds': a Decade of the Rosary at each of five numbered points arranged clockwise around the well, with each point effective for a particular category of ailment; the Hail Holy Queen at the head of the steps; and the Prayer to Saint Michael thrice repeated beside the well itself. This should take at least an hour and was to be repeated three times over three weeks for an effective cure. But there was no one else at the well today, and I sat to rest in the cool shade at the back of the courtyard. The sky above was streaked with thin cirrus and the countryside beyond the walls gave off a low composite hum of big agricultural machinery on the move.

More than 3,000 holy wells have been documented across Ireland.[5] There is some scholarly debate about whether they are truly ancient places that have undergone a 'transfer from pagan to Christian worship',[6] or rather a much later manifestation of a popular Catholic counterreaction to the Protestant Reformation.[7] But they have certainly been an important part of folk religion for hundreds of years. They might be visited as part of a private ritual, or among crowds of other worshippers on an annual 'pattern day'.

Whenever I visit a holy well, a ruined oratory, a cromlech, a stone circle, I find myself asking: *how did people get here? Which way did they walk?* None of these places was originally a discrete site – as they sometimes are today, islanded in the middle of a private silage field. Their presence extended into the surrounding landscape through a splay of radial pathways. The scholar Celeste Ray suggests that during the harshest colonial centuries when Irish Catholics were systematically excluded from ownership of land, they may have 'retained a sense of ownership of sacred sites that they visited secretly'.[8] Their movement across the fields to a well or grotto continued discreetly, regardless of who held the title deeds, and thus confirmed a sense of communal possession.*

The wells themselves were sometimes reputed to have resisted the landlord class, their water refusing to boil in Protestant kitchens.

---

* There was certainly some formal legislation against 'superstitious' gatherings at holy wells from the colonial Dublin Parliament at the height of its anti-Catholicism in the early eighteenth century; but later hostility to well-side pattern days actually came mainly from the Catholic Church, concerned by the associated 'drunkenness and debauchery' (see Harbison, *Pilgrimage in Ireland*, p.230).

At Killanne in Co. Wexford, a well was said to have changed its own location after the landowner barred access to pilgrims in the 1600s.[9] A later access dispute was recorded by an Ordnance Survey employee travelling through Co. Offaly in 1837. He noted that a well dedicated to Saint Colmcille in the grounds of the Durrow Demesne had 'been very much frequented until within these 2 years past' when the owner, Hector Toler, the second Earl of Norbury, 'prohibited access to the place'. Toler was now also trying to prevent locals accessing a nearby church 'thinking it too annoying to have them come so near his court'. However, the locals were 'determined not to be prohibited', and just a few days before the Ordnance Survey employee's visit, they had broken down the demesne gates to hold a funeral at the church. Toler should have paid heed to a local legend. It was claimed that his predecessor, Herbert Rawson Stepney, had blocked the well in a clumsy attempt to end local pilgrimage sixty years earlier. On the morning of 9 June, the anniversary of Colmcille's death and the date of the annual Durrow pattern day, Stepney found that 'his house was filled up to the roof with water and not one drop of it would go out of the doors'. It was only when he unblocked the well and readmitted the worshippers that the flood subsided.[10] Hector Toller, however, seems not to have conceded, and in 1839 he was shot and killed by an unidentified assassin while walking in his own woods.[11] Access to the well and church reopened and was maintained until the mid-twentieth century when the last of the Protestant landlords sold the place to new Catholic owners. Locals assumed that denominational sympathies would guarantee continued access, but instead the gates were firmly locked once more and remained that way until the place was bought by the state in 2003.[12] These days, the Durrow well draws a crowd on 9 June once more.

The pattern day at St Michael's Well in Lixnaw falls, naturally enough, on Michaelmas, 29 September. In the late 1930s a seventy-year-old local man, Tom Lawlor, recalled that 'Plays of all kinds, tinkers, thimble men, "Maggie Sticks [a kind of target game]," Pie shops and Shebeens were general features of the pattern'. There were roadside dances too, with the music provided by travelling pipers, the last of whom, according to Lawlor, was 'McCarthy the Piper'. This may have been Thomas McCarthy of Ballybunion who died in 1904, supposedly at the age of 105. At the end of the Lixnaw pattern day, Lawlor reported, McCarthy would retire to a nearby farmhouse, where 'dancing music [was] carried on to the small hours of the morning'.[13]

There was a printed sermon on the wall beside my resting spot, from a mass at a later pattern day, in 1998. It began with a reflection on the days when wells were a practical source of drinking water, as well as a place of prayer. 'There was never a road to a well,' it read; 'always a path like here in Ballinageragh – an aisle like the aisle of a church'.

* * *

Three kilometres out of Lixnaw on a straight road. My forward progress now had its own unpleasant and perfectly rhythmical metre, each step an iambic foot of discomfort: *dull ache at heel, sharp sting at toes, dull ache at heel, sharp sting at toes.* I was wearing the same model of cheap hiking boots I'd used for years. I preferred them to the more expensive brands precisely because they were soft, didn't need breaking in, gave me no trouble on long walks. I once took a brand-new pair to Morocco, still in their box, and wore them for a week-long trek in the Atlas Mountains without getting a single blister. But they were not designed for Irish roads. Rebecca Solnit suffered similarly, attempting a long-distance walk in Cork and Kerry in the early 1990s and discovering that to move on foot 'continuously along an extended contiguous stretch of land' in Ireland 'was not nearly as alluring as it looked on a map'. After three days of road walking, her feet 'felt like twin larks, these fragile metatarsal fans of bone being flattened and splintered more with every step'.[14] I'd had a week's rest after Dingle and was only nine hours into this next stage, but my own feet already felt like roadkill crows. *Dull ache at heel, sharp sting at toes.*

Where the road bent slightly, there was a field gate without any forbidding signage. I could see the line of the old railway just a few steps beyond it. Out of pained exasperation I climbed the bars, rolled under an electric fence, and found myself, for once, on a beautifully passable stretch. The line of the vanished rails here had become a green lane between hems of ash, sheeny yellow with celandines at ground level. I walked along it in a small blizzard of insects, then came to an old rail bridge across the River Feale. The river was fifty metres wide here, and the planking of the bridge was worn and springy underfoot. But the steel girders were solid. At the far side I sat down in the grass, took off my boots, and attempted a repair job on my blisters with a needle and some medical tape. The sky was taking an evening paleness at its edges and a breeze ran in from the northwest, wrinkling the surface of the river and stirring the yellow flag irises on the banks. Cattle lowed somewhere across the water.

I imagined for a moment that this had been the whole day: grass and soil and creaky bridges and places to rest in the green at the side of the path. But if that were true, I wouldn't have the medical kit and needle out of my pack. It was hard to hold off a sour resentment that even this narrow thread of notionally public land had been nibbled away, contested, barricaded, made mostly impassable. It was hard not to be resentful when the track vanished into a bank of thorns a few steps further on, and I had to return to the tarmac. Hard, too, not to be resentful on the approach to Listowel an hour later when I made a final attempt at a stretch of the track that had looked like it might be passable on the map but led only into a jungle of brambles and added two pointless kilometres to my day's walk. And it was very hard not to be resentful of the signs in the roadside gateways: 'Private Property', 'No Entry', 'Private Land', 'No Trespassing'.

* * *

What does it mean to 'trespass'? The concept behind the signs on the gateways was obvious: bodily entry without permission onto land held exclusively – literally *exclusively* – by someone else. But this was not the 'trespass' for which those doing the rounds at Lixnaw sought forgiveness, five times over, as they circuited the well.

In its original Latin, *transpassare*, the word does imply physical movement: 'to pass across' – though without any obvious suggestion of transgression (which in turn simply means 'to go across', *transgredi*, in the Latin root). But by the time it had passed, via Old French, into Middle English, 'trespass' seems mainly to have meant an act against a person or their chattels, their portable possessions. It entered the language of prayer during the Protestant Reformation through the work of the Bible translator William Tyndale. Earlier Latin and Greek versions of the Lord's Prayer typically asked forgiveness for 'debts' or 'sins'; but Tyndale made it 'And forgeve vs oure treaspases eve as we forgeve oure trespacers' – though he surely wasn't thinking about illicit entry onto private land when he did so. This raises an interesting question: did such a concept even exist in centuries past?

The very first path-makers, moving into a landscape which no one had ever previously crossed, did have a kind of freedom to roam (though they may not have felt that way themselves). But from thereon, individual pieces of land had particular human connections. During your daily round of hunting and gathering, you probably moved through country associated with your own community. But a longer journey – a seasonal migration, say – might require you to cross territory associated with other groups. That movement, then, was a kind of negotiated right; and it was important that it didn't interfere with other rights attached to the same territory – to fish or forage or build a homestead, for example. Indeed, this is how a public right of way still functions in the twenty-first century.* As hunting and gathering gave way to mobile pastoralism, and then to settled agriculture – probably around 6,000 years ago in Ireland[15] – the number of communities and individuals whose rights and claims were potentially implicated in a journey increased dramatically. But some possibility of movement across land that was not your own had to endure – to enable a mountain pilgrimage on a far-off peninsula, for example. Other rights associated with land, meanwhile, tended to become increasingly exclusive. Sometimes they were claimed by a group; sometimes they were claimed by an individual. In early medieval England, for example, all flotsam and jetsam cast up on the shore belonged to the king – though that didn't stop you going for a walk on the beach. But few land rights were truly universal.

Campaigners for a so-called 'right to roam' in England often use an idealised vision of 'common land' in their rhetoric, as if the whole country was a giant public park until the dastardly landlords carved it up for their sheep and their pheasant shoots. But most of the rights attached to individual patches of common land in Wales, England, Ireland and elsewhere were highly exclusive – and still

* There are, in fact, a few modern instances where the presence of a right of way *does* impact what the owner can do with their land. Under the Welsh and English system, a farmer is supposed to not keep a bull from a dairy breed – a Friesian or Guernsey, for example – in a field crossed by a public footpath. Bulls from the less aggressive beef breeds such as Herefords and Aberdeen Anguses are permitted.

are, where commons survive.* Even within a single community, not everyone had commoners' rights. Those with the lowest social status, or with the wrong type of employment or tenancy arrangement, might be excluded. And an outsider attempting to graze cattle or gather firewood – or, indeed, to practise the medieval equivalent of 'wild camping' – on a common might suffer violent punishment as a result. But on the other hand, the very existence of commons suggests that the concept of landownership itself as absolute and exclusive, equivalent to the possession of chattels, has not been around forever. Instead, there was a matrix of different rights, which different people might claim. A medieval English common was usually in some sense 'owned' by a feudal lord whose own tenure devolved from the Crown. But that ownership did not alienate the right of certain local peasants to cut turf or herd pigs there.† But what about walking? Did an outsider who *didn't* bring a cow, and *didn't* stop to gather firewood, have a right to walk across a common – or indeed a non-common? And how would an order not to 'trespass' have been understood in the pre-modern countryside? In Wales, England and other parts of Europe it is hard to say, for these were generally customary matters, seldom formally recorded;

---

* In medieval England there was also a category known as 'common waste' where rights were more or less universal. But it was the very poorest and least productive land, and it only amounted to a small proportion of the whole (see Patrick Galbraith, *Uncommon Ground: Rethinking Our Relationship with the Countryside*, 2025, p.22). In Ireland, the category of land known as *dírann úas cách* ('undivided land above all') or *an slíab coitchenn* ('the common mountain') may have had similar status – though the rights there seem to have been restricted to the freemen of the local polity, and extended neither to those from other territories nor to the local serfs (see Fergus Kelly, *Early Irish Farming*, 2000, p.406).

† A residual trace of non-absolute landownership occasionally surfaces when a piece of the countryside changes hands and the new owner discovers that others have confirmed rights to hunt or fish there, or that they have, in fact, bought a common where other people graze their sheep. In Wales and England, it also surfaces when the new owners of a country cottage discover that there's a public footpath at the bottom of their garden – a situation which does *not* arise under the much-vaunted and allegedly absolute 'right to roam' of Scandinavia.

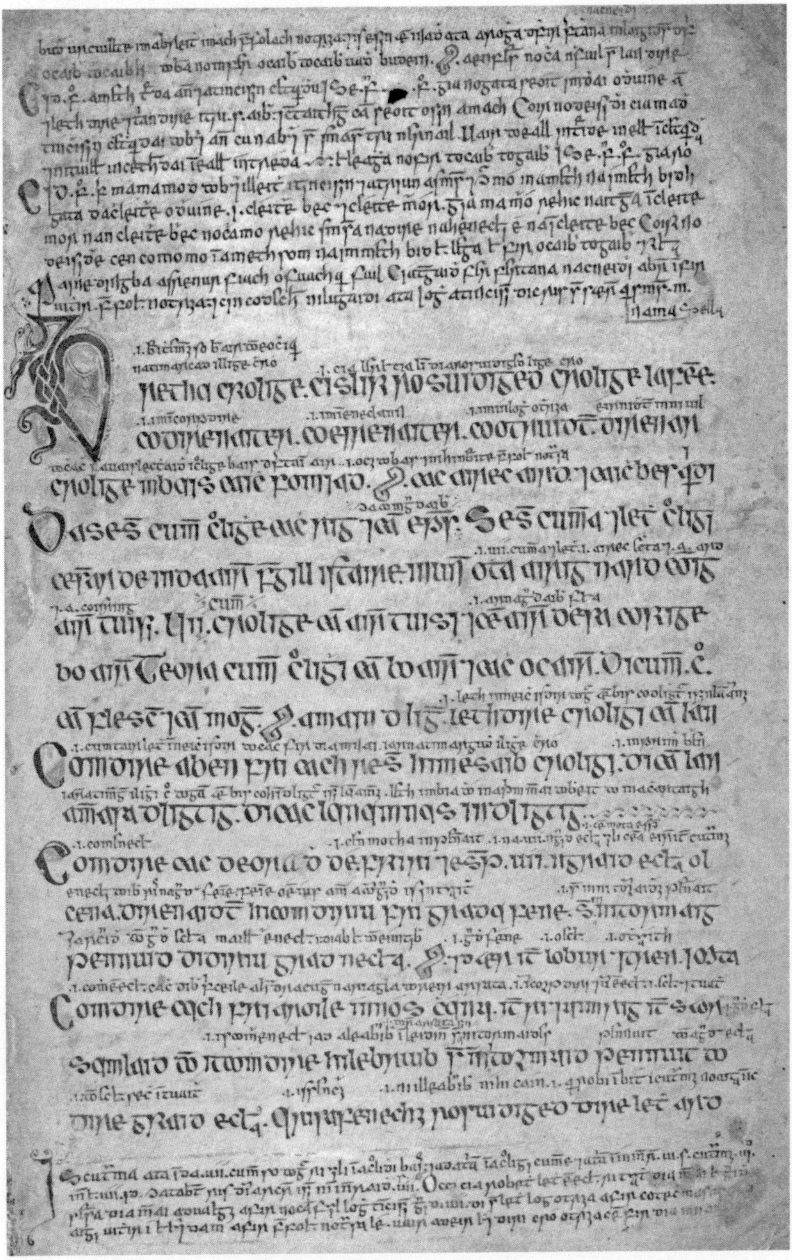

A decorated page from the *Senchas Már*, the single largest collection of old Irish law tracts, compiled in the eighth century and the legal texts that survive from the early medieval period are generally more concerned with the principles of kingship than with daily life. But Ireland is different, for a vast body of Irish civil law tracts survives, first recorded well over a thousand years ago. And they have rather a lot to say about 'trespass'.

The oldest surviving Irish law tracts were recorded in the seventh century, and they may have existed in oral form long before that. They are popularly known as the 'Brehon Laws' from an anglicised form of *breitheamh*, an Old Irish word for 'judge'. This is not the legislation of government nor of the ascendant Christian institutions. Instead, it is a legal framework for secular life, probably intended to be administered by a hereditary class of professional arbitrators (the *breitheamhain* or 'brehons' themselves). Ireland at the time had no centralised authority. Instead, the land was divided into over a hundred *túatha* or petty kingdoms. The three basic strata of society were the kings, the lords and the commoners. The commoners themselves were multiply subdivided into the free and the unfree. Near the top of the common pile was the *bóaire*, the 'cowman', a sort of yeoman farmer who held his own lands. According to an early eighth-century law tract, the *bóaire* was 'a man of three snouts: the snout of a rooting hog which banishes shame at all times, the snout of a bacon pig on the hook, and the snout of a plough under the sod, so that he is able to receive king or bishop or scholar or judge from the road'. The *bóaire* had a substantial farmyard – which would probably have been contained within what we'd now call a 'ringfort' – and kept a herd of twenty cattle.[16] Below the *bóaire*, there were smallholders, cottiers and the unfree serfs, tied by birth to the estate of a lord. The lands of the freeman commoners were ultimately granted by the lords, but there was no rent to pay.[17] Instead, the essential bond between the classes was clientship. This was a kind of mortgage system in which a lord granted capital – usually cattle – to a client farmer who made fixed payments in stock and service in return. The lord also undertook to defend the rights of the client.

Despite being controlled by no obvious central authority, the

Brehon Laws were remarkably consistent across Ireland. The Norman invasion of 1169 introduced a competing English system, but the Brehon Laws endured and at times resurged in parallel to church and English law. They were only fully abolished by the colonial authorities in the early 1600s.

The surviving legal manuscripts contain dozens of separate tracts, all penned before the ninth century. As the historian Robin Chapman Stacey writes, 'no other early medieval western European culture produced a body of legal literature that even comes close to the Irish material in volume and sophistication.'[18] They run to astonishing detail on the minutiae of daily life, covering everything from road maintenance to children's games, and at their heart is a system of strictly defined fines for every imaginable civil offence. These could be levied in silver, but more often in livestock – the major unit of wealth in early medieval Ireland. An adjudicator might be required to confirm the final specific payment; but in the meantime, the claimant could formally distrain or impound part of the defendant's property – often the animal involved in a particular offence.[19] Distrained pigs were to be shut up in their sty, sheep in their fold. Sometimes distrainment took on a more ritualistic manner. In the case of barren cattle, 'a stone is to be thrown over them thrice before witnesses', and in the distraint of a chained dog, 'let a stick be placed across his dog-trough, and a prohibition made that he be not fed.'[20] Ireland in the first millennium CE, it seems, was already a highly litigious society with an entrenched compensation culture.

In translation, the term 'trespass' appears frequently in the law tracts, used in the same sense as in the prayer: to describe offences against people and their things. In the original, this word appears in various forms, including *fogail*.[21] But there is an entirely different word – *caithchi* – which is also translated as 'trespass', and which explicitly refers to intrusion onto the land of another. But here's the interesting thing about land trespass in the Brehon Laws: it is almost always committed by an *animal*. There are lengthy passages on cow trespass, horse trespass, pig trespass, all of which have their requisite fines. There is even detailed legislation against trespass by bees. Crucially, however, all these animal trespasses involve damage or loss to the landowner. Trespassing livestock eat grass and trample crops; they break fences. Trespassing bees take the nectar of the landowner's flowers (though the Brehon Laws pragmatically avoid trying to legislate against that and restrict their attention to swarms). The occasional mentions of 'man trespass' seem mainly to refer to deliberate damage to crops and fences or violation of a distrainment. There are other offences against land: illegal mining, illegal sod cutting, illegal ploughing (unsurprisingly, a farmer was forbidden to plough his neighbour's fields). However, as the senior scholar of medieval Irish law Fergus Kelly notes, though there are references to the 'offences of hunting, fishing or food-gathering on private land', there is 'no suggestion that a person's mere presence is counted as an offence'. In fact, 'it looks as if a person crossing another's land may even acquire legal entitlements'. A passer-by who found a trespassing swarm of bees on another's farmland, for example, was entitled to a third of the honey.[22] There were also some eminently sensible limitations when it came to landowners' liability, and an onus on the walker to avoid injury while crossing private land. A passer-by who was attacked by a cow in *meracht a nuídlechais*, the 'madness of her newly-calved state', for example, had no claim for compensation against the landowner (unlike the owner's employees, who could expect 50 per cent of the standard compensation for any injury sustained in the attack).[23] And there were also clear protections of personal privacy: the apparent medieval right to roam did not extend to the immediate domestic space around the homestead. Anyone who entered a private yard without permission was trespassing, and if they went so far as to peer through the open door of the house, they risked a hefty one-cow fine.[24]

When I first came across these regulations – reading Fergus Kelly's book on the agricultural aspects of the early Irish law tracts, *Early Irish Farming*, at a quiet desk on the top floor of the university library – I was immediately struck by how sensible, how modern and how *familiar* they were. But my excitement quickly gave way to a familiar weary disappointment, a dutiful stifling of resentment: 1,400 years after the laws were first recorded, attitudes in Ireland are very different.

The supposed threat of litigation seldom arises in discussions of countryside access outside Ireland. But it *always* comes up here: *lads would be getting sued the whole time if they let people walk on their land.* At first glance, this seems a reasonable fear, given the remarkable prevalence of personal injury claims in Ireland in recent decades – and the astonishing size of some of the payouts. As well as the countless claims for trips and slips in shops and restaurants, there have been several cases related to countryside access. In 2019, a woman fell from her own horse while riding with a fox hunt in Co. Laois and took a High Court claim for compensation against both the hunt and the owner of the land they were crossing.[25] Still more notorious was the €40,000 award granted to a walker who gashed her knee after a fall on a boardwalk section of the Wicklow Way in 2013 and sued the National Parks and Wildlife Service for damages. Had the initial court decision stood, it would have had a chilling impact on public access to state-owned land like the Wicklow Mountains National Park. Fortunately, it was overturned on appeal[26] – and the High Court judge threw out the fox hunt claim.

In fact, landowner liability has always been strictly limited and was limited still further by a 2023 'voluntary assumption of risk' amendment to the 1995 Occupiers' Liability Act. Just as under the Brehon Laws, a landowner has a greater duty of care to an employee, or to someone they actively invite onto their property as a visitor. But their liability is minimal for a recreational user (or, indeed, a trespasser) crossing the land. That user voluntarily assumes the inherent risks involved in moving through the countryside. Indeed, to be successfully sued, a landowner would essentially have to *deliberately* injure a walker – or at very least knowingly expose them to a wholly unjustifiable risk.[27] There appears *never* to have been a successful case against a landowner by a recreational user since the original 1995 Act. However, it seems that very few people in

Ireland are aware of this, and the chimera of litigation arises every time countryside access is discussed. The other common refrain is, 'How would *you* like people wandering through your own back garden?' But again, just as under the Brehon Laws, the 'right to roam' provided by Scotland's Land Reform Act, Scandinavian *Allemansrätten* and access land in Wales and England *never* extends to the area immediately around a private dwelling.*

As for 'trespass' itself, in most places today it is a civil, rather than a criminal, offence – unless there are aggravating factors such as violence, deliberate damage to property or an ongoing campaign of individual harassment. This means that 'trespassers will be prosecuted' is generally an empty threat. An aggrieved landowner would need to take a civil case, and there would be little realistic prospect of successfully doing so against someone simply crossing the land on a country walk. In Ireland, however, there is a particular nuance. In 2002, the Housing (Miscellaneous Provisions) Act added an amendment to an earlier Criminal Justice Act, which criminalised anyone who might enter and – crucially – also *occupy* any land, and those who might 'bring onto or place on any land any object'. The notes about the meaning of 'object' made it clear what this obscure formulation was really about: '"object" includes any temporary dwelling [...] and an animal of any kind or description'.[28] This was legislation specifically targeting Ireland's tiny but much-maligned Traveller community.[29]

* * *

'Yeah, they'd have trouble with that,' he said with a roll of his eyes.

His name was Andy – a tall, dark-haired man with an accent

* Just about the only public access mechanism that does occasionally allow entry onto the fringes of domestic space is the Wales and England footpath network. It's not unusual for public rights of way there to run through farmyards – something virtually unheard of elsewhere. And occasionally they even run through private gardens. A householder can apply to have such a path reasonably rerouted in the interests of privacy, but it is an onerous process.

that seemed to waver between South London and South Africa, though it turned out he was originally from Jersey. He ran a bicycle hire business in Listowel, and I'd just asked him if he knew anything about plans to extend the greenway along the route from Tralee that I'd tried to walk the previous day.

'They claim there's a thing called "squatters' rights"', he said.

'Do you mean the houses built on the line?'

He rolled his eyes again. 'In Jersey you'd go to jail for that. You can't just *take* land that's not yours.' As Andy told it, you'd go to jail for rather a lot of things in Jersey – including being homeless and trying to claim asylum in the mistaken belief that you were in the UK. But he had a point. 'What makes me laugh', he said, 'is that they'd have had to get planning permission for those houses, so the council would have signed off on every one of them. And who's supposed to actually own that land now? Kerry County Council!'

Greenways on state-owned former railways are the closest thing Ireland has to a national footpath network. At its greatest extent in the 1920s, the rail network amounted to around 5,630 kilometres of track across the island. But most of the regional branch lines were closed during the twentieth century. This left several thousand kilometres of defunct track, still slicing long-distance across the countryside beneath a fuzz of overgrowth, and much of it still notionally in state ownership. The first full greenway to open was the Great Western Greenway in 2011, running between Westport and Achill Island in Mayo. It brought an estimated €7.2 million of increased visitor spending to the area within its first twelve months.[30] The forty-six-kilometre Waterford Greenway opened in 2017 and had a quarter of a million users in its first year. There is always a flurry of hostility from local landowners whenever a new greenway enters the planning phase, but the network has continued to grow: the Athlone to Mullingar Cycleway, the Boyne Greenway – and, since 2022, the Rathkeale–Listowel Greenway. Andy had been one of the first to take advantage of its business potential.

I'd limped miserably into Listowel the previous evening, against a heavily perfumed tide of locals heading for the racecourse. I was too weary even to nod in acknowledgement at the statue of John B. Keane on the main street. But I'd recovered somewhat overnight. It was the weekend, and the weather was good, so Cara and Róise had driven down from Galway to meet me. We'd spent the night at a busy campsite outside Adare, cooked sausages on a portable stove, had a couple of warmish bottles of beer. Róise bounced on the air mattress, and I complained about my blisters. In the morning, we'd driven back down to Listowel and met Andy in a car park near the river to collect two bicycles and a trailer for a toddler.

It was an uphill pull to begin with, through suburbs of neat white bungalows with laurel hedges, and then we were out onto the newest section of the greenway. It bent gently along the northern slopes of the valley of the River Feale, slicing through cool cuttings, green with ferns and overarching sycamores. It was Róise's first experience of cycling, and she sat bravely braced in the trailer – though she decided every couple of kilometres that it was time to be towed by a different parent. We weren't the only people out on the greenway this morning. A woman overtook us with three little boys, pedalling furiously on BMXs. Two older men came trundling past in the opposite direction, riding side by side in deep conversation. And every so often a sleek road cyclist flew past with clenched fists and bowed head.

At the old station in Abbeyfeale, where the walkers had gathered ahead of the face-off with the farmers in 2013, we bumped into Andy, waiting to collect bikes from other clients at the end of their ride. Cara and Róise took the opportunity for a lift back to Listowel in his van, and I pedalled on alone in the early afternoon heat. There was a depth in the countryside here: thick hedgerows, fat Herefords grazing in pairs in yellow meadows, a scent of silage – all of it out of bounds. My feet were off the ground, but I was still aching from the thirty-nine kilometres I'd covered the previous day, and as the land rose towards Barnagh, I found myself slowing to a wobbly crawl.

Ireland's greenways are always billed as 'multiuse trails', and 'hiking' is usually mentioned as a key activity in their literature. And I *had* seen a few dog walkers, a couple of hi-vis striders, where the route passed a village. But greenways are designed for cyclists, and the 'green' of the name is entirely figurative. The earliest Irish greenways were simple in their construction – a surface of tamped gravel on the old railbed and a bit of regular field fencing on either side where necessary. But more recently they've turned into multi-million-euro mega-projects complete with landowner-baiting compulsory purchase orders where no old railway is available. The Rathkeale–Listowel Greenway had a hard black surface, flanking fences, metal bridges and signs instructing you to dismount ahead of the road crossings. I was glad it existed, for sure; and I was glad to have been out with my family for a while on a bright June day, surrounded by fields and away from roaring trucks and speeding cars. But the greenway wasn't a *path*; it was still, ultimately, a strip of state-owned tarmac. And it would still have done just as much damage to my feet as the road if I hadn't been on a bicycle.

The hillsides on the final climb to Barnagh had a sun-bleached look, a faint hint of Spain. I passed a family – mother, father, two little boys – cycling in the opposite direction, and was absurdly lonely for a moment, though we'd another night booked at the campsite and a plan for a takeaway supper from the Adare chipper that evening. There was a busy café at the top of the rise, a bike-hire place, a children's play area and a long view over the flatlands in the northeast. Then it was a downhill run through tunnels of green foliage, past Newcastle West and Ardagh in the lengthening light, to a car park at the edge of Rathkeale where Andy was waiting in his van to collect the bike.

* * *

What would have happened if, instead of calling the gardaí, someone had raised a seventh-century *breitheamh* to deal with the stand-off outside Abbeyfeale in 2013? I suspect there would have been a few one-cow fines handed out, in any case. And the whole affair would probably have hinged on how the Brehon Laws categorised the old railway itself, what manner of 'road' they declared it to be.

The law tracts certainly deal with roads, and they subdivide them with characteristic precision. One text defines five specific categories, in descending order of importance. The largest road type was the *slige*. This name is connected to an Old Irish verb meaning 'to cut' or 'to fell', so it may have originally meant a path cleared through the woods[31] – a 'ride', perhaps. But by the time the law tracts were penned it meant a highway, which had to be wide enough to allow two chariots to pass freely in opposite directions, each drawn by a pair of horses. Below the level of a highway there was a *rout* (road), a *lámraite* (byroad), a *tógraite* (curved road) and finally a *bóthar*, a cow track. Another text lists seven road types, again with *bóthar* as the lowest. A cow track had to be wide enough to accommodate two cows, one standing lengthways and the other sideways. This was to ensure that a cow with an accompanying calf and yearling could comfortably pass another cow coming in the opposite direction.[32] By my reckoning, that measure comes to around two and a half metres – which makes the Rathkeale–Listowel Greenway a *bóthar*. But a cow track is *not* the smallest route across the countryside. It has its own diminutive: *bóithrín*, 'little cow track'. This is a word still in common use today as 'boreen' – the sort of narrow rural road on which you hope not to meet another car. And below *bóithrín* again, there must have been mile upon mile of simple footpath – *casán* or *cosán* in Old Irish[33] – leading to holy wells and churches and markets. The scholar Linda Doran argues that rather than 'thin strips of land with physical boundaries', many of the roads of medieval Ireland may themselves have simply been 'rights of way, sometimes with legal and traditional status'.[34] But the early law tracts make clear that the routes they discuss *did* have physical infrastructure requiring maintenance. Client farmers were obliged to mend local roads ahead of a visit by their lord, clearing ditches, filling potholes, cutting back encroaching vegetation and mending adjoining fences.[35] But a footpath tends *not* to have built infrastructure; it is maintained only through use.

Doran describes roadways as 'an ever-present but largely invisible feature of the history of medieval Ireland'.[36] But this seems an even more apt description of footpaths: hundreds of kilometres of them, enmeshing the countryside but now vanished on the ground and largely invisible in the archive. Their existence is barely hinted at here and there. Stiles are mentioned in the law tracts, providing pedestrian access to the fields.[37] And a fragmentary tract mentions a fine in silver for stealing a fistful of corn while walking on a path by a cornfield.[38] But footpaths themselves seem to have lain largely beyond formal legislation. At first this seems strange. These were laws that went so far as to differentiate between which sports injuries were ineligible for compensation (there was no pay-out to be had for an injury sustained at hurling, leapfrog, juggling or sandcastle building).[39] But there may be a simple explanation: as far as the people of medieval Ireland were concerned, the pathways through the woods, along the field edges, across the hillsides and over the ridges were an incontestable fact of nature. It would have been as futile to formalise them in law as it would have been to legislate against the trespasses of the bees.

This has probably been the universal norm throughout history: footpaths and general pedestrian access to the land lying well beyond the bounds of formal legislation. Public footpaths in Wales and England only crept into recorded common law via individual cases in the eighteenth and nineteenth centuries,[40] and only gained a proper footing in the statute books with the 1949 National Parks and Access to the Countryside Act and its successors, culminating with the Countryside and Rights of Way Act in 2000. Sweden's famous *Allemansrätten* may have existed as a custom since at least the medieval period, but it was only in 1974 that it entered the statute books and only in 1994 that it was enshrined in the national constitution.[41] It is reasonable to assume that of the millions of kilometres of footpaths functioning as public rights of way around the world today, the vast majority still have only customary status. And if public access to the countryside is confirmed only by custom, it is vulnerable – especially in a place where control of the land has been brutally and bitterly contested.

* * *

It had struck me forcefully during my second Keep Ireland Open AGM, with Michael Guerin sitting in the row behind me.

Peter Murtagh from the 'Friends of the Cliff Path' campaign in Greystones – the old seaside resort and commuter town, thirty kilometres south of Dublin – had the floor. There was a long-established coastal footpath running between Greystones and the neighbouring town of Bray, closely following the line of the railway around Bray Head. It had been in use for more than a century, had attracted around 300,000 walkers a year. But after a minor rockfall in 2021, Wicklow County Council had erected galvanised fortress gates and formidable 'no entry' signs at either end – even though they didn't seem actually to own the land. A council official had told concerned locals that 'that path is never reopening on my watch'. There'd been a social media campaign, stickers in the windows of local businesses losing out from the lack of walkers. Someone had bent back the bars of the gates far enough to let people scramble through, and there'd been a guerilla effort to clear the path of brambles. The Tánaiste, Simon Harris – who happened to be a TD for the local constituency – had got involved, but the council was still sticking to its guns. They'd been arguing for four years now. It was all fascinating, frustrating. But suddenly it struck me with a jolt: all this energy, all these hours and weeks and months of effort, all these calls to politicians, letters to the press – they were fighting for *just five kilometres of coastal footpath*.

There is another coastal footpath very close to my homeplace in Cornwall. You can get to it via a short right of way down the shallow valley below the house, and it runs through the strip of rough grazing between the final field boundary and the sea, on land owned by one of our neighbours. If you turn right when you reach it, you can continue along it for 400 kilometres, all the way to Minehead in Somerset; and if you turn left, you have 600 kilometres of almost unbroken right of way ahead of you. My head spun for a moment, and then I was back in Tailors' Hall.

'To the best of our knowledge,' Peter Murtagh was saying, 'the coastal walk is a right of way…' There was a mumble of dissent from the floor, and he opened his palms pragmatically. 'Well, it's contested as to whether it's a *public* right of way, but we think it is a *right* of way…'

'It's *not*,' I heard someone whisper to my left. I turned to look. It was Judy, the woman who'd told me last time that they'd never win.

This was all very strange when I thought back to last year's speaker from Shropshire, with her talk of definitive maps and *too many* paths. I asked one of the committee members at lunchtime: why wasn't it even possible to say definitively whether something was a public right of way? And why would something that had been regularly walked by the public for a century *not* be a right of way? Was there even such *thing* as a public right of way in Ireland?

'Ah, well! There *is*…' he paused and smiled ruefully. 'It's case by case; you have to go to case law, even back to English common law, to try to prove it's a right of way.' This, I realised, was exactly how things had been in Britain in the nineteenth century, before public footpaths gained proper status in the statute books. But there was a key difference: in twenty-first-century Ireland, the judgements seemed usually to go *against* the public.

In Ireland, as in other countries, you can – in theory – prove that a path is a right of way by demonstrating an established history of use without hindrance. But by one official reckoning, instead of simply gathering statements from a few locals confirming that they've been regularly walking that way since the early 2000s (as might be the case elsewhere), in Ireland you'd need to show that the path has been in public use 'since time immemorial'.[42] This is a very specific timeframe carried over from English common law: 'time immemorial' is the period before the end of the reign of Henry II in 1189. You might just about claim the route up Croagh Patrick as a right of way by this method, for the first written record of pilgrimage there dates from 1113 – but that's about it. A more likely basis for a claim is a 'dedication' – a statement issued by an owner permitting permanent and unlimited access across their land which should, in theory, endure even if the property changes hands. But proving the existence of a historical dedication is tricky, and court cases in recent years have set an impossibly high threshold of evidence.[43] It is extremely difficult to prove the existence of an old right of way in Ireland, no matter how long people have been walking it.

* * *

Grey and cool with a thin threat of rain in the air as we packed up the tent the morning after cycling the greenway. Cara and Róise dropped me back at the Rathkeale car park, waved me off and headed away north towards Galway. I'd be home to them by bedtime, all being well, breaking away from the walk for another week. But first I had to make it to Limerick.

When I first began to ponder a cross-Ireland walk twelve months earlier, the satellite images on Google Maps had shown a promising prospect here. A few kilometres north of Rathkeale, the old railway from Tralee joined another line, running between Limerick and the port at Foynes on the Shannon estuary. This line had only closed to freight traffic in the year 2000 – not quite long enough ago for it to have been carved up, built on, rubbed into the surrounding fields. On Google Maps, you could clearly see the old rails and sleepers, still in place. During the COVID-19 pandemic, Cara and I had walked another defunct railway in similar condition – the twenty-five-kilometre stretch from Athenry to Tuam, closed to freight in the 1990s. There'd been a few badly overgrown sections, and the span of the sleepers made for a slightly uncomfortable gait. But it had given us a rare chance to move on foot across a low-lying, agricultural landscape in Ireland. But since the last satellite image capture, everything had changed on the Limerick–Foynes line. It had been recommissioned for freight; the scrub had been cleared, the old track torn up and the ground re-levelled in readiness for new rails. There were earthmovers and JCBs at large, chained fence panels and very serious 'no entry' signs. I was facing another day on tarmac.

Somehow, it didn't sting as much as the first day out of Tralee. I *knew* I'd be entirely on roads this time, and I'd stick to the quietest lanes, the boreens, moving gingerly to save my feet. I'd cross the recommissioned railway three times, pass the stump of a castle like a broken molar in an empty field, see the fly fishermen below the bridge on the River Maigue whipping the sluggish water as if to rouse it to action. Coming into Limerick there'd be shopping complexes, roundabouts, lonely bus stops and shuttered pubs, a persistent whiff of cannabis and the rain beginning in earnest. At one point – near Cloonaduff, I think it was – a man with iron-grey hair and work trousers, pale with cement dust at the knee, greeted me as I passed a half-built house and asked where I was going. For the first time since Dingle, I overcame my bashfulness, said just Limerick for now, but then sketched out the bigger plan.

'Do you know the road? Ah, you do – you've a map. That's a grand plan – fair play!' And then, as if he wanted to make some kind of contribution but couldn't think what to offer: 'Do you need the toilet or anything?'

But before all that, I had to pass through Rathkeale itself.

There was a big church on a hill, and a flyer on a lamppost demanding the reinstatement of the Eighth Amendment of the Irish constitution, which outlawed abortion until 2018. Nearby, the litter of a wake the previous evening was spilt across the pavement. A black wreath on a white PVC door; dozens of empty Budweiser bottles on a plastic table beneath a tatty gazebo; a laminated image of the deceased, grinning and flashing his thumbs, thirty years old. A little further on I passed a young man changing the alloys on a souped-up car at the roadside. He gave a friendly nod. I was registering something here, but not yet processing the data.

Then the main street, and this was a very different place from Adare, twelve kilometres away. No thatched cottages, no tour buses bound for the Ring of Kerry. The place was grey and silent; a derelict cinema, boarded-up shops, everything closed except the tanning salon and the convenience store. There was no one about except for two young women, chatting outside the shop with a two-litre bottle of Coca-Cola positioned on the steps between them like an icon. Further on, I passed a guard, moving along the pavement with a slight swagger. I nodded, but he did not respond. What was the story here? Why wasn't I decoding what I was seeing? Then at the top of the street four big caravans crowding a little close, one with UK plates. And finally: *of course*. Rathkeale was a town with a large Traveller population. I remembered reading about it now: lurid tabloid headlines; the influx of returnees from Britain and Europe at Christmas; a place where some members of the 'settled community' claimed to have been forced out – though generally by the curious compulsion of Traveller families offering well over market value for their houses.

I walked on and out of the town on a quiet road. I was faintly unnerved, bothered by both my own slowness to register what I saw – and then by my having registered it at all. Hadn't I been here for more than a decade? Didn't I pick up on most of the cues, recognise the regional accents, code-shift successfully when I flew from Newquay to Dublin? Shouldn't I have identified exactly what sort of place Rathkeale was as quickly as someone raised in Ireland? But then, in working it out it even belatedly, was there a danger of adopting the sort of prejudices to which an outsider ought rightly to be immune – of striking a Faustian pact in the interests of belonging?

3

Between the Woods and the Water: Limerick to Portumna

Remember this. Remember it later, labouring along a busy Midlands roadside in the rain, wondering why you ever started on this journey. Remember it later still, at your desk or behind the wheel of your car, bearing the mundane worries and sadnesses that come, inevitably, in these middle parts of life. Remember being here alone on this mountain, Moylussa, at the end of this day – the outrageous privilege and good fortune of it – and it will all have been worthwhile.

A perfect platform for your little tent among the reeds and stones and sheep shit; the hiss of the camping stove; coffee cooling in a steel mug and the warmth of jacket and hat after the sweat of the day. Below, Lough Derg, pale and many-limbed, running in from the north and narrowing back to the form of a river between Killaloe and Ballina where the houselights are coming on in the dusk. On the far bank, late sunlight lying on the western slopes of the Arra Mountains, thick-hedged fields lapping up towards forestry and heath. Further off, the dark hulks of the Silvermine Mountains, swollen to Himalayan proportions at this uncanny hour. And further off again, in the northeast, the lavender line of Slieve Bloom on the Laois–Offaly border. The land is suddenly vast and open, and you have an eternity to walk across it.

Remember this – if you can. And if that doesn't work, then at least remember that of the thirty-six kilometres you walked today, only sixteen were on tarmac.

* * *

Leaving Limerick had the feel of a proper beginning. University semester and school term were over now, and Cara and Róise were heading off with Granny for a holiday in Spain ('Are you really sure you don't want to come?'). I had a couple of clear weeks ahead – time enough to walk myself to fitness, to find the rhythm of the days and, I hoped, to make it as far as the border, if not to the very end of the journey. And I'd changed my footwear. On Cara's advice I'd bought a pair of fancy running shoes with thick, spongey soles and lightweight uppers – better suited, I hoped, to walking on roads. (My hiking boots were tied to the outside of my backpack in anticipation of at least a few mountains and bogs ahead.) I'd come down on the train, spent the night in vacant student accommodation near the docks, and set out in a thin smirr of morning mizzle.

Limerick always feels to me – a visitor – like a real city in a way that the other towns of the west of Ireland don't: the grid of central streets with their four-way traffic lights; the glass-walled hotels along the waterfront; the urban fringes with their buddleias and piles of scrap metal behind rough block walls. It is a river town, built by Viking settlers in the tenth century close to the upper tidal limit on the River Shannon, and even today it feels like a place that looks resolutely downstream, towards Shannon Airport and the estuary, away from the byways of the hinterland. But above Limerick, the river stretches upstream for 360 kilometres, all the way to an aquifer-fed pool in Co. Cavan. The Shannon would guide me northwards, into the Midlands, in the coming days.

The way out of town ran along the old Park Canal, built in the eighteenth century to carry water traffic across the peninsula formed by a long northwards bend of the river. The old towpath was tarmacked, busy with bikes and e-scooters heading in from the suburbs upstream, a few early joggers and dog walkers. In an urban area like Limerick, walkers and cyclists are given dedicated space in a way that they seldom are in the countryside: walkways through parks, alleys too narrow for cars, canal paths, the very pavements flanking the streets. There are probably more kilometres dedicated to pedestrians within Limerick City than in the whole of the surrounding county that shares its name. However, as a speaker at one Keep Ireland Open meeting I attended – the former Green Party TD Steven Matthews – had pointed out, even these may not always be true rights of way. The example he'd given was of a footbridge across a railway. It might appear to be a permanent feature of the cityscape, essential to thousands of daily journeys on foot; but the people who use it typically have no confirmed *right* to pass that way.

Where the canal rejoined the river, the path bent away to the right through a tunnel of sycamores. The tarmac gave way to well-compacted gravel. Five little shacks with whitewashed walls and crooked chimneys stood on the banks here with rowboats moored in the reeds below. This was once the highest point on the Shannon directly navigable from the sea. For ten kilometres upstream, as far as a spot called World's End near the village of Castleconnell, the Shannon winds through braided channels and modest rapids. A century ago, the winter flow here was a thunderous spectacle.

A visitor in 1923 described it as 'a miniature Niagara' where 'the Shannon is raging mad – racing, leaping, seething, foaming like a thing possessed'.[1] But today the river passes through Castleconnell at a sedate and artificially constant ten cubic metres per second all year round. Millions of litres – all the discharge of Lough Derg, the run-off of a thousand bogs and the contribution of myriad tributaries – have been spirited away.

Across a road bridge and past blocks of empty student flats half-swallowed by the summer greenery; along the line of another canal that once carried boats around the Castleconnell rapids, and on to a quiet road. Swampy meadows extended on either side, hedgerows grown into linear jungles, monstrous stands of giant hogweed twice my own height – the sort of country you could never 'roam' across without a path or a road. The mizzle cleared and the soundscape of the morning broadened: birdsong, dogs barking, distant agricultural machinery. And then, at the end of a long straight lane, a huge sheep-cropped embankment reared ahead. I scrambled up to the top and there below me in a wide, wind-ruffled channel was all the missing discharge of the Shannon.

In the late 1920s, the English travel writer H. V. Morton passed this way. The son of a Birmingham newspaper editor, he'd started his writing career in his father's newsroom, then rapidly moved on to Fleet Street, scoring a major scoop for the *Daily Express* with an eyewitness account of the official opening of the tomb of Tutankhamun in Egypt in 1923. But Morton's real success arrived in 1927 with the publication of *In Search of England*, a travelogue about his forays through the English countryside in a Morris Oxford car. It was a major bestseller. He followed it up with a similarly titled book about Scotland, and then turned his attention to Ireland. He was perhaps the first author to be properly famous *as* a travel writer, well ahead of Peter Fleming, Eric Newby and Bill Bryson. A new Morton travelogue routinely shifted 200,000 copies in the first edition, and he sold well over three million books in his lifetime. He was also – as private letters and diaries have posthumously revealed – a vicious antisemite and enthusiastic Nazi sympathiser.

Nazism, he believed, was the necessary 'first stage of a spiritual revolution'.[2] Many distressed fans have expressed surprise at the apparent disconnect between the warm and sensitive narrator of the books and the unpleasant attitudes of the actual man. But if you pay attention, you can spot the warning signs. Morton's emphasis in his travel books is often nostalgic; his search is for the pastoral and the picturesque. This, surely, is exactly why he had such appeal in the 1920s and 30s for a British readership largely inhabiting an industrialised urban world. He presented them with a comforting vision of the countryside – the mythical locus that people always convince themselves is threatened by liberal elites and the sinister forces of internationalism.

Unsurprisingly, Morton found much to appreciate in the Ireland of the late 1920s: the white cabins with green half-doors; the cattle herded through village streets. Less than a decade after the violent upheaval of the War of Independence and the Civil War, he claimed that in Ireland 'the candles of the eighteenth century are not burnt out', and that it was a 'country of herdsmen and horsemen' where there was 'no real pride in machinery'.[3] But on the lower reaches of the Shannon, he simply couldn't avoid the technological present. Somewhere near the spot at which I was now standing, Morton had 'looked down into a mighty excavation':

> an artificial valley in which men the size of flies swarmed over a rocky bed or stood on ledges working, tending strange bucket excavators and all manner of uncanny machines which moved on caterpillar wheels. The valley was criss-crossed by railway lines. German engines and German trucks full of rock moved busily down there.[4]

Morton was looking down into what would soon become the headrace canal for the world's largest hydroelectric power station.

The idea of an electricity generation scheme on the lower reaches of the Shannon had first been mooted at the turn of the century. But in 1923, a twenty-six-year-old engineer named

Thomas McLaughlin, who had worked on construction projects in Germany, approached the government of the Irish Free State with a fresh proposal. At the time, most of Ireland outside of Dublin and Cork was without mains power, but McLaughlin had an idea for a hydroelectric plant big enough to electrify the entire country.

The Shannon hydroelectric scheme became the ultimate prestige project for the new state. There was a certain amount of grumbling about the £5.2 million cost – more than a fifth of the entire national budget at the time. But the Shannon Electricity Act was passed in 1925, and work began four months later. The building contract went to the giant German engineering firm Siemens-Schuckert, with Thomas McLaughlin as managing director of the project. His plan involved damming the Shannon above the Castleconnell rapids and diverting the main flow into an artificial twelve-kilometre headrace feeding three huge turbines built into a second dam at Ardnacrusha, with a shorter tailrace below to return the water to the natural channel just north of Limerick. By the time of Morton's visit, the whole valley between Killaloe and Limerick was crisscrossed with temporary railways, strung with powerlines and humming with the sound of generators and machinery. Vast quantities of equipment had been shipped in directly from Germany – 30,000 tons of heavy plant machinery, 40,000 tons of coal and 400 tons of explosives, according to Morton's guide, a German engineer 'in a Norfolk jacket and tweed cycling knickers'. Four thousand Irish labourers and 300 German machine operators and engineers were working three shifts a day. Alongside the site were two temporary townships – 'Irish Town' and 'German Town', the latter complete with German schools for the workers' children and 'delicatessen stores in which you can buy liver sausage and Sauerkraut'.[5] Meanwhile, beyond the valley, work was underway on a national grid of powerlines and substations to carry the turbines' output around the state. Foreign commentary on the project tended to take a predictably patronising tone: to 'the white cabin whose inhabitants have never seen a bath', wrote Morton, had now arrived 'the possibility of heating water by pressing a button'.[6] But at its opening in 1929, it was the largest hydroelectric plant on earth and one of the biggest engineering projects of the 1920s. Throughout the mid-1930s, the Ardnacrusha plant supplied 80 per cent of the state's electricity needs. It is still running with modernised turbines a century later, but its contribution to current Irish electricity demands is just 2 per cent.[7]

As well as the displacement of millions of cubic metres of water – and a catastrophic impact on the salmon stocks of the river – the scheme brought radical changes to landownership and access in the lower Shannon valley. The 1925 Shannon Electricity Act and its follow-up legislation granted extraordinary powers – initially to the Minister for Industry and Commerce, Patrick McGilligan, and then, from 1927, to the new Electricity Supply Board (ESB). The 1925 Act allowed the minister to 'impound, hold up, divert, take, and use the waters of the River Shannon and any river or stream tributary thereto and any lake, pond, or canal thereon or connected thereto' and to 'embank, dam, dredge, deepen, widen, straighten, divert, and otherwise alter the River Shannon or any river or stream tributary thereto'. But it also allowed him to 'compulsorily acquire (either permanently or temporarily) any lands or premises' and to either compulsorily acquire, terminate, restrict, or otherwise interfere with 'any easement, way-leave, water-right, fishing right, or other right existing over or in respect of any lands, premises, or water'.[8] The twelve-kilometre headrace and the two-kilometre tailrace sliced through countless roads, boreens and footpaths and gobbled up entire farms. But the project also had an unexpected consequence for modern access.

When I first began to contemplate a route across Ireland, scrolling back and forth across the Google satellite images, I'd been unsure whether I'd find a way through here. After all, the embankments of a hydroelectric feeder canal are just the sort of place you might expect to find 'no entry' signs anywhere in the world. But once I got onto the ground and unfolded the map, I saw that the southern embankment was marked with a dotted red line identified as the 'Lough Derg Way'. And now, standing here at ten o'clock on a brightening morning with a soft breeze ruffling the water and a view of the twin church towers of Cloonlara in their thicket of trees two kilometres to the northeast, I found a small sign warning of eight-metre depths and fluctuating levels, but nothing to forbid my progress on foot. I could walk this way because these embankments were state land; and the state body concerned, the ESB, had *chosen* to permit public access.

* * *

The day unfurled gently under clearing skies. The sun came out as I passed Cloonlara, with a scent of freshly mown grass. A cormorant beat downstream, low over the water, and the big hills of Tipperary reared ahead. The 'Lough Derg Way' seemed little used. There was only the faintest darkening of the grass along the top of the embankment to indicate the passage of feet, and I saw only one other walker – a woman with incredibly long blonde hair, slapping along in flipflops outside O'Briensbridge, two tiny dogs trotting behind, one white and one brown. I came off the embankment here and sat for an hour in a village café with violet lobelias in terracotta pots and an avaricious rook prospecting for leftovers. I ate a panini and read H. V. Morton's account of the valley in the 1920s. A sound of lawnmowers drifted over the housetops.

Two kilometres upstream, I came to the upper dam at Parteen where the headrace canal splits from the original channel. The clouds had crept back in, and the breeze had stiffened. Small wavelets slapped against the greyed concrete of the dam and swallows skimmed across the water. I was sad to have to leave the embankment and take to the road. The ten kilometres along the water's edge had been good walking: a level, forgiving surface that allowed tiredness to gather gently without discomfort. The next five kilometres to Killaloe on a quiet road raised a faint ache in my heels and a powerful weariness, but no sharp sting this time – the new running shoes were doing their job.

Killaloe was caught in the perpetual five o'clock of a hot summer afternoon. I retreated into the cool silence of the thirteenth-century

Cathedral of St Flannan on its riverside ledge: a scent of roosting bats and old basketwork, the whitewashed walls greening in the corners. Like most of the older church buildings of Ireland – those that weren't destroyed or abandoned – this place had been taken over by the minority Protestant denomination in the sixteenth century. The plaques on the walls commemorated a vanished world: Purdons and Parkers and Ponsonbys; sons lost in the Napoleonic and First World Wars; and a medical attendant for the Killaloe dispensary who died in January 1848, exhausted by his 'exertions during a season of unparalleled distress'. It was still an active church, the current dean a woman.

The first Christian establishment at this pinch-point on the Shannon where Slieve Bearnagh and the Arra Mountains slope steeply down to the water is credited to the sixth-century abbot Molua, also known as Lughaidh or Dalua. He gives his name to Killaloe itself: *Cill Dalua*, 'Dalua's Church'. Molua was born a century after the arrival of St Patrick, when monastic centres were popping up all over Ireland. He built a monastery on a river island downstream from Killaloe (the island was submerged when the valley flooded after the construction of the Parteen Dam, and St Molua's Church was dismantled and rebuilt in the town). His disciple, St Flannan, became the first Bishop of Killaloe, and presumably oversaw the building of the original riverside cathedral here. It flourished for several hundred years, for this strategic crossing point on the Shannon was the seat of the Dál Cais *túath*, which was headed in the late tenth century by Brian Boru, the closest thing Gaelic Ireland ever had to a real 'high king'. He took the crown of Dál Cais after his brother's death in 976, and within a couple of years was claiming the overlordship of the whole Munster region. After a series of alternating conflicts and partition arrangements with the Uí Néill dynasty which dominated the northern half of Ireland, he eventually extracted an acknowledgement of outright over-kingship. But this did not make Brian Boru an all-Ireland king in the sense of a head of state with administrative control over a single block of territory.

Rather, he was the ultimate warlord in a warlord society[9] and after his death at the Battle of Clontarf in 1014, Ireland reverted to a ceaseless jostling of petty kingdoms. And then, in the following century, the Normans arrived…

* * *

I'd half-intended to find a B&B in Killaloe. But the long midsummer evening stretched ahead and my feet were doing nicely in the new shoes, so I pushed on, back out of town. Fuchsias in the thick hedges, red cattle in reedy fields and dark banks of conifers on the high ground ahead. Beyond the last hillside bungalows the tarmac gave way to a wet green lane that became a pale forestry track on a clear-felled pass. A steep trail struck away up the western flank of Moylussa, the highest summit of Slieve Bernagh at 532 metres. Now I really was tired, leaning heavily on my trekking pole and still in a muck-sweat despite a sharpening breeze. Eventually the trail levelled out on to the boggy crown of the mountain and became a narrow boardwalk of staple-studded timbers. It ended at a marker stone in an ulcer of mud. A huge round of country opened in all directions: the pine-darkened swells of Slieve Aughty running northwards, the white lobes of Lough Derg, the distant line of Slieve Bloom and the heavyset mountains of Tipperary closer at hand; and then in the northwest, beyond the defunct windfarm at Derrybrien and the blue whalebacks of the Burren, a faint suggestion of the Maamturks and the Twelve Bens, a hundred kilometres away in Connemara.

I'd thought that I was in that lonely part of the evening when a solo walker intent on sleeping outdoors is without human coeval. But Moylussa was a busy mountain tonight. As I rested at the summit, two young women in skimpy sports gear turned up with a pair of energetic black labradors. They were from Killaloe, had powerwalked up for the exercise.

'We're very lucky, having this on the doorstep.'

They asked where I was heading, and I explained, rather hesitantly, the full scale of my itinerary.

'Are you doing it for charity?'

'No,' I said, and felt immediately guilty. 'It's just for the challenge, really.'

When they'd gone, I retraced my steps to find a place to camp out of the wind. A lean man with dark hair and black-framed glasses was striding up the first stretch of boardwalk towards me. I stepped aside to let him pass, but he stopped and grinned at me.

'So, you must be the man who's walking from Dingle to Belfast. What possessed you to do a mad thing like that?' He'd met the two women heading down, and they'd told him about me. His name was Mike. He was an engineer. He'd been working in Killaloe that afternoon and was taking the opportunity to bag a few summits before heading home to Co. Cork. He seemed to possess an almighty surfeit of energy. When he'd finished on Moylussa he was planning to cross the Shannon and head up the mountain above the Graves of the Leinstermen in Tipperary. He'd brought a headtorch, expecting to be out in the hills long after dark.

'That's ambitious in one afternoon,' I said.

'Says the man walking to Belfast!' He'd been a great hillwalker in his twenties, he said, and then got back into it recently when his divorce proceedings started.

I found a perfect platform among the reeds below the trail for my tent. I boiled water for coffee then sat there with my arms wrapped around my knees, telling myself to remember this moment while a dinner of instant pasta bubbled on the stove. I spotted Mike, far below, heading for the next summit, then a dog walker in lime-green turning off the forestry track. A mountain biker laboured halfway up the summit trail then turned for the downhill run, and other transient voices drifted across the slopes, late into the evening.

* * *

'Top of the morning to you!'

It was such a preposterous greeting, delivered with a straight face, and he was such an improbable figure that I wondered for a moment if this was some kind of setup – an obscure joke arranged by Mike and the women from the summit the previous evening. It was before eight o'clock in the morning and there were no houses nearby. I hadn't expected to meet anyone here, let alone a Samuel Beckett lookalike proffering cod-Irish salutations in a soft American accent.

I'd woken in a coppery wash of early sunlight, Lough Derg molten below and a patina of dew on the mountainside. I shook the condensation from the tent, then headed back past the summit marker and onwards to a boggy track that ran down the northern face of Moylussa and into the dense blocks of forestry on the lower slopes. A dawn stillness lingered here and the birdsong was muted. A rabbit skipped across the track ahead of me, and a little while later a hare powered away up a side-cutting. I'd put my hiking boots on to cross the mountain, but where the gravel gave way to mossy tarmac I sat down on my pack to change back into the running shoes. And that's where he appeared, stalking up the lane with his hands folded behind his back: rake-thin and remarkably tall. He wore bright white tennis shoes, ill-fitting blue jeans and glasses with blue-tinted lenses. His hair rose in stiff white bristles. The Beckett resemblance was uncanny.

Top of the morning? What do you even say in response to that?

'How are you?' I mumbled.

He looked down from his great height. 'Ah. Changing the shoes.' Perhaps I was just as unexpected and inexplicable to him.

'I had those on for the mountain, but these are better for the road.' I motioned to the damp boots and then to my feet, trying to explain.

'I didn't even know there was a mountain here.' It turned out that he'd arrived in darkness the previous evening, straight from the airport. He was staying in a cottage a few kilometres down the road and had gone out to stretch his legs while his companions were still asleep. It was his first time in Ireland: 'It's so *green*!'

I asked if he was on holiday, but he shook his head. 'I do outreach work for my church.'

He lived in Fiji, he said. Decades ago, someone had gifted his 'spiritual teacher' a small island there, and they'd built a retreat.

The island had been a copra plantation before they arrived, and there were villagers. 'But we built them a new village and took over their old one. They are very happy with us. We all get on together.' He kept calling his organisation 'my church' – an American reflex, perhaps, which didn't have quite the same ring here in Europe. But I asked him its name and when I looked it up later it was a neo-Hindu thing, founded by a white rishi in California in the 1970s. I asked if Fiji was a good place to live.

'Oh, I love it.' There was a gentle sincerity in his way of speaking, a softness, a strange hint of melancholy. These days, he spent six months of the year travelling, promoting his church in Australia, Europe, North America. He'd be in Ireland for a week, was staying with members nearby.

'Do you enjoy the travelling?' I asked.

'Oh, I love it.' The same phrase, the same softness. But Fiji, he said, was home. 'I've been there for thirty-eight years – most of my life now.' He paused for a moment; and then, as if the realisation had come to him right there at the end of a forestry track in the west of Ireland: 'I was quite a young man when I went out there.' Something about the surprised, faintly mournful way he said this opened a small rupture in my heart.

He asked what I did for a living.

'Oh, how interesting! Is it Irish literature you teach?'

'Some,' I said, 'but not specifically. A bit of Joyce and that.' It would have been weird to mention Beckett, I decided.

'If I had my time again,' he said, 'I think I'd study writing.'

A couple of kilometres down the lane there was a ramshackle farmyard with a rusty blue tractor parked beside an asbestos-roofed shed, and across the road a cottage with a faintly hippyish look: windchimes and bright plant pots – the sort of place where followers of a Californian guru might live. *Top of the morning*, he'd said. *Is it Irish literature you teach?* I don't think he'd noticed anything in my own accent, hadn't known that we were both foreigners here.

The lane ran on down into the green country between the Slieve

Bernagh and Slieve Aughty uplands. Hedges thick with fuchsias, common vetch, honeysuckle; a warm wind shifting the leaves of the sycamores. Small decaying farmyards, beef cattle dozing in rumpled meadows and the lane a strip of blueish tarmac with weeds growing down the middle. This could almost have been the Cornwall of my childhood were it not for the stark white new-builds in road-front plots, the sporadic roar of Ryanair jets banking in for Shannon Airport and the fact that the ash trees were dying. 'Ash dieback' – the effect of a fungal pathogen *Hymenoscyphus fraxineus* – was first detected in Ireland in 2012, having arrived from mainland Europe. But this summer was the first time its impact had been impossible to miss. While the sycamores and hawthorns and elders and all the other plants of the hedgerows were in fullest leaf, the ashes had a wizened, sickly look. The fungus is airborne. It infects a tree through its leaves then chokes its internal xylem and phloem – the vascular system of the vegetable kingdom. An infected ash will rally anew each spring with a burst of regrowth around the lower trunk. But in the end it succumbs. The disease will probably kill most of the ash trees in Ireland within the next couple of decades.

I came to a white cottage at the roadside where two women – one in her sixties, the other much older – were setting bedding plants into the wall.

'Where are you headed?'

'Up towards Belfast, eventually.'

'Well!'

The younger of the two was glad to see that I was wearing running shoes: 'The road is awful hard on your feet in walking boots.' She'd walked the first stage of the Camino in Spain the previous year, couldn't wait to return.

'Join me on the way to Belfast now, if you like!' I said.

'Well, Ann,' she nodded at the older woman, 'will we?' And for a moment I thought they really might.

The map gave the name of this area as Caherhurly – a telling placename. And scattered across the sheet like chickenpox were tiny red circles. 'Caher' is one of several common placename elements indicating the historical presence of a ringfort; and each of those little red circles represented a surviving ringfort, still discernible in the twenty-first-century landscape. There were once at least 50,000 ringforts across Ireland, and the modern maps still record more than 40,000 of them. In places – and especially in the west – the land is so densely pocked with them that you can find half a dozen within a couple of square kilometres of farmland. Most have an internal diameter of around thirty metres. Those built of banked earth are usually called *lios*, anglicised as 'lis', or *ráth*, anglicised as 'rath' (I noticed a 'Rathbane' on the map, a few kilometres east of Caherhurly). Those built mainly of stone are called *caiseal* (anglicised as cashel) or *cathair* (anglicised as caher or cahir). The term *dún* and its anglicised variants turns up here and there too. Ringforts are not really forts – and certainly not military structures. They are simply the surviving perimeters of the homesteads and small farming communities that were once scattered across the countryside. The bank would probably have been topped with a fence or a ring of living thorn bushes (which had more to do with keeping the cattle in and the wolves out than with any endemic culture of violence). Within the protecting circle stood huts for the residents, pens for the livestock. When I later searched the detailed nineteenth-century map of the area for Caherhurly itself, it turned out to be a largeish ringfort, 700 metres north of the road. It was still there today, marking the junction of four fields and hidden beneath a small spinney.

The vast bulk of the ringforts that survive today were occupied in the second half of the first millennium CE. After that, for whatever reason, most of them were abandoned. People moved out, moved on. There are similar structures where I am from in Cornwall; and in places the Irish words come back out of the Cornish landscape like a muffled echo: *cathair* and *dún* and *lios* becoming *ker* and *din* and *lis* in Cornish. But the Cornish ringforts are older. They were mainly occupied from the Iron Age through to the Romano-British period. Around the seventh century, just as the peak of ringfort use in Ireland began, the last of them were abandoned in Cornwall, left as litter in the landscape as people resettled in unenclosed clusters of cottages and barns. These converse cultural shifts – into the ringforts in Ireland, out of them in Cornwall – are not properly understood by archaeologists and historians. But the change roughly coincides with the period of the Plague of Justinian – a terrible wave of bubonic infection, vectored by rats, which began in the eastern Mediterranean around 540 CE, and which surged and resurged across Europe for the next two hundred years. The plague killed millions and had pronounced impacts on trade, agriculture and politics. It seems reasonable to suspect that it may also have had an impact on the way people occupied the Irish and Cornish landscapes.

Much is made today of the supposed protection afforded to old ringforts in Ireland by superstition. So many of them survive, it is said, because country folk consider them the dwelling places of the fairies. Indeed, they're sometimes called 'fairy forts', and to damage one, so we're told, would be to invite a curse. But old things get left in any landscape. A small earthen bank hardly interferes with the grazing of cattle; and even when the land is given over to tillage it might be easier to plough around one small and stony irregularity than to level it out. People sometimes needlessly invent rationales for the actions of their forebears, then half-ironically adopt them for themselves.

But it is certainly true that ringforts, with their readymade perimeters, their sense of an established place, were sometimes used as burial grounds for unbaptised children. This is another feature that shows up frequently on even the modern 1:50,000 map – not a symbol this time, but a tiny red-inked word: *cillín*. The name means 'little graveyard', and there are around 1,700 of them recorded across Ireland, mostly in the west – Cork, Kerry, Clare, Mayo and, above all, Co. Galway where there are 480 recorded *cillíní*. They became a constant quiet presence from the early seventeenth century as the Catholic Counter-Reformation hardened the church position on older Canon Law.* An unbaptised or stillborn child, destined for an eternity in Limbo as far as the clerics were concerned, was denied burial in the consecrated graveyards. So *cillíní* developed as an informal alternative.

Not everyone buried in a *cillín* was an unbaptised child. Adults deemed ineligible for a resting place in consecrated ground might end up there too. The cost of official interment or the distance to the nearest proper churchyard might have been other reasons for a *cillín* burial. And surely many children whose entire existence was kept a private matter went into these quietly accepting places, these small pockets of sadness secreted in the fabric of the countryside. Some were still in use until the 1960s, when the Second Vatican Council, Pope John XXIII's liberalising ecumenical congregation of church leaders, finally took the cruellest edges off Catholic teachings.

Most of the *cillíní* you see recorded on the maps lie within farmland, and as with the holy wells, I find myself wondering: how did people get to these places? How did they move across the land towards them? The archaeologist Marion Dowd – she of the 12,000-year-old bear bone – points out that *cillíní* are sometimes found close to a topographical boundary – a cliff edge, a field corner, a crossroads; liminal places – and that burials usually happened at night. It was typically the child's father or some other male family member who undertook the solemn task, moving alone through the darkness. These journeys, Dowd writes, 'must have been laden with shame and anguish', and the darkness allowed for 'a private outpouring of grief'.[10] But it also heightened sensory inputs other than sight: the sound of the breeze through the thorns, the unevenness of the ground beneath slow-moving feet, the chill of the night air on wet cheeks. The path to a *cillín* needed to be readily navigable in low light. It might make use of a field boundary,

* The marked prevalence of *cillíní* in the west of Ireland may be because of the influence there of the Franciscan Order, who were firmer in their interpretation of Canon Law than the Jesuits who dominated further east.

a stream, a ridge as a guideline, discreet but unmistakable. And the embankment of an old ringfort provided a particularly clear indication that you had crossed the threshold of a space consecrated by time and custom, if not by ordained men.

If you come across a *cillín* today, you'll sometimes find the ground within its perimeter stippled with small, upended stones: simple markers scratched out of the soil itself in the process of digging a grave under cover of darkness. Perhaps a story about fairies is an easier explanation for a taboo on destroying ringforts than an unspoken understanding that there might be tiny children buried there.

* * *

Midday heat in Tuamgraney – the kind of weighted heat that only comes of a day that also contains rain. I stepped off the road to rest in the cool silence of St Cronan's Church. The western nave had bare walls and a visitors' book. It was built in the mid-tenth century on the site of an earlier monastery, probably established in the early sixth century as part of the flurry of church-building up and down the Shannon, centred on the great riverside monastic centre at Clonmacnoise. The working part of the church was in the chancel – a simple Romanesque barn of a place with high rafters, added in the twelfth century. This was another ancient church annexed by the Anglicans. There was still a service here on the fourth Sunday of each month, which reputedly made it the oldest church in Ireland in continuous use.

Onwards into Scarriff, past the ruined workhouse and the fishing-tackle shop and the Spanish-owned chipboard factory. The breeze had gained an ill-tempered edge and I could sense the coming rain. There was something slightly sad about the village – though it might have just been the weather and my growing weariness after the long morning of road walking. An old man in the shop nodded at my backpack and trekking pole: 'You're heading to the mountains. You'll be wanting a drop of poitín for that.' Instead of poitín, I got a coffee from a café across the way and sat to drink it on a bench in the square. A silver-haired German woman waiting for a prescription from the pharmacy sat down beside me and asked, in a rather interrogatory way, where I was going. I asked in return if she lived here in East Clare.

'Only for ten years,' she said, with a certain defensiveness. I knew that there were many German residents in these hills, in renovated cottages and self-built chalets on quiet boreens among the Sitka spruce plantations – mostly older people now, though many had been quite young men and women when they came out here. I often wondered what it was they'd been looking for in this part of Ireland – and whether they'd found it.

'Can you tell me', I asked, 'why so many people from Germany have ended up living around here?'

'I don't know,' she snapped; 'I don't talk to the other ones.'

I'd been presumptuous, asking her to generalise about an imagined community to which she did not believe she belonged. I smiled apologetically. 'I'm sorry. But why did *you* come here?' She could have simply thrown the question back at me. Instead she muttered something about 'being individualistic'.

'I was in Kerry before I came here; but it became too touristic.' She stood up abruptly. 'I think my prescription will be ready now,' she said and marched off. I did look rather touristic myself, I realised, with the hiking boots tied to my backpack.

The afternoon grew heavier, darker, as I followed a quiet lane that curved northeast along the outer flank of the next range of hills. There were bungalows with laurel-hemmed gardens to the left, and wild strawberries in the hedge to the right. I stopped to pick a few, hoping that the tiny gobbets of sweetness would power me on to the roadhead. As I approached the last of the bungalows a little white dog, something like an albino Yorkie, came skittering eagerly towards me, then stopped abruptly, gave an outraged half-bark and retreated towards a woman standing in the road outside the house.

'He thought it was Sean. I said, "There's Sean coming now!" and away he went; but we were wrong about that, weren't we?' She was in her fifties, with short dark hair. I was the second walker with a backpack and camping gear she'd seen in recent days. Last week it had been a man from Ennis, heading for Gort across country.

'And he'd left his phone behind and everything, wanted to be out of contact for a few days. Not very sensible, like – I hope you've your phone? You have? Well, that's good, now. He came to the door looking for water. He'd looked on Google before he started and he knew this was the last house to get his water bottle filled. Would you be needing water? Would you like a cup of tea?'

This was her husband's homeplace, she said. She'd been here for twenty-five years but had only really explored the area for the first time during the COVID-19 pandemic.

'I've four boys,' she said, 'so it was good not to be dropping them off everywhere all day long for once. I did a loop for exercise' – she waved a hand in the direction of Lough Derg – 'down into Mountshannon. And I got my husband to cut a track up onto the land, up onto the bog, like. There's great walking here. My husband is a hillwalker. He'd go away down to Carrauntoohil; but I say there's no need for that; we've it all on the doorstep. Are you sure you don't need water, now?'

She asked why I was walking, and I tried to explain about the countryside where I'd grown up – the mile upon mile of public footpath through the fields. She recoiled slightly, a small backward jerk of the head.

'Oh, very different, *very* different.' She made it sound as if I'd described something obscene. 'You can't do that here. That would be *trespass*!'

The rain came on at the edge of the open ground and I sheltered for half an hour in a gimcrack shed full of mouldering hay and empty feed-sacks. When the weather cleared, I went on along a rutted track. An old man came past at the wheel of an ancient Massey Ferguson with bowed axles. He saluted me gravely, and a little while later I saw a distant figure footing turf on a tawny slope. And then I was across the Clare–Galway border and out on to the high ground of the Slieve Aughty range: a tussocky sweep of purple moor grass sliced abruptly by dark walls of spruce. A male hen harrier, battleship grey, erupted from the heather and whipped away eastward. Fragments of lark song carried in the roaring air and there were deer slots everywhere. This was open country that you could, just about, 'roam' across, high-stepping over the tussocks. But you'd certainly default to any available path, and I found myself following deer tracks in search of a sheltered place to camp. A mid-moor outcrop marked by a lone lodgepole pine looked promising. But there was a very active badger sett beside it in a garden of bright green bracken, and I didn't want to disturb the inhabitants. It was nearly ten o'clock now. The light was fading and the wind was fierce and wet. It pushed me on eastward, reluctant but unresisting, into the gloom of the forestry. I pitched my tent by a log-pile at the head of a stony track with darkly regimented spruces soughing and creaking in every direction.

* * *

The Slieve Aughty range is a huge and boggy blot, rising from the banks of Lough Derg and stretching for around twenty-five kilometres west towards Gort, north towards Loughrea and south towards Scarriff. The range doesn't really deserve the name 'mountains': it is a series of broad ridges underpinned by old red sandstone, blunted by past glaciation and topping out at the 400-metre mark.

In 1887, an American journalist travelling through the area to report on the rent strikes, evictions and general agrarian unrest then unsettling the Irish countryside – and we'll get to these topics later – described an incredibly barren landscape:

> Around us are low, long rolling hills, flecked with every color from orange to bluish black, closely spotted with gray heaps of stone and chequered with bare stone walls; beyond rise higher hills, golden brown against a silvery sky; and in the valley are long peat dikes and one tiny patch of emerald grass, with two cows and a few solitary sheep. Each successive amphitheatre of hills is more barren and

> more stony than the last. Stones lie on every side as thick as in an ancient graveyard or a glacier moraine, and where the stones are fewer there is bog.[11]

But Slieve Aughty doesn't really look like that today – and nor did it look that way in earlier centuries.

The name – *Sliabh Eachtaí* in unanglicised Irish – is linked to the myths of the Tuatha Dé Danann. These stories were first recorded in the early medieval period by Christian scribes who gave them a quasi-historical gloss, though it is often claimed that the Tuatha Dé Danann actually represent the religious pantheon of pre-Christian Ireland. In mythical fragments, Echtge Uathach, the daughter of a Tuatha Dé Danann king (there's some confusion about exactly which one), was gifted the hill country west of the Shannon by her suitor, a royal cup-bearer named Fergus Lusca Mac Ruidi. The hills thus took her name: *Sliabh Eachtaí*, 'Echtge's Mountains'. Fergus had land aplenty, but no livestock, and Echtge brought him two cows as a dowry. He placed one on either side of a river, close to what is now the main road across the range from Gort. In time, the cow that grazed on the southern bank produced three times as much milk as its northern counterpart and so Fergus was able to identify the most fertile part of his holdings. The river is still called the Owendalulagh, from *Abhainn Dá Loilíoch*, the 'River of Two Milk Cows'.[12] An Ordnance Survey official in the late 1830s recorded a version of this story, and noted that the locals pronounced the name of the range 'as if it were written Slia Bacht-te'. He thought this was 'a remarkable corruption',[13] but it is very much how people still pronounce 'Slieve Aughty' today.

Throughout the nineteenth and well into the twentieth century, Slieve Aughty was a largely treeless expanse. But the abundance of placenames with the prefix 'Derry' – from *doire*, 'oak grove' – plainly suggests that this was not always the case. A fourteenth-century chronicler wrote of 'Echtge's dense woods of lofty foliage pleasant and fresh', and the eminent early twentieth-century antiquarian Thomas Johnson Westropp gathered solid placename and archival evidence of 'the enormous oak forest that, even in the fourteenth century and certainly down to Tudor times, ran round the flanks of Aughty, and covered the lower slopes of its hills'.[14] What happened to this vast woodland is part of a millennia-long saga of deforestation in Ireland.

The popular modern myth has it that the first humans arrived in a land entirely blanketed with woodland, much of it now claimed as 'Celtic Rainforest'. This sylvan paradise endured until the arrival of English colonists who, in the Elizabethan era, rapidly destroyed the lot – partly to build their own warships and partly to deny Irish rebels a hiding place. This is an oversimplification. As the incised bear bone from the Ennis cave proves, the earliest humans in postglacial Ireland actually arrived *ahead* of the trees, and their successors lived through long centuries of afforestation, which peaked between 8,000 and 6,000 years ago when around 85

In the imagination of the Tudor-era colonial authorities, Ireland's woodlands were an ungovernable haunt of rebels, such as Ruaidhrí Óg Ó Mórdha, the Lord of Laois, depicted here hiding among the wolves of the forest by John Derricke in his 1581 book, *The Image of Irelande, with a Discoverie of Woodkarne*

per cent of the place was covered with trees.[15] The lengthy process of deforestation then began – some of it humanmade as land was cleared for agriculture, some of it caused by the encroachment of oxygen-poor blanket bogs, which was at least partly prompted by climate change.

Though periodic shifts of population and climate allowed for temporary reafforestation, by the Bronze Age, woodland cover was probably down to around 50 per cent. And the process of reduction continued. By 1600, only around 12 per cent of Ireland was wooded – a situation similar to that in England in the same period.[16] A rapid bout of deforestation got underway at this point, but little Irish timber ever went into English warships, and far from enthusiastically destroying Ireland's woods, the Elizabethan authorities actually attempted to control the exploitation of what they recognised as a valuable resource – though with little success. The tremendous upheavals in landholding patterns produced by colonialism encouraged asset-stripping. The sustainable coppicing practices used in English woodlands were never deployed here. Instead, individual colonists and private companies disregarded official edicts and clear-felled their Irish holdings to produce pipe staves and construction materials for export. Surviving Irish landholders with little faith in the future did much the same.[17]

Much of the initial destruction of the Slieve Aughty oakwoods – as elsewhere in Ireland – was to provide charcoal for iron-smelting, 'with an extravagant disregard for the future supply position', as one historian puts it.[18] In the eighteenth and early nineteenth centuries, meanwhile, a rapidly increasing population and changes in the farming patterns on the bigger holdings pushed increasing numbers of people into once sparsely populated upland areas like Slieve Aughty. In fact, between 1770 and the eve of the famine in the early 1840s, numbers of rural dwellings increased five times faster on the less fertile uplands than on the long-settled and cultivated lowlands.[19] Small farmsteads sprang up in mountain valleys, and the land around them was cleared for fields. The unbroken higher ground, meanwhile, was used for booleying, a form of localised transhumance in which cattle were taken out of the infield and on to the high commons during the summer months to make space for crops and haymaking. It seems to have mostly been young people, and especially teenage girls, who went to the mountains with the cattle and stayed in the rough booley huts while the adults remained below to work the fields.[20] The booleys were a blurry, liminal zone between home and away, the cultivated and the uncontrolled, childhood and adulthood – a place of long summer evenings after the milking and butter-making was done. You can see their traces in Slieve Aughty today in a few ruined hutments and a scattering of placenames: Boleyneendorrish, Boleycurheen, Boleybeg. The agricultural settlement of the uplands rapidly did for the surviving hazel and birch scrub.

By the 1790s, as little as 1 per cent of Ireland may have been wooded.[21] Today, however, forest cover is back at late Tudor levels – around 11 per cent. But this is very different woodland to that described in the annals and echoed in the placenames.

The first attempts at commercial state forestry in the 1890s were unsuccessful, but a properly organised forestry programme got underway the following decade and survived revolution and civil war. Between 1922 and 1939, the government forestry service planted some 24,000 hectares of commercial woodland.[22] The pace of planting accelerated in the second half of the century, and by the 1980s over 5 per cent of Ireland was under forest – and 78 per cent of that total was owned by the state.

Today, Coillte – the semi-state forestry enterprise established to take on all government forestry concerns in 1988 – owns 7 per cent of the entire landmass of the Republic of Ireland. But it's a very particular 7 per cent. The financial and emotional premium placed on farmland in independent Ireland, and the limits on the price the forestry service was allowed to pay for land in the early decades, meant that only the least agriculturally productive parts of the countryside could be acquired for afforestation. The flurry of late twentieth-and twenty-first-century tree-planting took place almost entirely on the bogs and mountains, land ill suited to dense tree growth. Foresters cut drainage channels on waterlogged slopes and plough the scraw into what look like giant potato ridges. These are then planted with fast-growing North American conifers – Douglas fir, lodgepole pine, and above all Sitka spruce (which accounts for more than half of all Irish woodland).[23] The planting is done at an incredible density – up to 5,000 seedlings per hectare – to ensure long straight trunks. Spruce plantations are thinned at fifteen years, and are ready for final harvesting from thirty years. The standard approach at this point is clear-felling. An entire block of forestry is lopped down and hauled away, leaving a grim waste of stumps and stripped branches, which is abruptly replanted with the same species – a practice originally demanded by the 1928 Forestry Act, which required owners to replant all land within twelve months of felling.[24] Commercial conifer plantations are relatively effective for carbon sequestration; but they are terrible for biodiversity. And they are grim places to spend the night alone in a small tent.

* * *

It was a cold awakening, with rain spattering thinly on the tent and the spruces swaying and moaning outside. I packed up and pulled on my wet weather gear and headed north.

Slieve Aughty is one of the largest chunks of the Coillte estate in Ireland. Well over half of the whole range is under commercial forestry, and the map here is patched with angular dark green blocks, interspersed with smaller shards of open country. This makes it one area with good public access to the countryside – in theory, at least. Though Coillte is still a commercial operation first and foremost, these days it makes much of its secondary role as a provider of public recreation, with various gravelled trails in designated 'forest parks', and a 'Woodlands for Health' programme. It was Coillte who installed and maintained the boardwalk to the summit of Moylussa.

I was far from any officially gazetted 'recreation site' here, but I wasn't trespassing: Coillte claims to apply 'an open forest policy which means everyone is free to visit any of our forests according to the Leave No Trace Principles'. This, then, makes a fragmented 7 per cent of the Irish countryside notionally open to the public – a proportion only slightly smaller than that part of England designated as access land. But there's a crucial difference which Coillte makes plain on its own website: 'All access to our forests is by permission only'.[25] There is no *right* to walk the forestry tracks or to stumble over the clear-felled hillsides. As on the ESB-owned banks of the Shannon, this is permissive access, granted at the owner's discretion and apt to be arbitrarily withdrawn. It creates a certain subtle dynamic, knowing that you are accessing the countryside only on sufferance: it emphasises the idea of land as a kind of chattel in which all rights lie exclusively with the owner. A Keep Ireland Open member explained to me that a Coillte official once told him they had 'no interest in creating rights of way' – and why would they in a culture where landownership is always absolute?

This is the other important point that the permissive access arrangement on Coillte land reveals. Coillte is a semi-state body, as are the ESB, Bord na Móna, the Office of Public Works and the National Parks and Wildlife Service. Where a semi-formal arrangement for countryside access – only ever permissive, never by right – exists here, it is generally on land belonging to one of these bodies. And so, in Ireland, there is an implicit understanding that the public are only allowed onto *public land*. This is also how land access is conceived – albeit rather more overtly – in the USA (where the federal government owns around 28 per cent of the entire landmass, and a clear majority of it in certain western states such as Utah and Nevada), which is why the American tourists I used to guide around Cornwall struggled to process the concept of a public footpath across privately owned farmland. But it is not the norm in the rest of Europe, where the rights of access and ownership are usually at least partly disaggregated.

* * *

On this cold, wet morning it was hard to be suitably grateful for Coillte's beneficence in permitting my presence. I'd hoped to cut northwest through the forestry lands to hit the road as close as possible to the village of Woodford. But the 1:50,000 map was of little practical use in this frequently altered landscape and even a compass bearing was hard to maintain in the disorientating maze of overgrown rides. I teetered across a pole over a drainage ditch and picked through the tussocks at the edge of a recently clear-felled and replanted block. The new saplings had simply been dumped out onto the freshly churned ridges without being dug in. I drifted further south than I intended, and came out onto a thin road running north from Mountshannon. But there was a good strip of cattle-trampled roadside grass to walk along, and I marched north through the flying showers. To the east, the broad expanse of the Derryoober Bog swept away towards Lough Derg in the lemony light. The name might mean something like 'the working oak grove' – a hint, perhaps, of a managed woodland here long ago. But it was the largest expanse of open ground I'd seen all day. Coillte can take in no further land for forestry in Slieve Aughty, for the whole area has been gazetted as a Special Protection Area, specifically for merlins and hen harriers. What's left of the open ground is supposed to be preserved to provide them with habitat. But it doesn't seem to have done much good. The male harrier I disturbed the previous evening probably belonged to one of fewer than six breeding pairs recorded in Slieve Aughty during the most recent survey, down from twenty-seven pairs in 2005.[26] The one species that does thrive here is Japanese sika deer, introduced to Ireland in the 1860s on the Powerscourt estate in Wicklow.

Closer to Woodford: more forestry; small fields, abandoned and vanishing under reeds and willow carr; a scattering of derelict houses and a few stark newbuilds, pristine concrete rising from patches of rubble. A dead water rail lay at the roadside, its beak blood-coloured against the wet tarmac. Beyond the village, a van halted alongside me. The nearside window came down and the driver leant across.

'Can I give you a lift?' He was a moist-mouthed older man.

It was an unseasonably cold morning, but I grinned and shook my head. 'Ah, no – that would be cheating!'

He asked where I was from and where I was going. I was close to home here, and I told him that Cara taught in a village school nearby.

'Would she drive a red car? She would? Sure, I see her on the road every morning!'

He wished me luck and drove on, and a little while later I broke away from the road on to another Coillte property. But this place was different from the grimly angular plantations on the higher ground. It was a much older mixed woodland. Parts of it had been here since at least the early nineteenth century. The southern portion of the wood was marked on the map as Derrylahan and the larger northern section was called Rostura: the ubiquitous 'oak grove' again, plus ros, 'wood' – the old names still matching the current landscape, for once. There were blocks of regimented spruces within the body of the wood; but they sat among stands of much older beech trees and a few surviving oaks. Where Coillte had recently felled a section, they'd removed the conifers but left a scattering of spindly beeches. They'd grown absurdly tall as they strove for light among their densely packed neighbours and were now waving hysterically, unaccustomed even to the lightest breeze.

The map showed a track that I thought would carry me nicely to the northern side of the wood. But it was unused, grown in thick with scrub and barricaded with long-fallen beeches. My boots were quickly waterlogged, and then so were my shorts. A crash to the right, the flash of a cream-coloured rump, a brief backward glance of contempt, and a big sika deer vanished into shadow. The way became ever more tangled, and finally I could only move forward on my hands and knees, brambles snagging at my pack, my knuckles sinking into buttery mud. I came out at last in a burst of brittle sunlight on a clear track where a man with wild white hair and a tangled beard was wrestling a short log from a stack towards a battered quad bike. The German accent of his greeting was obvious; but I thought better of repeating the question I'd asked of the woman in Scarriff. I did, though, ask if he lived nearby.

'Only for forty-eight years!' he said. But his English was strangely patchy, and I got the impression that he didn't often speak to other people. He talked at me without heeding my own attempted interventions, the ideas emerging in fragments.

'The Germans – the split is still there, east and west, and they are going more far right! They never learn! They called it Nazism, and then they called it communism – and now? And America – what is it? Four hundred million people think the world is only 5,000 years old…' He wore grubby checked pyjama bottoms and a faded blue shirt, unbuttoned to the chest. His face under the flying white hair was shiny, polished by wild weather. 'And France – they are even more far right!'

'Well,' I said, motioning at the woods and the sky, blindingly bright now, with tiny cloud bundles rushing across like panicked sheep; 'at least we have the clouds, the trees…'

'Pah!' He threw his head back dismissively. 'But this is all rotten too. The ash is all rotten from the inside.'

I said I hadn't seen much ash on my way through the wood.

'Yes – because I took it all out! Forty years cutting, cutting, cutting.' He thumped his chest fiercely. There was a battered crutch leaning against the quad bike. He was still clutching the log with his other hand and I offered to help, but he waved me away, and when I walked on, he called after me: 'Stay out of hospitals!' I could hear the monologue continuing until I was out of earshot.

A lane past a farmyard and a herd of glossy Friesians in a sloping field, then a muddy track on to a patch of bog. Birch and willow at the edges and Jenga stacks of turf drying in little plots. I sat down in the reddish grass and cooked instant noodles for lunch. I was out of the Coillte-owned country now, moving into the agricultural lowlands. But a flush of positive possibility came to me. If I could find enough places like this – the odd unsurfaced bog road or muddy track through a wood, even just for a kilometre or two each day – perhaps it would be enough to temper the long stretches of road walking that lay ahead.

The final ten kilometres today were almost entirely on tarmac, however, through a thickening succession of pistol-crack squalls. I limped into Portumna at four o'clock with a wet wind at my back and water sheeting from the cracked gutters on the main street. It felt more like early November than late June.

A DETOUR: TWO THINGS

The winter has come on very abruptly.

It's a couple of months now since I finished my trans-Ireland journey, but its shape is still finding proper form in my head. To aid the process, I've stuck a large map to the wall of my office and marked it with the line of my route. It wobbles and wanders a good deal; but at a scale of 1:450,000 it has an unexpected fealty to the original diagonal desire line. It looks like I knew where I was going. I'm pulling together the ideas now too: the things I knew before I started and want to crosscheck; the fresh historical digressions prompted by a particular encounter along the way; the questions arisen at random in a wet field gateway and scribbled down in my notebook to follow up when I returned to my desk.

This weekend, though, I'm taking a break. We've loaded the car and driven an hour north to an annual gathering in a village on the Galway–Mayo border that bills itself as an 'unconference'. A friend has been nagging me to sign up, reckons it will be my sort of thing. And he's right. It's nothing like the traditional academic conferences I've attended, with their formally delivered papers and terrible coffee. There's a theme – 'legacy', this year – and anyone is welcome to join and to share their ideas. The attendees meet in huddles in cafés, halls, pub backrooms. You can't generally bring a three-year-old to a conference, but Róise is welcome here and she potters about merrily while the grown-ups are talking.

There's a storm rising. The last browned leaves are tearing from the agitated treetops, and every so often the wind flings curtains of rain across the village. The idea of ever having camped out on a mountainside seems fantastical. It's a good day to be indoors, talking.

The first session I go to is in the tourist information centre, an old courthouse. It's cold and everyone keeps their coats on. The chair of the session is a local man, and he hands out packets of sweets then gives a little preamble on the 'legacy' theme. He mentions a story from the famine of the 1840s still remembered around the village, about a starving woman dying in a gateway near his own homeplace. It's usually told, he says, as a simple validating example of the horrors and injustices of that era. But lately he's been thinking about it more uneasily, wondering why no one helped the starving woman, why she ended up in a gateway while his own ancestors didn't. I've been quietly wondering about related questions myself in the last few weeks.

I wait until the third session – in a pub function room with an ornate white fireplace and dark furnishings – to share my own 'presentation'. It's about footpaths, of course. I talk about the idea of a path as a feedback loop of legacy and renewal, the idea that footpaths exist only if people continue to use them, and that people continue to use them only if they exist. I say a little about Le Corbusier and his pack-donkeys. And I try, rather clumsily, to give a synopsis of the historical points I've been thinking about while staring at the map of Ireland on my office wall: the Brehon Laws, the traces of a lost footpath culture in nineteenth-century Irish literature, the fact that Ireland probably has the worst provisions for countryside access in Europe.

The idea of the 'unconference' is to keep things short and have the chats afterwards. The other people in this session besides Cara (who's heard it all before) and Róise (who's making a castle of chairs in the corner) include a retired academic, a technology researcher, a professional storyteller and a woman who does something serious and business-related – corporate law, I think.

'That's fascinating,' she says, in the way people do when they don't entirely agree with you. 'But two things. Firstly, never mind the Brehon Laws all those hundreds of years ago; this is a very litigious country today and there would be a lot of personal injury claims if people had access to private land.'

I briefly open my mouth like a landed fish, wanting to explain about the recent changes to the Occupiers' Liability Act. But she has a second, more important point to make. 'The English have always *had* their land,' she says, 'so maybe it doesn't matter to them if other people walk all over it. But *we* had it taken away from us and we had to fight to get it back, so it's different here.'

PART TWO

Our Land

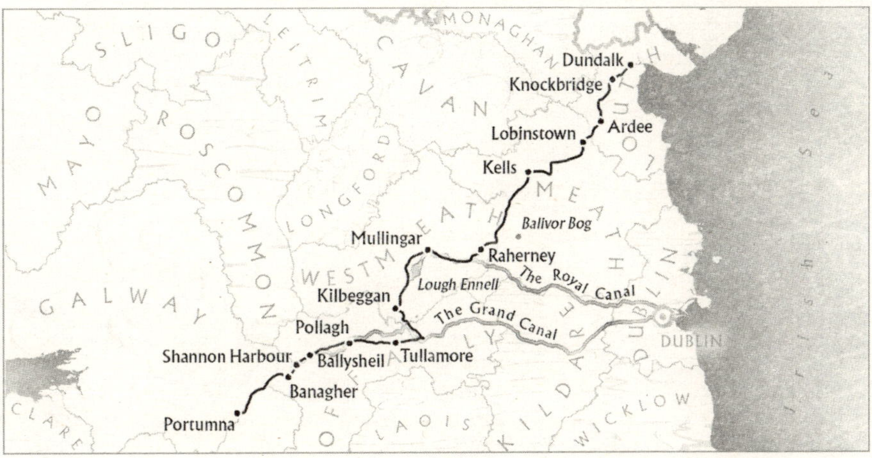

4

River Ghosts: Portumna to Banagher

Imagine the scene:

A wood in the boggy northern reaches of Tipperary – not the unbounded wildwood of myth, for it is 1603 and little more than a tenth of Ireland is under forest cover now. A pocket of old growth then, surrounded by bogs and pasture lands with the reedy callows of the Shannon to the west. It is the dead of winter, 7 January. Imagine the ceaseless creak and moan of the place, the grey lichen wet on the trunks, the sodden leaf litter underfoot and the low turmoil of the sky seen through the branches above.

Between the trees, men and women: several hundred of them; cold, frightened, exhausted, seven days' hard march from home with the country hostile all the way. There is a smell of horseflesh grilled over smouldering campfires, and in a clearing, men frantically bending withy poles, hacking at felled timbers, stretching the hides of a dozen newly slaughtered horses. They are trying to build a boat. Watching over the scene, their leader, Donal Cam O'Sullivan Beare, forty-two-year-old Lord of Beara and Bantry and Chief of the Name of the O'Sullivan Clan. He belongs to the old Gaelic aristocracy, the aristocracy of the *túatha* and Brian Boru which has endured and at times even flourished during four centuries of English involvement in Ireland, but which is now in final headlong flight – though Donal Cam himself probably doesn't recognise that yet.

How has it come to this?

The earliest beginnings of English – and later British – colonialism in Ireland are customarily dated to the Norman invasions of the twelfth century. But this is a retrospective assessment. The Anglo-Norman state itself was barely crystallised at the time, with blurry boundaries stretching across the English Channel into the duchies of northern France. The Normans were initially invited into Ireland as mercenaries during a struggle for control of the Gaelic kingship of the southeastern Leinster region in the 1160s; and their 'conquest' was by no means comprehensive. Nonetheless, in 1171, Henry II made himself the first English king to set foot in Ireland. He received submission from several Gaelic lords, made substantial grants of territory in Leinster to Anglo-Norman barons and gave his youngest son John the title 'Lord of Ireland'. John was popularly known as 'John Lackland', given his apparent lack of inheritance; but he ended up on the throne himself in 1199. The English monarch was thenceforth officially King of England and Lord of Ireland. But this was a tenuous and incomplete colony.

The English Crown was represented in Dublin, with a semblance of direct control in the immediate surrounds and a network of

Anglo-Norman lordships stretching southeast through Leinster and into Munster. But you didn't have to travel too far before any discernible English influence frayed away. Vast swathes of the north and west – almost the entirety of Ulster and Connacht – remained wholly Gaelic in culture and kingship. And the Anglo-Norman lords themselves rapidly did that thing that would horrify colonialists in other parts of the world in later centuries: they went native. They retained an enduring, if rather peculiar, sense of 'Englishness' across the generations. But at the same time they married into the surviving Gaelic aristocracy, took on their lifeways and their language, and even gave Brehon Law precedence over the English legal system. And they periodically went into revolt. These 'Old English' as they were later known were 'degenerated and growen almost meare Irishe, yea, and more malicious to the Englishe then the very Irishe them selves' according to one sixteenth-century critic, Edmund Spenser.[1] The Crown authorities were unnerved by this aristocratic creole culture and made futile attempts to reverse the process – most notably with the infamous 'Statutes of Kilkenny' of 1366, which officially banned any notional English subjects in Ireland from further intermarriage, outlawed the use of Gaelic language and dress, forbade recourse to Brehon Law and even banned participation in hurling matches. The statutes were largely ignored, and by the end of the fourteenth century any meaningful English colony was restricted to the 'Pale' – the rough arc of settled territory around Dublin, hemmed by a protective ditch (the 'Pale' itself) and running from Dundalk in the north, inland as far as Kells, down to Naas and back out to the coast at Dalkey. But things would change with the coming of the Tudors.

The 1533 English break with Rome had little immediate impact in Ireland, for Henry VIII himself was no committed Protestant reformer. But it did have political consequences. The rationale for the original 'Lordship of Ireland' was a papal bull of 1155, licensing the English king to annex Ireland in the name of eradicating the idiosyncrasies of the indigenous Gaelic church. But with papal authority now rejected, the legitimacy of the lordship looked decidedly shaky. A related problem was that of subjecthood. Technically, only the 'English' in Ireland had ever been subjects of the English Crown. The Gaelic lords, not to mention the many thousands of ordinary Irish people living in their territories, were not. A solution was proposed by Henry's lord deputy in Ireland, Sir Anthony St Leger. He arranged the 'Act for Kingly Title', which did away with the lordship and made Ireland a kingdom under the English Crown. As for the Gaelic lords, they were to formally surrender their territories to the Crown and submit to royal authority, at which point the lands would be handed straight back with a feudal charter and a newly minted peerage – a policy known to modern historians as 'surrender and regrant'.* A whole swathe of clan chiefs thus became viscounts, barons, earls – anything below the rank of duke. They were also supposed to stop speaking Irish and start conforming to English customs, though this was rather hard to enforce, and surrender and regrant actually helped to narrow the cultural distinction between the Old English and the Gaelic aristocracy.

The Protestant Reformation rapidly took hold in England after Henry's death in 1547, but in Ireland the process failed – though *why* it failed is still a matter of debate. The idea of a conscious Ireland-wide resistance to an English imposition is a pleasing one for modern nationalists; but the endurance of Irish Catholicism may have had more to do with language barriers and a lack of resources. In 1562, the Scottish-born Anglican Bishop of Kildare asked to be removed from his post due to his inability to communicate with his Irish-speaking congregation.[2] There was no Irish translation of the New Testament available until 1603, and no translation of the Old Testament until the 1630s.[3] The most obvious active hostility to the

* The policy had no particular name during its sixteenth-century application; the term 'surrender and regrant' was coined in 1913 by the historian Willam Butler (see Christopher Maginn, '"Surrender and Regrant" in the Historiography of Sixteenth-Century Ireland', in *The Sixteenth Century Journal*, Vol.38 No.4, 2007, pp. 955–974: 955).

Reformation actually came not from the Gaelic Irish, but from the Old English – who quite reasonably saw it as yet another attempt to interfere with their 400-year-old tradition of cultural hybridity. They – and some of the more recently elevated Gaelic peers – removed their sons from English colleges and started sending them instead to institutions in Spain and Italy, binding them into the pan-European Catholic networks and shifting their allegiances still further from England.

The reign of Elizabeth I saw a series of Irish rebellions. In the 1560s and 70s, the Desmonds of Munster – an Old English dynasty descended from one of the original Norman invaders – rebelled in their home region, prompting a ferocious English response. The following decade, the trouble came at the other end of Ireland in Ulster – always the least anglicised of the four traditional provinces. And this time it was led by a member of the old Gaelic aristocracy. Hugh O'Neill was the son of an Ulster chief who had been appointed the first Earl of Tyrone under the terms of surrender and regrant. He had been raised in an English household inside the Pale and had spent time in England in his youth. He appeared at first to be a reliable military ally of the Crown authorities. He organised the massacre of shipwrecked survivors of the Spanish Armada on the Ulster coast in 1588 and actually took enthusiastic part in the brutal suppression of the Desmond Rebellion. But in 1595 he switched sides, joined a rebellion kickstarted the previous year by several other Ulster chiefs and was proclaimed 'The O'Neill', clan Chief of the Name in the Gaelic tradition. Years of guerrilla warfare ensued. The Ulster chiefs were joined in their confederacy by Gaelic lords from other parts of Ireland, but the Old English remained mostly aloof. Despite his earlier treatment of Spanish sailors, O'Neill now looked to England's enemies in Catholic Spain for support. After much lobbying, a Spanish fleet arrived off the coast of Ireland on 21 September 1601. Unfortunately for O'Neill, it made landfall not on the west coast of Ulster as he had requested, but more than 300 kilometres away at Kinsale in Co. Cork, and the 3,300 Spanish troops were immediately besieged by English forces.

O'Neill scrambled southwards to launch a poorly coordinated relief on Christmas Eve. It was roundly rebuffed. The Spanish surrendered and O'Neill and his surviving troops fled back north. This left their southern allies – most notably Donal Cam O'Sullivan Beare – in a difficult position.

Like Hugh O'Neill, O'Sullivan was a Gaelic lord who had initially seemed well able to negotiate the dual worlds of Englishry and Gaeldom. His O'Sullivan ancestors had come originally from Tipperary. But they were displaced by the Normans in the late twelfth century and moved south where they bifurcated, the larger branch of the clan settling in South Kerry and the smaller taking the Beara Peninsula, a jagged, mountainous promontory jutting into the Atlantic on the modern Cork–Kerry border. When O'Sullivan's father was murdered in 1563, the title of Lord of Beara and Bantry was passed to his uncle, Eoin, in accordance with the old Gaelic tradition of tanistry. This was the succession principle which had given Brian Boru the crown of the Dál Cais back in 976, a kind of rough meritocracy in which leadership passed not automatically to a biological heir, but to the male relative deemed most capable by other senior clan members. The English authorities in Dublin initially acknowledged Eoin's ascent. But when Donal Cam came of age in the 1580s, he petitioned for a change, pointing out that English law demanded primogeniture in matters of aristocratic title. Evidently he made a convincing argument, for the authorities recognised him as the new Lord of Beara and Bantry – a decision they must have regretted when he joined Hugh O'Neill's rebellion a decade later.

After the rout at Kinsale, O'Sullivan retreated to his fastness at Dunboy Castle on the Beara Peninsula – the last rebel redoubt in the south, which Crown forces besieged in June of 1602. It fell after a weeklong bombardment. The besiegers also seized Dursey Island at the westernmost tip of the Beara Peninsula and reputedly massacred the noncombatants who had been sheltering there.[4] O'Sullivan himself was away from Beara at the time, conferring with the surviving rebel leaders in Ulster. But he returned and spent the late summer and autumn in low-level skirmishing around Cork and Kerry. There were rumours of a second Spanish fleet; but it never arrived.[5] Crown forces steadily gained control of the region. Other local Gaelic lords threw their lot in with the victors; a bounty was placed on O'Sullivan's head and pardons were promised to any who deserted his camp. With the onset of winter, his support dwindled. At one point, a large body of Connacht men who had been fighting with him slipped away under cover of darkness and headed for home.[6] And so, on 31 December 1602, with all other options exhausted, Donal Cam O'Sullivan Beare set out northwards, hoping to rendezvous with Hugh O'Neill somewhere in Ulster. He had around a thousand followers of whom 400 were soldiers. The rest were unarmed camp followers, men and women. O'Sullivan's own wife Elena, their children and most of the other noblewomen of the clan were taken into the mountains by a loyal retainer and hidden in a booley hut in the Coomarkane valley west of Glengarriff – and fed on scraps of meat stolen from an eagle's nest, according to legend.[7] They were later spirited away to safety in Spain.

The most detailed account of O'Sullivan's retreat across Ireland in the winter of 1603 was written by his younger cousin, Philip O'Sullivan Beare, a couple of decades later. Philip did not take part in the journey himself. He was twelve years old at the time and had been sent away to Spain the previous year. But his father Dermot and mother Johanna were there throughout the journey and Philip became a close associate of his cousin during his later Spanish exile. As a teenager growing up among the heat and the orange trees, he must have heard countless stories of this grimmest of marches, had each skirmish and bleak campsite firmly fixed in his imagination. His narrative certainly has the granular detail of an oral history.

* * *

On the first day out of Glengarriff, the O'Sullivan party skirted the Shehy Mountains for forty kilometres and saw in the New Year at a camp near the head of Lough Allua. A thousand people sounds like a substantial crowd; but it quickly diminishes when considered against the scale of a landscape. Imagine them with the big hills of their own Beara home country at their backs: bundled belongings, a few laden donkeys, a handful of horses, some of the soldiers labouring along in armour or settling and resettling heavy pikes on aching shoulders; the mud, the winter weather coming at them sideways.

At lunchtime the following day they stopped to pray to Gobnait, saint of the bees, at her shrine in Ballyvourney. But it did little good, for they were harassed throughout the afternoon by men of the MacCarthy clan whose allegiance had flipped back and forth between rebels and Crown but who were now firmly against O'Sullivan. That night they camped somewhere towards Kanturk where 'the natives annoyed them throughout the whole night rather by yelling than hurting'.[8] The whole country seemed to be against them now, and the following days were marked by near-constant attack – sometimes by Crown forces and their allies, sometimes by locals hurling missiles and insults at their flanks. In the Golden Vale, the rich farming country of Tipperary, their route wavered first to the northeast and then to the southwest. They sat out a nocturnal storm in the woods of Aherlow, marched with nothing to sustain them but 'plants and roots and leaves of trees' and broke into a fortified grain store at Donohill and 'set themselves to feed on meal, beans, and barley grains, like cattle'.[9] This explains the seething hostility that they encountered as they headed north. All this country had been through years of violence and famine. It was the dead of winter, and a thousand strangers descending on the neighbourhood was a serious threat to your own precious supplies. The best bet was to give them no welcome, keep them moving on.

On 5 January, O'Sullivan's party passed into the Slieve Felim mountains and managed to break through a blockade of troops belonging to Thomas Butler, the Earl of Ormond – scion of a venerable Old English family but nonetheless a staunch Protestant and Royalist, having been raised at the English court. That evening, O'Sullivan camped in a tiny hillside graveyard at Latteragh. There was a fort occupied by Ormond's men just 150 metres to the west, and the fugitives were fired on throughout the night. They left at dawn in a hail of musket fire – the 'daily salutation with which the enemy honoured him; a farewell as they drew off at night; a greeting as they turned up in the morning' – and descended towards the banks of the Shannon where O'Sullivan 'seemed to be landed [...] in a very tight corner, as he could not cross the broad and navigable river [...] since the enemy had removed all boats and ships, and warned every ferryman under the severest penalties not to carry him over'.[10] And thus to that muddy wood, where, with all the outrageous creativity of the desperate, O'Sullivan's men killed twelve of their horses and set about trying to build a boat from the carcasses.

Philip O'Sullivan Beare gives a detailed account of the boat's construction:

> Two rows of osiers were planted opposite each other, the thickest end being stuck in the ground, and the other ends bent in to meet each other's vis-a-vis, to which they were fastened with cords, and so formed the frame of the ship turned upside down. To this frame the solid planks were fixed, and seats and cross beams were fitted inside. Outside it was covered with the skins of eleven horses, and oars and dowels were fitted on. The keel was flat, both on account of the material used and in order to avoid rocks and stones. It was twenty-six feet long, six feet broad, and five feet deep, but the prow was a little higher in order to stem the tide.[11]

They were two days camped in the wood, chewing at the gristle of the slaughtered horses and labouring on the boat. At first light on 9 January they carried it down to the riverbank at a spot called Portland. A smaller coracle-type craft foundered midstream on its first crossing; but the main boat floated successfully. It could carry thirty people at a time. The surviving horses were tied to the stern and swam in its wake. The eastern banks of the Shannon here were controlled by the MacEgan clan, who held an old Norman fort nearby. The MacEgans were an ancient Gaelic family, hereditary

Brehon Law experts. But their current head, Cairbre, was also the Queen's High Sheriff of Tipperary.[12] While the ferrying process was underway, a party of Cairbre MacEgan's men, led by his son Donnchadh, attacked, and in the panic the fleeing camp followers swamped the boat and sunk it in the shallows. Once the attack was rebuffed, they refloated it and made the final crossings. A few stragglers managed to swim across the river – in its full winter flood and surely only a few degrees above freezing. On the western bank O'Sullivan ordered the boat – the boat they had laboured on for two full days – destroyed, lest it should fall into enemy hands.

They were out of Munster now, into Connacht. But if they had expected a warmer welcome in these western lands, they were to be disappointed. At midday, they looted a deserted village for grain and malt beer – which 'seemed, to their parched palates and hungry stomachs, regular nectar and delicacies'.[13] And in the afternoon they won an improbable victory at Aughrim against a well-armed company under the command of an English general, Henry Malby. O'Sullivan led his exhausted and outnumbered troops away from the enemy and into a bog in a classic feint, before abruptly wheeling about for a counter-charge: 'This sudden and unexpected volte-face struck terror in to the royalists, and when ordered to fall into line some fled to the rear ranks and, one following another, they wheeled round in a circle'. Malby himself was killed in the ensuing ruckus. But O'Sullivan knew that this could only be a temporary success, and he fled on northwards into the evening, 'with such haste that he left some soldiers worn out on the road, and overcome with sleep'.[14]

The final days of the retreat take on a feverishly fantastical quality in Philip O'Sullivan Beare's retelling. As they move ever northwards, into Roscommon, rain falls so heavily that the fugitives are 'scarcely able to bear the weight of their soaked clothes'. They flounder into banks of wet snow. They find themselves benighted in a forest so dark that they can only stumble about 'as if blind, following only the sound of familiar voices'. So depleted are their ranks by death and desertion that no more than sixty remain capable of bearing arms and even they fall away hour by hour. They kill the last of the horses and use their hides to replace the boots worn out on the road. One of O'Sullivan's lieutenants, Seán na gCath, the O'Connor Kerry, finds his feet so ruined that he can barely stand.[15] But by delivering a forceful address to his own body, 'he struck his feet against the ground, and squeezing out the matter, pus, and blood, he got up and began to march with the rest'. The daily attacks continue from all sides. And then, at the very last, an ethereal figure 'clad in a linen garment, his feet bare, his temples bound with a white wreath' appears on the path. He has heard of their flight, heard of their unlikely victory at Aughrim and has come to guide them the final twenty-five kilometres to safety in the fort of Hugh O'Neill's ally Brian Oge O'Rourke, Lord of West Breifne in Leitrim, which they reach in darkness on 14 January. Of the thousand who set out from Glengarriff two weeks earlier, just thirty-five remain: eighteen armed men, sixteen camp followers and one woman, Philip O'Sullivan Beare's mother Johanna.[16]

Donal Cam O'Sullivan Beare later continued north in search of Hugh O'Neill with the idea of regrouping for a fresh campaign. But by the time he reached the woods of Glenconkeyne north of Lough Neagh, where he'd heard that O'Neill was holding out, it was all over. On 30 March at Mellifont in Co. Louth, O'Neill had submitted to the English Crown, unaware that Elizabeth I had died six days earlier to be succeeded by her more sympathetic nephew James I. The terms were generous enough anyway: O'Neill had to sever all links with Spain and give up his Gaelic title; but he kept the earldom of Tyrone. He held on for a few more years, at uneasy peace with the Crown authorities in Dublin. And then, on 14 September 1607 he and a clutch of other notable former rebel lords departed from Rathmullan in Donegal on a French ship bound for the continent. This was the so-called 'Flight of the Earls', seen in retrospect as the symbolic end of the old Gaelic order in Ireland. O'Neill died in Rome nine years later. Donal Cam O'Sullivan Beare, meanwhile, received no royal pardon nor regained his territory and reportedly lived for a time as an outlaw in the mountains of West Cork. In 1604 he got away aboard a Spanish ship captained by an exiled poet from Kerry and arrived in Spain that autumn.[17] He stayed there for the rest of his life. The court of King Philip III gave him a pension and the empty title of Count of Berehaven. He was murdered on the street in Madrid in 1618 after intervening in a duel between his cousin and memorialist Philip and a man named John Bath, another Irish exile, this time of Old English stock.[18] An elegy by the poet Domhnall Ó Dálaigh declared that with his passing there remained 'no man of the Gaelic company capable / Of resuming the struggle against the foreigners'.[19]

There is a portrait of O'Sullivan painted during his Spanish exile: a slender, flamboyantly beruffed figure with finely arched eyebrows and flying moustaches, every inch the European Catholic nobleman and not the sort you could easily imagine cobbling together a boat from withies and rawhide in the cold and the mud of a Shannonside wood.

* * *

On the western bank of the Shannon, seven kilometres upstream from Portumna and a little way north of the place still known as Portland, there is an information board, marking the approximate site of O'Sullivan's crossing in 1603. It is illustrated with a cut-out facsimile of the Spanish portrait, somewhat faded behind the birdshit-specked Perspex. You pause here, lean on your pole, scan the text.

Reeds bend; a breeze runs down along the water. You try to imagine the scene – the ceaseless creak and moan of the place, the grey lichen wet on the trunks; try to conjure the breadth of the river in winter flood, before the constricting embankments were raised. And for a moment the ferocious reprimand of the past comes at you hard: that you might have the temerity to complain of blisters and aching heels, to wish for something other than instant noodles for lunch, to make a hostile countryside of a few 'no trespassing' signs. But isn't that always the way? You wonder, too, about the roads they followed in that bitter winter, the boreens and horse tracks and footpaths, wonder how many of them are still passable today.

Beyond the reeds a big white pleasure boat rumbles downstream towards Lough Derg, a man in sunglasses at the elevated helm. You wave; but he is focused on the river, doesn't see you, and you head on northwards with no one to note your passing.

* * *

The angry weather had cleared overnight, leaving an early coolness that was almost autumnal. For the first hour out of Portumna I walked with my jacket on and my hood up. By the bridge at the eastern end of town where the Shannon flows out into Lough Derg, a sign pointed north away from the road on to the 'Hymany Way' – which takes its name from the anglicised form of Uí Mháine, an old Gaelic lordship of this region. This was in turn part of the larger 'Beara–Breifne Way' – stitched together from existing walks and cycleways in a rough approximation of Donal Cam O'Sullivan Beare's route. For the next fifteen kilometres I'd be off-road, following the west bank of the Shannon.

When I'd first encountered officially waymarked walking trails like this in Ireland, I'd been puzzled. If there were no real public footpaths, then how could such routes exist? And if you were allowed to walk *here*, then why weren't you allowed to walk *there*? But the mechanisms of access were beginning to make sense now: I could thank the 1925 Shannon Electricity Act for these fifteen kilometres. Even this far upstream, the Shannon had been embanked during the building of the hydroelectric plant at Ardnacrusha. A narrow strip of riverside land still belonged to the ESB, and as a state body they had granted the public permissive access to walk along the embankment. And a few short stretches of the route further north skirt privately owned fields, which have also been opened up through permissive arrangements with the owners. But a note on the information board at the start of the trail warns walkers that 'both the Hymany Way and the Beara–Breifne Way are closed to the public for one day each year, the 31st January'. I was puzzled by this, and sent a message later to Sport Ireland, which oversees this and other trails, trying to find out why. The answer should have been obvious: the annual closure 'serves to prevent any argument that the land has become a right of way'. You *can* walk the banks of the Shannon here; but there is no guarantee that the way will remain open in years to come if any of the landowners change their minds.

The recent rain had brought the country to its fullest fecundity. Everything was at the brink of fermentation even as the last buds were opening. Waist-high cocksfoot grass and a pale froth of meadowsweet along the ditches; mallards, skimming swifts and the yellow pennants of the water flags. But there was an off-note in the midsummer song: the ash dieback here was the worst I'd seen. A line of youngish trees, deliberately planted, rose from the blueish reedbed between the embankment and the water. They were ghastly, almost entirely bare, like the starving stragglers of a defeated season. And where the embankment bent away from the main channel to admit a tributary, a bigger, older tree rose in grim silhouette. It had clearly been suffering for years. The failed regrowth of previous summers made a bony lattice around its quinfurcated trunk and the ivy was surging hungrily from below.

This year, the fading lifeforce had produced only isolated leafage towards the ends of the upper branches, and even that had a wilted, sickly look, hanging about the skeletal form in rags and tatters. A monstrous revenant; a river ghost.

A slow heat came into the day with a rising breeze and all the low country around the Shannon began to seethe with it. Seven chestnut horses grazed in a yellow smear of buttercups and a buzzard turned and mewled over a fifteenth-century church on a hillock above the floodplain at Friarsland. Big white pleasure cruisers slid past in the main channel every so often, but the Hymany Way itself was empty, with only the faintest band of darkened grass meandering along the embankment top to show that anyone had ever walked this way. I passed no one else on foot until the grass turned to tarmac by the weir at Meelick.

This, I knew from the map, was the end of today's off-road walking. I was aiming for Banagher, nine kilometres upstream, beyond which I could get onto the old towpath of the Grand Canal. But the only way through was along the road. I'd been on level, easy ground all the way from Portumna; but a subtle weariness had mounted that made me baulk at the prospect of two hours on tarmac in the afternoon heat. I sat for a long while on the grass beside Meelick Quay, half-hoping that a boat heading north might pull in so that I could hitch a ride. There wasn't much here: some parking spaces by a small farmyard; a couple of picnic benches; a boy fishing optimistically with a flimsy collapsible rod; and a derelict cottage under the trees on the opposite bank. There were no nearby towns, but there was a 'walk' here recorded on Google Maps – a couple of kilometres, out along a tarmacked walkway, across the top of a crescent-shaped weir, down to a lock – and back. Cars pulled up by the farmyard: families with baby buggies and kids on plastic scooters; older couples with dogs on extendable leads. How far had they driven to get here? I watched them heading off towards the weir, and when I started to recognise those returning in the opposite direction, I forced myself to my feet and walked on.

This was heavy farming country without the usual roadside

bungalows. Cattle pasture stretched away to arrow-straight hedgelines. The sky was yellowish overhead and in almost every gateway a black-and-white sign was fixed with cable-ties to the galvanised bars: 'NO CYCLEWAY' with the 'NO' in an extra-bold font. There'd been a proposal to bring a cross-country greenway, stretching from Dublin to Galway, through this way, and it had clearly been ill-received by some of the local farmers. The lane was part of the existing Hymany Way, and anyone walking or cycling this way would see the signs, receive their barrage of hostility.

I came out onto the bigger R356 where a sign informed me that it was still seven kilometres to Banagher. This was a bad road for walking. There were no verges and it bent constantly left and right so I couldn't see the oncoming traffic. The cars that came through did so at speed and I was forever flinching into the hedges and switching skittishly from side to side to avoid the blindest spots of the bends. At times the river showed blue through the trees to the right, and the grey roofs of Banagher came into view when they were still tauntingly distant. By the time I reached the bridge across the Shannon, I was exhausted. I shambled across with the sun at my back. A man with snowy hair riding a bicycle with a short fishing rod held across the handlebars slowed up as he came level with me, tried to chat about the day, the weather. But I barely had the energy to answer. On the eastern bank I hobbled down a quiet side-lane to a guestroom with creaking laminate floors in a low-slung bungalow near a ruined nineteenth-century battery with a few replica cannons angled back across the water. I was out of Galway and into Offaly now, out of Connacht and into country that the English authorities had tried in the sixteenth century to remake in their own image.

* * *

There had been English settlers in Ireland since the first Norman invasions. The original transfer to Anglo-Norman ownership of territory that had once been the fief of a Gaelic lord didn't necessarily involve immediate upheaval in the culture of the countryside. But

Victorious English soldiers returning from an encounter with Irish forces during the upheavals of the 1570s with prisoners, seized livestock and severed heads, as recorded by the artist John Derricke in his 1581 book, *The Image of Irelande, with a Discoverie of Woodkarne*

in the sixteenth century the idea emerged that rural Ireland needed to change. The English concept of an inferior Irish other had been around from the start. They were both barbarous and lazy – like every subject people in every colonial imagination. And with the successful Protestant Reformation of England their otherness had gained a sectarian component. If only the Irish natives could abandon Popery and pastoralism, take up tillage, Anglicanism and the English language, then everyone would be much better off. This idea emerged partly from a sincere if grossly patronising sense of a 'civilising mission'. But it was also, bluntly, about control. A countryside remodelled on the ideal of an English shire, with a beneficent lord of the manor presiding over compact villages where dutiful peasants laboured industriously in open fields, would surely be less likely to erupt into armed rebellion every few decades. But the Irish would need to be led to this halcyon state by example – and thus the idea of 'planting' the land with English colonists emerged.

The first concerted attempt to create colonial 'plantations' in Ireland took place in Laois and Offaly in the 1550s. These boggy Midlands counties lay just beyond the original Pale, and their traditional O'More and O'Connor lords had long harassed the English-administered country towards Dublin. Concerned Tudor officials began lobbying for the active seizure of O'More and O'Connor territory, the establishment of a network of garrisons to pacify the countryside and the importation of new freeholder farmers 'out of England'. This, according to William Thomas, clerk of the Privy Council during the brief reign of Edward VI, would help transform the Irish themselves from 'rude, beastly, ignorant, cruel and unruly infidels, to the state of civil, reasonable, patient, humble, and well-governed Christians'.[20] A similar approach had worked in the marches of Thomas's own Welsh homeland, after all. A 'Settlement of Laois and Offaly Act' was duly passed in 1556. Laois was renamed 'Queen's County' and Offaly became 'King's County'. But the project was not a great success. Too few settlers were enticed over from England, and the O'Mores and O'Connors maintained a low-level insurgency from the fringes of their erstwhile territory for decades to come. If you really wanted to remodel the land, it had become clear, you needed to lay waste to it first – which was precisely what the victorious Crown forces did to Munster in the early 1580s in the wake of the Desmond Rebellion.

Perhaps 7,000 people were killed in the fighting and its immediate aftermath, many by summary execution. Lord Grey de Wilton, the English lord deputy and commander of the Crown forces, declared in his own report to Elizabeth I that he had overseen '1,485 chief men and gentlemen [on the rebel side] slain, not accounting those of meaner sort, nor yet executions by law and killing of churls, which were innumerable'.[21] His troops had also burnt the crops, killed the cattle in the fields and destroyed homes and grain stores. As many as 48,000 people – around 10 per cent of the entire estimated Irish population at the time – may have died in the ensuing famine.[22] An infamous description of Munster in this period comes from the pen of one of Wilton's deputies, Edmund Spenser:

> The proof whereof I saw sufficientlye ensampled in those late wars in Mounster; for notwithstandinge that the same was a most ritch and plentyfull countrye, full of corne and cattell [...] weare brought to such wretchednes, as that anye stonye herte would have rewed the same. Out of everye corner of the woode and glenns they came creepinge forth upon theire handes, for theire legges could not beare them; they looked Anatomies [of] death, they spake like ghostes, crying out of theire graves; they did eate of the carrions, happye wheare they could find them, yea, and one another soone after, in soe much as the verye carcasses they spared not to scrape out of theire graves; and if they found a plott of water-cresses or shamrockes, theyr they flocked as to a feast for the time, yett not able long to contynewe therewithall; that in a shorte space there were none almost left, and a most populous and plentyfull countrye suddenly lefte voyde of man or beast.[23]

This passage – which Spenser ends with a spectacular piece of victim-blaming, claiming that the mass mortality among the people of Munster was 'all by the extreamytie of famyne which they themselves hadd wrought' – is much quoted, and usually uncritically presented as eyewitness testimony. But a certain scepticism is required. Spenser was an accomplished poet after all, author of *The Faerie Queene*, and he took a particularly creative approach to his *A View of the Present State of Ireland*. Rather than straight reportage, he presents it as a dialogue between two Englishmen. Irenius, who has recently returned from Ireland, tells his friend Eudoxus about what he saw there. The 'I' of Spenser's account does not belong to the author himself, then, but to a fictional narrative device. And there's something about the rhetoric: the starving Irish natives moving on all fours, foraging like beasts and, above all, practising cannibalism.* It is not the only such account from the colonial

* Spenser was by no means the first foreign writer to accuse the Irish of cannibalism. In one of the very earliest references to Ireland, the Greek geographer Strabo wrote that 'its inhabitants are more savage than the Britons' and that 'they count it an

centuries in Ireland, and even when the writer is appalled at the suffering and full of sympathy for the victims there is a certain latent inference: look at these people! Surely no *English* peasant, even in extremis, would allow themselves to sink so low! But it is a rhetorical trick that betrays itself – for if the starving Irish appeared less than human, then what on earth did that say about those whose deliberate actions had brought them to such a state?*

Whether or not people really ate corpses, the violence and the famine in Munster certainly cleared the way for an ambitious new plantation project. The territories of the Desmond earldom were confiscated, and 298,653 acres were reapportioned to so-called 'undertakers' who *undertook* to develop the land on specific terms. They were to bring in exclusively English tenants, remove any surviving Irish, practise English commercial agriculture and build English-style model villages governed by English law and custom. Each undertaker was limited to a holding of 12,000 acres (with a few exceptions, such as Walter Raleigh, who got 40,000) – vast as an agricultural estate but, it was hoped, not big enough to allow the emergence of de facto princedoms like those of the grandest Old English families.

As in Laois and Offaly, the reality of the Munster Plantation didn't quite match the ambition of the plan. There was still a shortfall of willing English settlers, and many undertakers lacked the capital to build new villages and properly overhaul the management of their estates. Some simply left the surviving Irish tenants in

---

honourable thing, when their fathers die, to devour them'. The Irish also, he noted, 'have intercourse, not only with the other women, but also with their mothers and sisters'. Strabo had never visited Ireland himself, and he added a blunt disclaimer to his lurid allegations: 'I am saying this only with the understanding that I have no trustworthy witnesses for it.' But he put the idea out there, and stories of Irish cannibalism persisted, right up to the mid-nineteenth-century famine years.

* In a mirrored response, a later Irish nationalist author might quote Spenser's passage but 'omit the most revolting part of it' – the accusation of cannibalism among the starving Irish – and thereby mitigate the dehumanising impact (see Sullivan, *Bantry, Berehaven and the O'Sullivan Sept*, p.16).

place. But between war, famine and plantation, the fabric of the Munster countryside – always the most fertile part of Ireland – had been significantly altered in a very short period. And the next major plantation project would bring about even more profound changes – ones with eternal consequences.

The 1607 flight of Hugh O'Neill and the other former rebel earls confirmed in the eyes of the English authorities that they had never ceased to be traitors, even after the Treaty of Mellifont. And so their vast territories in Ulster – half a million acres – were seized for the Crown. Ulster had always been the least anglicised part of Ireland, but now it was to be planted on an unprecedented scale with the explicit stipulation that new settlers should outnumber the native Gaelic population of the province. The land was portioned up and handed to corporate bodies and private undertakers. A corporation of City of London guilds got the whole of Co. Coleraine (hence its rebranding as 'Londonderry') while the various individual undertakers got holdings typically no larger than 1,000 acres – again, a measure intended to prevent the rise of over-powerful magnates. One-fifth of the confiscated land was reserved for the so-called 'deserving Irish' who had fought for the Crown against O'Neill. But unlike in the previous attempted plantations, this time large numbers of immigrants were successfully encouraged to settle (though still not quite as many as had been hoped). Some were from England, but most were staunchly Calvinist Scots. And still more Scots came in under private settlement schemes to the easternmost Ulster counties of Antrim and Down, which were not part of the official plantation. By the mid-seventeenth century, almost a fifth of the population of Ireland was of recent immigrant background, and nearly half of that fifth was to be found in Ulster. All in all, around 100,000 Scots and English settlers had moved in over the course of a century. It was probably the single largest population movement within Europe in the period, easily comparable to the contemporary Spanish settlement in South America.[24] And in Ulster it embedded all manner of tensions and resentments – no longer simply among a tripartite gentry class, Old English, New

English and Gaelic, but also at the level of the small tenant farmer and the landless labourer.

These resentments erupted in 1641. A limited rebellion planned by the surviving Catholic gentry of Ulster – intended to force Charles I to grant them religious toleration and secure title to their lands – rapidly morphed into a bloody popular revolt among those dispossessed by the plantation process. Thousands of Protestant settlers, particularly those of English background, were murdered, burnt out of farmsteads, hunted off their lands by those they had earlier displaced. Meanwhile, the Old English gentry finally threw their lot in with the Gaelic lords. Whatever the personal identities involved, meaningful cultural distinctions between the two groups had greatly diminished. In the seventeenth century, they were all politically marginalised Catholics with the title to their estates perpetually insecure. In November 1642, they formed a Confederate Association and established a shadow administration at Kilkenny in the Old English heartlands of Munster. The Confederates always insisted on their ultimate loyalty to the Crown; they just didn't like the political conditions to which they had been subjected within Ireland. But by now that English Crown itself was descending into fatal crisis with a ferociously Puritan Parliament in the ascendant. And the destructive force that would descend on Ireland after Charles I's execution in 1649 would outdo everything that had gone before.

* * *

I knew nothing about it when I walked through. I didn't notice it that evening, scribbling in my diary and scanning the maps over a bowl of chowder and a pint of Guinness in a quiet pub near the bridge in Banagher. And I still had no idea when I marked up the whole route on a large wall map back at home afterwards and started to match sections of the route to planned topics and chapters. It was only much later that I spotted it: a name on a digitised version of an old Ordnance Survey sheet.

The writing had ground to a halt for the day. I should have turned off the computer, folded the tattered maps, closed the notebooks, stacked the reference books neatly at the back of the desk and gone for a walk. But instead, I kept nibbling at the edges, picking needlessly at minor references. I found myself idly wondering when the weir at Meelick was built (between 1841 and 1844, it turned out; longer ago than I'd expected), and then wondering whether the island it connected to the western bank – the one where the families with the buggies and the scooters walked – had a name. It seemed not; but the search had led me to the nineteenth-century Ordnance Survey. And there on the earliest six-inch map, surveyed in the late 1830s shortly before work on the weir commenced, was another river island nearby, a rough rhomboid containing a battery to guard the channel. This island did have a name, and it was a name that might as well have been that of the devil himself as far as the popular narrative of Irish history is concerned: 'Cromwell's Island'.

Oliver Cromwell landed in Ireland with his New Model Army in August 1649 intending to wipe out all remaining Confederate and Royalist resistance to Parliamentarian supremacy. But the expedition also had a motivation of vengeance for the events of 1641. In the aftermath of the initial uprising, the authorities in Dublin gathered evidence from hundreds of those who had been caught up in the violence. As well as eyewitness testimony, these depositions also contained a good deal of hearsay. The most lurid sections were soon circulating in England, accompanied by gruesome engravings depicting demonic Irish Catholics herding terrified Protestants into rivers and spearing English babies with pitchforks. This, combined with the zealous Puritan flavour of Parliamentarianism, had produced a Cromwellian invasion force primed for unrestrained sectarian violence. They first besieged the port town of Drogheda, north of Dublin, which was occupied by a mixed force of Confederates and Royalists under the command of Arthur Aston, a one-legged Englishman from a recusant Catholic family. After a three-day siege, Cromwell's men stormed the defences and in his own words, 'being in the heat of action, I forbade them to spare any that were in Arms in the Town'. Even of those who submitted, 'their Officers were knockt on the head, and every tenth man of the Soldiers killed, and the rest Shipped for the Barbadoes'. Almost 3,000 soldiers and an unknown number of civilians were killed. Cromwell himself was firmly 'perswaded that this is a righteous Judgement of God upon these Barbarous wretches who have imbrued their hands in so much innocent blood'. With the Drogheda massacre he had firmly established himself as the ultimate colonial bogeyman of popular memory in Ireland.

Another siege and another massacre followed at Wexford, and the New Model Army was soon surging through Munster. Cromwell himself returned to England in the early summer of 1650, leaving his son-in-law, Henry Ireton, to conduct a three-year mopping-up campaign (Ireton himself succumbed to illness near Limerick before the job was complete). But more than the massacres, it was Cromwell's political policy towards Ireland, developed back in Parliament, that would have the lasting impact.

The island in the Shannon at Meelick wasn't really Cromwell's own. The name probably emerged from a folk memory of a victory by Parliamentarian troops in the autumn of 1650. By this stage, Henry Ireton had already extended his control up along the banks of the Shannon – which would soon become the Rubicon in his father-in-law's grand scheme for a reconquered Ireland. But in early October, a Confederate and Royalist force under the command of the Old English Marquess of Clanricarde, Ulick Burke, snuck east across the river near Athlone for a hit-and-run operation. They got almost as far as Birr before retreating to Meelick. This was a complex section of the Shannon, braided into multiple channels and dotted with several dozen low and scrubby islands. Burke's men took up a position on one of these islands where there were already some defensive structures. In the previous century, it had been described as a spot which 'ten men might keep against a thousand'.[25] But at nightfall on 25 October, Parliamentarian troops forded the river under the command of Daniel Axtell, a veteran of the slaughter at Drogheda the previous year. They caught the defenders by surprise and killed around a thousand of them in the ensuing rout. Ulick

Burke reportedly later declared the defeat 'so unhandsome I am not willing to have any written records of it'.[26]

Perhaps local people in later generations vaguely remembered that a battle with Parliamentarians had taken place on an island that they called Gutáile in Irish – and so it became 'Cromwell's Island' for anyone who asked about it in English. The battery marked on the old map belonged to a much later period, that of the Napoleonic Wars, built as a pair to a Martello tower on the opposite bank. But an Ordnance Survey researcher, visiting in 1838, recorded that an old man he spoke to at Meelick remembered seeing the ruins of an earlier castle on the island before the battery was built.[27]

The weir was constructed in the 1840s, with an adjoining 750-metre canal and a lock named for the new British queen. These were intended to make it easier for boats to pass through this awkward section of the Shannon. Ahead of the work, the Board of Works made payments to the Marquess of Clanricarde, the friars of the nearby church and the Board of Ordnance who occupied the battery 'for land at Cromwell's Island, required to be taken for the improvement of the River Shannon'.[28] The Board of Ordnance manned the Martello tower for another fifteen years, with the commander complaining that the only access was now via the Victoria Lock – 'a very inefficient mode of communication with a military post' – and that the lock keeper repeatedly accused his men of trespassing.[29]

The work on the weir and canal had changed the geography of the river. Cromwell's Island is there on the map revised in 1891, with the defunct battery still marked. But its outline has changed. The surrounding channels have narrowed and small islets have started to merge into bigger blots of land. The island is still named on the next revision in 1913. But by the time the final large-scale map was published in 1944, it had vanished entirely, the name erased, and the island itself melded into the western banks. The ESB embankment now ran across the site of the old battery. I'd passed right over it myself, paused to watch the buzzard turning over the reptilian stonework of the old church, then walked on, unaware of the river ghosts beneath my feet.

5

The Wet Centre: Banagher to Tullamore

'You're wet!'

She was leaning from the open window of the pub at Shannon Harbour where a sign on the pavement advertised takeaway coffee: a woman with thick blonde hair pulled back into a loose ponytail. Her name was Shirley.

'I am,' I said, 'so I think I deserve a coffee.'

'You do. And will you come in and dry off in the bar?'

It felt extravagantly early to break off from the walking: I was only an hour out of Banagher. But the morning was unexpectedly wet. I'd slogged north on a bungalow-strung road through grey cataracts of rain, and I was shivering inside my damp waterproofs.

'Sure, why not.'

'Come in, so.'

There were foreign banknotes pinned to the wall behind the bar – dollars and dinars and baht and kip – and a rack of crisps and chocolate by the door. Shirley and her husband had bought the place two decades earlier after a career in the public healthcare system. 'I left a secure job in the HSE to run a pub,' she said with a grin. 'Mad thing to do!' But they'd made it through the post-2008 financial crisis, and through the COVID-19 pandemic too. You had to be willing to try new things to keep a business going in a tiny village like Shannon Harbour, she said, and these morning openings with the coffee hatch were a recent experiment. But they hadn't been getting much business, and she and the young barmaid – a local student, home for the summer from her first year at university in Northern Ireland – were bored, glad of a customer to talk to. They asked if I was walking to Dublin, which was a slightly uncomfortable question, for I knew I was drifting off-trajectory here.

All the way from Dingle, my route had maintained some kind of connection to the 400-kilometre desire line striking across the map of Ireland from Dunmore Head to Burr Point. It had wavered in places; but none of the deviations had been wilful. And there'd always been something to go on, something to provide appropriate direction for each day's walk: the Dingle Way, the old Tralee–Limerick railway, the banks of the Shannon. But at Banagher, it felt like I'd run out of road – or rather I'd run out of everything but road. The next major staging post on the diagonal was Mullingar – fifty-seven kilometres away as the crow flies, and that crow's trajectory should have taken me across the M6 motorway halfway between Tullamore and Athlone. But there were no more riverside embankments, no defunct railways or modern greenways and no large blocks of Coillte-owned forestry in the vicinity of that line, only roads. But there was the Grand Canal, striking away eastwards an hour's walk north of Banagher.

The canal – stretching 117 kilometres from Dublin to the Shannon – opened in 1804, after half a century of tricky construction work. The last commercial cargo barges travelled its length in the 1960s; but it is still navigable – as the clutch of dark narrowboats and pale pleasure craft moored along the banks at Shannon Harbour made clear. And the old towpath is designated 'The Grand Canal Way'. It was irresistible: an off-road way through, even if it wasn't running in quite the right direction. And anyway, for the first twenty kilometres out of Shannon Harbour, the canal did edge towards the northeast. I could walk it for a day at least and convince myself that I was still on track.

Shirley went into the little room behind the bar to make my coffee, and while I waited, I asked the student barmaid why she'd chosen to go to university in the North. She lowered her voice and said with a conspiratorial half-smile, 'You don't need so many points to get into college up there.' She was studying pharmacy in Coleraine – near to the site of the earliest known human settlement in Ireland at Mount Sandel. She liked living there, was glad that she'd chosen a small town and not Belfast. She liked the people too, she said, but she was always struck by their ignorance of the Republic.

'Like, sometimes I ask them to guess where I'm from, and they always say Dublin or Donegal, because those are literally the only places they know. If I say I'm from Offaly, they're, like, "Is that a town?"'

The other thing she found strange, she said, was the persistent need to know what you are, denominationally, in the North. 'It's like they can't really relax until they know,' she said. 'Here no one cares; like, literally, no one cares. And, actually, there are some Protestants here; but no one even thinks of it as a difference. Up there, if you're from the Republic they just assume you're a Catholic – but they could be wrong!'

Shirley returned with the coffee, and the friendly interrogation flipped back towards me: why was I walking? Where was I walking? Where would I stop tonight? One of the reasons for these experimental morning openings, Shirley said, was the prospect of more traffic along the towpath. It was being upgraded for cyclists and was supposed to connect, eventually, to the planned Dublin–Galway Greenway. I said that I'd seen signs of opposition to that route on the walk up from Meelick the previous day. She rolled her eyes – to the left, to the right and then straight up: 'I'll say no more about that,' she said; 'I'll say no more.' But at least the Grand Canal route itself was progressing. The transport minister was due to open it officially as a greenway at the end of the summer, and they'd just finished tarmacking the entire towpath between Tullamore and Shannon Harbour. Shirley must have seen my face tighten as she told me this, for she grimaced apologetically.

'I don't know if that's good news for you or not…'

But a canal has two banks, and there was good news: they'd only tarmacked one side. When the coffee was finished, I went back out into the drizzle and got onto the northern bank. It was a grassy

A view of the Grand Canal and its towpaths soon after its opening, by the Dutch artist Gabriel Beranger

before Cromwell's invasion. But the O'Sheils were still in place in the early 1650s and found themselves targeted for removal. They did not, however, have to traipse all the way to some barren valley in Connemara. Instead, they were assigned a few parcels of land a day's march west across the Shannon, close to the route that Donal Cam O'Sullivan Beare had taken on his march north half a century earlier. At some point during the upheaval, someone transcribed the 'Book of the O'Sheils', the family's medical bible, built up over generations and containing both traditional Irish plant-lore and commentaries on famous Greek and Roman physicians, as well as on the more recent work of the Dutch anatomist Andreas Vesalius.[9] Perhaps the transcriber was a family member, trying to preserve a concrete record of an old tradition now that they had gone from clan physicians to middling farmers. There are still Sheils living in East Galway today.

Ballysheil itself ended up with a Protestant family named Judge, and sometime around the turn of the eighteenth century they demolished the old towerhouse and replaced it with a modern, two-storey mansion. The Judges were not aristocrats, but they seem to have been solidly respectable members of landed Protestant society. One scion of the family became High Sheriff of King's County, and a daughter of the house, Martha, married the Anglican Dean of Killaloe in 1783.[10] In 1803, Samuel Judge built a bridge across the new canal to preserve access to his house. But in the next generation, the family fell into bankruptcy – through gambling according to local legend. After decades of litigation, in 1852 the estate went to the Fox family from Wicklow.[11] They seem never to have lived at Ballysheil and by the end of the century the house was in ruins. A widowed Mrs Fox was remembered locally in the following century as a harsh landlord who 'would not allow you to sow corn in the one field, years in succession [...] would not allow you to burn [invasive] scutch grass [and] would not allow you to shoot game on the land'.[12] There were still Judges living nearby in the 1900s, but they were Catholics, small farmers, and any connection to the earlier family is unclear.

And so now what's left of Ballysheil House stands at the end of a long field north of the Grand Canal. Eight blind windows and a mirage of a roof, the spectre of an ivy-strangled ash tree to the fore and a grey horse grazing away to the left. Perhaps there are still a few medicinal herbs growing along the faint line of the old bawn.

* * *

The afternoon softened gently and the dampness went from the air. There was an ease to the walking, the ground perfectly level and lightly vegetated underfoot – the kind of terrain you can walk across hour after hour without fatigue. Occasionally a cyclist whizzed past on the new tarmac across the canal, a few dog walkers and women striding ferociously in pairs. I enjoyed the smug perversity of eschewing the hard surface, walking on the wrong bank, and as the lengthening distance from Shannon Harbour spooled out behind me, I felt an old familiar pleasure rising in my chest, one that I hadn't really experienced on the walk until now.

The countryside opened to the south and the Slieve Bloom mountains showed in the distance, bringing a sense of vastness after the constrained horizons of the morning. The canal ran into the edges of the derelict Derries Bog. A tramline crossed the water here, with a clever swivel mechanism to carry the track across the canal without permanently blocking the way for boats. But commercial peat extraction had ceased here twenty years ago, and the bare black ground was vanishing under a scrub of gorse and birch. The fox-red rails of the old tramline streaked away north into an ocean of knapweed and ribwort plantain.

Onwards: an overgrown section of towpath; electric-blue damselflies dancing in the reeds; a confetti of meadow brown butterflies and the livid scarlet flash of a six-spot burnet. A red tractor appeared ahead, halted beside the canal with its engine running. I felt a sudden instinctive apprehension: I wasn't entirely sure if I was allowed to be walking on this bank. But the young lad in the cab gave me a hearty thumbs-up as I approached. Just beyond the tractor, an older man in a beanie hat appeared to be standing on the surface of the canal. It was only when I came level that I saw through the reeds that he was balanced in his boxer shorts in a little sled boat. His bare legs were pale and hairless and he was fiddling with a length of rope that linked the sled to the tractor, grinning at the cackhandedness of the operation.

'I thought for a minute you were walking on water,' I said, and his grin widened.

'Only Our Lord can do that!'

'Well, that's what I was wondering: was I meeting the Messiah in Offaly? What are you doing?'

'Putting this back where it's supposed to be!' He motioned merrily to the sled. It was rocking back and forth on the weedy water as he half-crouched to maintain his balance. 'It's easier this way than hauling it out, like.'

'Well, good luck with that,' I said sceptically, and he laughed.

'The new walkway brought you something you never thought you'd see – the Messiah in Offaly!'

A few hundred metres further on, the towpath widened to a band of rutted mud. Late sunshine came through the thinning cloud, low at my right shoulder, and with it a sudden beneficent warmth. Heavy green country stretched away on the level in all directions; no cars, no other people, and the distant hills purplish in the new light. The swell of pleasure that had gradually filled my chest through the day burst out. Here, at last, I had a sense of being *in* the countryside rather than confined to its tarmacked and gravelled peripheries; a sense of freedom – taken for granted on the footpaths of Wales and England but unaccustomed in Ireland – to make distance across the land on foot. It made me giddy. I turned in the track, walked backwards for a few steps to feel the sun against my face. I knew it couldn't last, but it carried me happily into the canal-side village of Pollagh where a late mass was broadcasting through loudspeakers fixed to the wall of the church: 'I believe in the Holy Catholic Church; I believe in the Holy Communion of saints…' The priest had a strong South Asian accent.

I was hoping for a cold soft drink, but there was no shop near the canal so I went into the little pub instead. A small crowd of drinkers huddled at the end of the bar, focused intently on a Galway–Dublin Gaelic football match on the wall-mounted TV. Each man nodded in curt acknowledgement as I edged awkwardly past with my laden backpack. I took the first empty seat at the bar and ordered a pint of Guinness and a packet of crisps. The barmaid had long black hair and a loose black cardigan over a hot-pink tee-shirt. She nodded wearily at the silent drinkers when she handed me my pint.

'You'll get nothing out of them,' she said. 'There's nothing more boring than a match.'

I drank in silence. There was an open turf fire blazing on this hot June afternoon, a portrait of Michael Collins in uniform pinned to the cellar door, and his Hollywood counterpart, a young Liam Neeson, up above the fire. Endless group portraits of Offaly GAA teams filled the other wall spaces. I finished my drink and pinched the last crisp crumbs from the seams of the packet. Dublin were up by four points, but the match still had half an hour to play. As I made ready to go a short man with iron-grey hair came past on his way from the toilet. He pointed to my backpack.

'You must be a homeowner.'

I didn't know what he meant, whether it was an ironic quip. 'Homeowner?'

'Homeowner! Where are you headed for?'

He was wildly enthused when I explained, told me I could camp in the field behind the next pub at Rahan if I lied to the landlord and told him I was a keen golfer. He followed me out of the pub with a younger friend in shiny sunglasses, and they fumbled at a pair of bicycles chained to a bench. They'd cycled out from Tullamore earlier in the day and had been in the pub all afternoon.

'My name's Cross Cassidy and I'm not on the Internet so don't look me up,' he said (I did; he wasn't). 'And this here is Bryan on his very expensive bike. We're half-drunk and we're cycling to Tullamore!'

'Make sure you fall to the left, lads,' I said as they wobbled towards the greenway – which had switched to the northern bank here.

'Fall right, is it? Into the ditch? Jeez, I don't know, Bryan...' and away they went.

* * *

Twenty minutes later, south of the canal and out onto Pollagh Bog: a sudden heart-lift in the slanted evening light.

Willow scrub and birches, and then a great expanse of open ground stretching ahead. A hare streaks away, burnished by the low sun. Ocean-blue striations of standing water between dark corrugations of milled peat; a festival crowd of bog cotton, each white head nodding to the beat of the breeze; and common horsetails sprouting green from the black ground like something alien, something from the earliest beginnings of life. There is a sense of elevation here that is not entirely an optical illusion. The trees at the southern edge of the bog look as though it would take a full day to reach them, and Slieve Bloom, twenty kilometres beyond, appears as a high sierra a week's march away. A heron turns awkwardly in the distance. And back and forth over the bog pools: lapwings, beating the brittle blue air with their ill-fitted wings, mewling and mewling and mewling.

You know that this is a ravaged place, only five years into its recovery after half a century of commercial peat extraction. But with the birds, the hares, the late sunlight it feels fabulously life-filled, and a fine place to end what has, unexpectedly, been the best day's walking of the journey so far. There is a good camping spot behind a stand of young birches on a little hillock. The tent pegs slide beautifully into the yielding black ground.

* * *

During the Last Glacial Period, when almost the whole of Ireland was under ice, the glaciers rooted their way across the land like a herd of blue-grey pigs, pushing up lines of rubble with their snouts and smearing the solid ground beneath their bellies with gravelly matter known as 'drift'. Where water flowed through hidden channels beneath the ice, the drift was sifted and graded, the rocks rumbled together and rounded. When the icecaps retreated, the drift material originally deposited in the base of the channels was left behind as long ridges in the postglacial landscape. These ridges are known in Irish as *eiscir*, a name passed on to geographers worldwide as 'esker'. The eskers seem curiously humanmade: meandering banks, wandering across fields or heaving unexpectedly through the woods. Spotting one, you might wonder if someone has been at work with a bulldozer. One distinct band of eskers begins near Dublin and stretches west through northern Offaly and all the way to Galway Bay. It is not exactly a single ridgeway, more a stop-start system, a series of creases and wrinkles in a tight-stretched sheet. In places it splits, wandering away to dead ends or detouring into scenic diversions. But taken as a whole, the esker band provided prehistoric travellers with a natural causeway across the low and boggy midriff of Ireland. It was known as the *Eiscir Riada* (anglicised as 'Esker Riada') from the Old Irish *ríad*, for riding or driving[13] – probably of livestock in the original sense. So *Eiscir Riada* might mean something like 'the drove road on the glacial ridge'. It may have been used as a cross-country route as far back as the Mesolithic.

In the spaces between the eskers, the glaciers had carved out shallow basins, which, filling with meltwater, formed a matrix of lakes and pools in the treeless postglacial landscape. These were poorly oxygenated and seldom properly flushed by moving water. Rather than decomposing, any dead vegetation that fell to the lakebeds accumulated. From around 9,000 years ago, the lakes shallowed and became reedbeds. And then, as more and more vegetable matter fell into the oxygen-poor shallows, the reedbeds became squelchy expanses of sedge. The water just below the surface was increasingly acidic and cut off from the enriching minerals of the groundwater. Soon enough the sedge grasses gave way to a low scraw of sphagnum moss, floating on the semi-liquid mass of poorly decayed material below. A bog had been created. But this is where the process known as 'paludification' achieves a kind of awesome horror: it did not stop at the original surface and shores of the lake. The ceaseless life-cycle of the moss itself contributed to the accumulating peat beneath the scaw, and the bog *continued to grow*, monstrously, upwards and outwards. It gradually asphyxiated and consumed any surrounding woodland, piled layer upon layer of barely decomposed matter and dragged the water table ever higher. The scraw of the deepest raised bogs could lie twelve metres above the original lakebed.

Much of the low-lying Irish Midlands ended up under these great wet cankers. They were an ominous presence for those who lived around them, and a challenge for communications to be traversed only by the laborious construction of wooden *togher* bog roads. They couldn't be cultivated and they were dangerous for grazing. In the Bronze Age, people surely recognised the bogs as unstable and ever expanding, slowly eating their way into the cultivated land. They placed votive offerings into their black pools. But the bogs also provided a ready source of fuel. Peel back the scraw, carve out the fudgy black matter beneath and stack it to dry in the wind and you have something like homemade coal. For thousands of years, turf-cutting for domestic fuel went on at the edges of Ireland's bogs; but they were so vast that it made little impact on their overall extent. The bogs, more than any hill, were a challenge for the builders of the Grand Canal. Cutting a stable, watertight channel through metre upon metre of wet black peat proved impossible and the engineers found that bypassing a bog entirely was the only practical solution. Looking back at my own route, I could see the way the canal bent north and south to skirt the bog at Derries. In 1810, a Commission for Bogs was established to try to work out how to make the boglands commercially useful. They mapped a total of 1.2 million hectares, evenly split between the raised bogs of the Midlands and the shallower blanket bogs of the mountains. In places, deep drainage channels were cut, which lowered the water table and turned bogs into pasture. By the mid-nineteenth century, some 30,000 hectares had been reclaimed,[14] but even today, around 16 per cent of the Irish landmass is under bog – the third-highest proportion of any nation in Europe, after Finland and Estonia.[15]

Major commercial exploitation of the bogs began in the twentieth century. A Turf Development Board was established in 1934, and reconfigured with an Irish-language name, Bord na Móna, twelve years later. Like the state forestry service, the Bord made compulsory purchases of large blocks of so-called marginal land. The new extraction process was very different from domestic turf-cutting. The bogs were drained, the scraw peeled back across vast acreages and the peat below milled by enormous harvesting machines, loaded onto industrial tramways and fed into peat-fired power stations or made into briquettes for domestic use. Bord na Móna later added potting compost made of macerated peat to its output. Its operations brought an economic revival to places like Offaly that slowed, if not entirely halted, the ceaseless rural emigration and brought a sense of community identity linked to heavy industry that had seldom existed in Ireland. But they also produced uncanny black deserts in place of what had once been the nesting sites of hen harriers and curlews.

For Seamus Heaney, Ireland's turf cutters were pioneers to match the European settlers of the American West, striking forever inwards and downwards.[16] But the 'wet centre' is *not* bottomless: in places the Bord na Móna operations have cut 9,000 years of accumulated peat right down to the 'lack', the original bedrock or glacial drift below. And there has been a belated recognition that undamaged bogs are by far the most important carbon sinks on earth. Because the dead plant matter does not decay, bogs actively lock up huge quantities of carbon. Globally, peat bogs hold more than double the amount of carbon contained in all the world's forests.[17] But of course, if you drain and disturb a bog, that carbon is released. As Ireland scrambles for its climate targets, Bord na Móna is winding down operations even on the bogs that have not been worked out down to the lack, trying to diversify into renewable energy, recycling, waste collection and skip hire. Some decommissioned bogs have simply been abandoned; others are being actively restored and rewetted, the drainage channels plugged, the surface recontoured and reseeded. Hundreds of jobs have gone, and places like Pollagh now have an atmosphere faintly reminiscent of the former tin-mining region where I grew up in Cornwall: post-industrial but still avowedly rural – an atmosphere created here from scratch in little more than half a century.

Between 1814 and the formation of Bord na Móna in 1946, almost half of the raised bogs in the Midlands had already been cut away by hand to fuel the open fires and stoves of private homes. But in the second half of the twentieth century, domestic turf-cutting declined significantly. The ready availability of electricity and fuel oil – not to mention Bord na Móna briquettes – left fewer and fewer people with an appetite for hard labour by hand on a bog. But there was a resurgence of private cutting in the 1980s with the advent of mobile mechanical turf hoppers.[18] Instead of snicking away with a *sleán*, the sharp-edged spade designed for cutting neat slabs of turf, you can call in a contractor with a JCB, dig out great chunks of wet peat from the turf face and feed them into a tractor-mounted hopper which excretes the matter in reconstituted black sausages. Once sliced, these are sometimes still footed – stacked for air-drying – by hand. But it's easy enough to produce an excess. While some families with traditional turbary rights on bogs keep up small-scale turf-cutting for purely personal use, mechanisation also allowed any number of unregulated private commercial operations. A clumsy attempt to end the practice by outlawing all sales of fuel turf in 2022 turned turf-cutting into a distinctly Irish offshoot of the global culture wars – with the use of heavy industrial machinery on fragile wetlands cast as an ancient native tradition. Illegal harvesting continues, even in Special Protection Areas.

There's something else about the bogs. The Bord na Móna holdings are, like the Coillte forests, quasi-state lands, and they're seldom marked by 'no entry' signs at the margins. Some of the actively restored bogs now have boardwalks, and a few old tramlines have been turned into walking trails. Even private bogs are often divided among multiple owners and so, like the mountain commons, they may escape the excluding signage of the individually owned fields.

Heaney saw the bogs as an Irish answer to the unfenced American prairies. They *are* largely unfenced, the sort of landscape that would be automatically designated access land in Wales and England. And though I didn't know it yet, they would become cherished stations on what remained of my journey, all the way to the foot of the Cooley Mountains. On each day's walk to come I would scour the map and the satellite image for the blurry thumbprint of a bog somewhere close to my projected line northwestward, knowing that it would provide an island of open land, a place to move off-road even if just for a few kilometres, and a discreet place to camp somewhere among the tussocks.

* * *

I heard a thunderous passing as I lay in the tent at first light. It might have been the ghost of a giant Irish deer, roused from the black depths of the bog. But when I scrambled out of my sleeping bag and tugged up the zip of the fly sheet, I saw only a fresh set of hare-prints skirting my campsite and angling away to the southeast. The bog was colder and greyer in the dawn, the pools pale and wind-ruffled. But the lapwings were still mewling overhead, and another hare bolted from the tussocks as I headed back to the road.

I'd lost count of the hares I'd seen on the journey so far. The first had come before I even reached the formal beginning: loping up the track ahead of me as I made my way from the Blasket visitor centre towards Dunmore Head on the first morning, the pale fluff of its lower hindlegs showing. At low speed, its movement suggested a thing made of cogs and springs rather than muscle and bone. But twenty minutes later there'd been more – a brace, racing away across a sheep field on the approach to the headland – and at full tilt they appeared neither mechanical nor animal, more like small celestial bodies. After that there were hares near St Malkedar's Church, hares at the edge of Tralee Bay, hares on Moylussa, hares on the banks of the Shannon. Every time I saw one it brought a small thrill. They seem like a thing you're not *supposed* to see – creatures of another dimension. Their unexpected size, measured against the reference point of a rabbit, is one part of it; their ability to materialise in the middle of an apparently empty field is another. It's easy to see why traces of medieval apocrypha hung about them for so long. As late as the eighteenth century serious scientific treatises were still reporting that hares could change sex over winter and that they occasionally grew antlers.

There's an added personal exoticism for me in a view of a hare: there were none to be found in the far west of Cornwall when I was growing up. Our countryside was alive with rabbits, but no hares. I saw pictures of them in my nature books: amber-eyed, cat-faced creatures of patrician bearing. But I could only imagine what it would be like to encounter one. The first I ever saw erupted from the cougar-coloured grass of a big field on a friend's farm on the Lizard Peninsula, Cornwall's southernmost extremity, when I was twelve or thirteen. The shock of its size and speed and sudden strangeness never left me. Even years later when I lived in the English Midlands for a while and came to expect hares on every walk, I never entirely got used to the way they'd explode from their hidden forms, and I often took a moment to work out what that *huge* thing was, streaking along the hedge-line like a gazelle. But these had been brown hares, naturalised immigrants perhaps brought to Britain from mainland Europe in the Iron Age or the Roman era. Those I saw on the Pollagh Bog were Irish hares, by some reckonings the only mammal unique to Ireland.

Irish hares are a subspecies of the mountain hare, which is found, with minor variations, in upland areas across the entire Eurasian landmass. But the Irish variety is the only mountain hare to make itself properly at home in the lowlands (it's possible that the British variant, the blue hare of Scotland and the Peak District, also inhabited the lowlands until displaced by the slightly larger brown hare). The Irish subspecies is also the only mountain hare that does not change its pelage to match the winter snow – though if subjected to extreme conditions, the scientists say, they still 'possess the genetic machinery' to turn white.[19] What a phrase! What a possibility! Imagine it: one severe winter, strange reports drifting in from the countryside; unexplained sightings, dismissed at first; shaky mobile phone footage of fast-moving objects in the snow. And then, at last, confirmation on the evening news: the hares – all of them – have turned white.

* * *

I should really have broken away north from Pollagh towards Clara and Kilbeggan. But the canal path exerted an easy seduction. I got back onto the unsurfaced northern bank via the Thirty-First Lock at Cornalaur and drifted on towards Tullamore.

There's something about Offaly, some quiet, understated attraction for an outsider. I feel it every time I cross the county border from Galway: the crass ostentation of the modern domestic architecture west of the Shannon gives way to more modest bungalows and older cottages. The glittering SUVs are replaced by cars with plates from the early 2000s, and the pubs like the one in Pollagh come without 'traditional' décor chosen from a catalogue in the Celtic Tiger years. And there's often an easy-going openness to even the briefest of encounters. I felt the Offaly charm particularly strongly, walking beside the canal on this quiet morning. A fine soft rain fell for a while, then cleared to watery sunlight. There were signs nailed to trees and gateways – 'Pollagh Gun Club, members only', 'Rahan Gun Club, members only', 'Ferbane Gun Club, members only' – but the towpath itself was open.

A field full of old-fashioned rectangular haybales, footed like turf, and dozens of rooks squalling overhead; a herd of Friesians in deep ryegrass; the sound of a cockerel crowing away to the right; and a church bell ringing for morning mass somewhere behind. Near a pair of cottages, abandoned but not yet derelict under a big sycamore, an old man, upright on an old bicycle, rattled out of a sideroad and on to the towpath. His grey hair was smartly combed and his brown trousers neatly creased. He raised a hand in greeting across the canal: 'Howya going on?' H. V. Morton's quest for an imagined rural ideal was dogging me dangerously at this point; but I couldn't help thinking of all the American and German tourists, nodding dutifully to ersatz trad music in Dingle and Doolin. If they ever asked me for travel advice, I'd send them here.

At Ballycowan, another ruined house rose beside the canal, a huge broken tooth of a thing with six tall chimneys, ivy washing up the walls and the joist supports of the upper floors sustaining only air. Jackdaws chattered irately from the high gables. This was another place that had been caught up in the churn of the seventeenth century. The original castle here was part of the territory of the Gaelic Ó Maolmhuaidh clan, but it seems to have fallen into English hands as part of the original sixteenth-century plantation of King's County. The current castle was built by Sir Jasper Herbert and his wife Lady Jane Finglas, reputedly in 1626 – though the Ballycowan lands and other property in the vicinity seem to have been regranted to Herbert in 1637.[20] Jasper Herbert was of recent English extraction, but crucially – and fatally – he had converted to Catholicism, possibly to marry Lady Jane.[21] He participated in the 1641 uprising, and so found himself in the firing line when Cromwell arrived in Ireland. According to local folklore, Ballycowan was shelled by Cromwellian forces and has been in ruins ever since.[22] It was certainly confiscated under the terms of the Act for the Settlement of Ireland.

As part of the planned restructuring of Irish landownership, relatively modest parcels of confiscated land were handed out to the soldiers of the victorious Cromwellian army – over 30,000 of them.[23] The idea was that they should settle, farm as they would in Surrey or Somerset, and help to anglicise the Irish countryside. But it didn't work out that way. Of those who stuck with their new holdings, some ended up marrying Irish women and raising Irish-speaking children. But nearly two-thirds of the Cromwellian soldiers simply sold their windfall and went straight home to England with the proceeds.[24] With all this land suddenly entering the market, the post-Cromwell years proved a ripe time for would-be magnates among the new Protestant elite.

Sir Jasper Herbert's forfeited lands at Ballycowan were initially granted to a Captain Samuel Bonnell, but he sold them on to

Charles Coote, the first Earl of Mountrath, whose father had arrived in Ireland in 1600, taken part in the Siege of Kinsale on the winning side and ended up with extensive plantation lands in the Midlands. Coote was an ardent anti-Catholic and an enthusiastic participant in the Cromwellian campaigns. He expanded his estate significantly in the aftermath with purchases such as Ballycowan. A generation later, during a period of temporary respite for Catholics following the restoration of the English Crown, the second earl (also named Charles) had to see off multiple claims from aggrieved heirs – including Jasper Herbert's son Edward – trying to recover their ancestral holdings.[25] These descendants of the Catholic landowners removed from their estates in the 1650s were the generational bearers of a burgeoning narrative of dispossession, of lands stolen by the English from their rightful owners (even if some of the complainants, like Edward Herbert himself, were themselves of English descent and pining for property that had previously been taken from someone else). More even than the earlier plantations, the Cromwellian Settlement would become the origin myth of this narrative. But it was by no means the end of the saga of dispossession.

Most of Ireland ended up firmly on the Jacobite side after the Catholic James II was ousted from the English throne and replaced by his Dutch son-in-law, William of Orange, in 1688. This was hardly surprising, given that three-quarters of the Irish population was still Catholic, and it led to another bout of large-scale violence. The ousted James travelled to Ireland from his exile in France and raised an army which besieged the Protestant stronghold of Derry. But in June 1690, William himself arrived at the head of the largest invading army in Irish history. The Williamite forces won decisive battles at the Boyne and Aughrim and sealed their victory with the Treaty of Limerick in October 1691. By many reckonings this marked the ultimate completion of the English conquest of Ireland. But for the Protestant landowners who overwhelmingly dominated the reconstituted Dublin Parliament (which was ultimately subordinate to London), the Limerick treaty was unconscionably lenient towards what they saw as ever-rebellious Catholics. From 1695 they began to enact a series of explicitly anti-Catholic Acts which came to be collectively known as the 'Penal Laws'. Under the earliest of these Acts, Catholics were banned from owning horses or weapons worth more than five pounds. Later laws forbade them from sending children under twenty-one abroad for schooling – a strategy to weaken old links with Catholic Europe. Gatherings at holy wells were declared unlawful; Catholics were banned from working as teachers or serving as legal guardians to Protestant children; and interdenominational marriage was outlawed. Both Catholics and Protestant Dissenters were effectively barred from civil and military office, and a final Penal Law Act in 1728 stripped the right to vote from even the vanishing number of Catholics who had previously met the necessary criteria.

The Penal Laws pushed everyday religious practice into the open air. The Anglican Church of Ireland had taken control of the old-established chapels and cathedrals, and the monasteries had been broken up. Catholic priests were required to register, pay a bond to ensure good behaviour and stay within their home county, and any who remained unregistered risked deportation. But there was relatively little direct persecution and the Catholic Church managed to retain its essential institutional structures throughout the era of the Penal Laws.[26] Unofficial worship was widespread – in homes, barns or simply out in the open with a 'mass rock', a natural boulder or a stone rescued from a demolished church, serving as an altar. These unregistered holy places accrued their own network of access routes. Known in Irish as *cosán an aifrinn*, 'mass paths', they threaded their way across the countryside through fields and woods towards mass rocks and other makeshift gathering sites. Walking these paths – and those that led to the holy wells – became a quiet act of resistance, even if few of their users actively thought of it that way. Some mass rocks remained in occasional use even after Catholic emancipation (the Penal Laws were gradually rolled back in the later decades of the eighteenth century, and the 1829 Roman Catholic Relief Act completed the emancipation process across Britain and Ireland). Today, however, many of the surviving sites lie out of reach on private land.

In 1704 the most notorious of the Penal Laws, the 'Act to prevent the further Growth of Popery', was introduced – which revealed that the whole business was, once again, really about landownership. Catholics were now entirely banned from buying land. Those wishing to take out a lease were limited to a term of thirty-one years; and most importantly of all, inheritance practices were tightly controlled. Any surviving Catholic landowners were explicitly forbidden to practise primogeniture. Instead, they were bound to follow a procedure known as gavelkind and to divide their lands equally among the male heirs. Gavelkind was, it should be said, the traditional mode of inheritance in precolonial Ireland, where the automatic passage of either properties or titles to eldest sons had never been the norm. Even small leaseholders tended to subdivide their little tenancies among their children when they reached adulthood. But the 1704 Act made this the law, rather than the custom. The last survivors of the old Catholic landholding class – the Gaelic lords and especially the Old English (who, with their hybrid culture and identity, were more likely to have practised English-style primogeniture) – could now expect to see a decent estate splinter into worthless fragments within a couple of generations. There was one get-out clause: if an eldest son converted to Protestantism within three months of his father's death he'd get the entire inheritance. The Penal Laws may not always have been strictly applied in their finer detail, but they helped to complete a process which had begun a century and a half earlier: by the middle of the eighteenth century, possibly as little as 3 per cent of all Irish land remained in Catholic ownership.[27]

The plantation projects in the Midlands and Munster and the Cromwellian Settlement of the 1650s had all, ultimately, failed. They had been supposed to anglicise the countryside, to turn the Irish into dutiful English Protestants by way of coercion and example. Instead, with the final refinement of the Penal Laws, they produced a system of colonial apartheid. Everywhere outside of Ulster, the vast majority of the population remained Catholic. Those Catholics, whether their ancestors were Gaelic lords, Old English aristocrats or penniless cowherds, were now legally marginalised and obliged to pay rent to an elite Protestant minority largely descended from seventeenth-century arrivals, the so-called Anglo-Irish 'Ascendency' whom the Catholics could convincingly tell themselves *had stolen our land*. The landscape itself recited the narrative. Rising from the fields were the ruined towerhouses of the old landholders, while here and there among them an imposing demesne wall sheltered a new Palladian mansion.

* * *

Close to the ruin of Ballycowan Castle, the towpath ran past a gate fixed between concrete pillars. Its iron bars were neatly painted scarlet. The field beyond had been cut for silage in recent weeks and a small herd of half-grown beef cattle were picking over the yellowish stubble. Affixed to the gate was the familiar sign: 'TRESPASSERS WILL BE PROSECUTED'.

On the approach to Tullamore the fresh tarmac of the greenway switched again to the northern bank, but I crossed over and managed to stay on grass and dirt tracks all the way to the edge of the town. A thickening stream of dog walkers and cyclists on the other side of the canal; a brief flurry of rain then a hot breeze under a leaden sky, bending the canal's heavy trim of rushes. A church tower appeared in the distance, and then another ruined castle, right beside the canal.

I was deeply weary now, and my heels throbbed, the persistent low-level pain of the long-distance walker returning. But perhaps that's part of the attraction of these long journeys on foot: the motivating promise of relief at the end of the day. It kept me going, anyway – under road and railway bridges, past rows of faded houses, boarded-up pubs, tattoo parlours and Indian takeaways and into the friendly bustle of Tullamore in time for an early finish, a sausage-and-rasher bap and a large pot of tea in a café on Bridge Street.

6

Translations: Tullamore to Mullingar

A rainy afternoon in Mullingar; a room in a B&B beside the railway and the weedy curve of the Royal Canal. When a Sligo-bound train comes past the teacups rattle on the dresser. It's midsummer, but it feels like October. Dusk has arrived six hours ahead of time, and beyond the window the green dome of the Cathedral of Christ the King is vanishing into a sad grey smear. Wet walking shoes are upended on the radiator and the flysheet of a soggy tent is slung across the shower rail.

The rain has got into everything. My sleeping bag is clammy when I unfurl it to air in the narrow space between the bed and the wall. The page-ends of my notebook have swollen obscenely. Even the money in my wallet is damp. And the folds of the maps, packed into a side pocket of my backpack, have acted as capillaries and made the sheets into fragile grids. I spread them to dry on the bed: Ordnance Survey Ireland maps 41 and 42 and 35.

I'm over halfway there now, two weeks' walk and 421 kilometres from Dunmore Head. It must be – what? Another 250 kilometres from here to Burr Point? But looking down at the wet maps I'm struck by an insurmountable sense of defeat. I scan my projected line northeast across Meath and Louth, and I can see *nothing* to go on – nothing but roads, endless roads, marked yellow and orange, running hither and thither, splintering and converging, promising only blisters and blind bends. I wonder seriously for a moment whether I should give up, go home. But I've started, and I'll have to finish.

And then I wonder how I'll write about this when the time comes. How to describe a tiny crisis in a guestroom on a wet weekday afternoon in July without sounding sourly self-indulgent? Should I breeze past it, ignore and omit? Make myself the hardy outdoorsman who can walk a thousand miles without a blister? The lone enraptured male concerned only with the literature and philosophy of the landscape? Adopt the relentlessly cheery tone of the 'amiable companion' that reviewers of travel books always seem to favour? And then there's a bigger question: who am *I*, here, in *this* place, to complain about having nothing but tarmacked roads to walk upon?

* * *

Two hundred and fifty-four years earlier – to the day, as it happens, though I only realised this much later – a twenty-eight-year-old Dutch-born Englishman named Richard Twiss set out from Dublin on his own tour across Ireland.

Thanks to the scurrilous opprobrium later heaped upon him,

reliable biographical details are hard to come by; but Twiss was certainly born in 1747 and raised in Holland where his father was some kind of wealthy expat merchant. He seems to have been sent to London for a private education, during which he picked up some skill as an artist and a fiddle-player, but perhaps not the proper manners of a gentleman. Once he came of age, he decided to spend the generous allowance drawn from his father's fortune (reputedly £100 a month, an amount with a purchasing power akin to £16,000 today) on travel. He wandered widely around Britain and Europe, ticked off the essential sights of the Grand Tour and spent most of 1773 in Spain and Portugal. But far from travel exerting an improving influence on this rather wayward youth, Twiss 'went out a booby, and returned a dogmatic coxcomb' – at least as far as one of his later critics was concerned.[1] Correspondence from the aristocratic English expats in Madrid whose hospitality he exploited certainly suggests that he was an annoying houseguest, 'a great vulgar' and 'a compleat gigg' with a tendency to overstay his welcome.[2] He was pompous, overbearing and 'fond designedly of getting into scrapes'.[3] And he was rumoured to be an incorrigible womaniser and a frequenter of houses of ill repute. However, he was also a very entertaining travel writer with a snappy prose style, a caustic sense of humour and a penchant for wilfully provocative judgements. His debut, *Travels Through Portugal and Spain in 1772 and 1773*, published in 1775, did well and went through multiple editions, even if readers properly familiar with Spain had little good to say about it. He next turned his attention to Ireland, which was emerging as a suitable alternative to mainland Europe for English tourists and travel writers – sufficiently wild and exotic to be worthy of attention, but with the practical benefits of British governance and widespread use of English.

Twiss departed from London in May 1775, passed through Bath (about which he had little good to say) and Bristol, and flashed enough cash at Aberystwyth to convince the captain of a small sailing boat to detour from his intended port of Caernarvon to

Dublin. He disembarked there 'after a pleasant passage of forty-three hours'.[4]

Twiss spent a month in the capital, making various excursions into the surrounding countryside, and then, on 9 July, he set out on a 1,254-mile circuit of the country in a hired post-chaise – a compact carriage pulled by a pair of horses, upon one of which the driver rode. He travelled first along the east coast through Dundalk and Newry to Belfast, then skirted the northernmost shores before heading into Donegal. In Newry he 'found nothing to observe […] but two shabby bridges',[5] and he didn't think the Giant's Causeway was worth the journey. But the sight of salmon leaping the falls on the Erne at Assaroe near Ballyshannon enthralled him, and he 'remained hours in observing them'.[6] He also particularly enjoyed his next stop as guest of the Anglo-Irish baronet Sir James Caldwell at his castle near Lough Erne. Wandering the lough's shores, Twiss felt 'a kind of pleasing melancholy' and decided that this little-visited spot compared favourably to Loch Lomond and Lake Geneva. A few weeks later, after traversing the Midlands and skirting the eastern banks of the Shannon, he arrived in Killarney and saw its much more famous lake. He did not think it surpassed Lough Erne's charms.

Twiss does not seem to have been particularly interested in history or politics, but he made various interesting social observations as he travelled. Outside of Dublin, he noted that the standard dwelling was a cabin 'made of dried mud, and mostly without either chimney or window' and that there 'is generally a small piece of ground annexed to each cabbin [sic], which produces a few potatoes; and on these potatoes, and milk, the common Irish subsist all the year round'.[7] On the east coast, he noted that 'the brass coins of the Isle of Man' were common currency, and near Dunleer he spotted 'about a dozen bare-legged boys' sitting at the roadside outside a cabin 'scrawling on scraps of paper placed on their knees' – an indication of the way an unofficial 'hedge school' system was already operating to bring basic literacy to over half of the male population and around a third of females by the late eighteenth century.[8] And as he headed back towards Dublin from Killarney, Twiss noted that the 'counties of Kilkenny, Waterford, Wexford, and Carlow, are over-run with ruffians called White-boys':

> These are peasants, who do not chuse to pay tythes or taxes, and who in the night-time assemble sometimes to the number of many hundreds, on horseback and on foot, well armed, and with shirts over their clothes, from whence their denomination is derived, when they stroll about the country, firing houses and barns, burying people alive in the ground, cutting their noses and ears off, and committing other barbarities on their persons. The objects of their revenge are chiefly tythe and tax-gatherers, and landlords, who attempt to raise their rents; they never rob; neither do they molest travellers.[9]

This was actually a fairly accurate account of the Whiteboys – right down to the mutilations and the burying alive.

By Twiss's day, centuries of dispossession coupled to a rapidly rising population had primed the Irish countryside for discontent. But a simplified narrative of a few thousand Anglo-Irish aristocrats directly lording it over millions of impoverished, cabin-dwelling Catholics masks a more complicated actuality. The peasantry itself was multifaceted and riven by its own internal tensions. In the upper echelons were the descendants of the old Catholic landowning classes occupying large leasehold farms and employing numerous labourers who lived as subtenants on tiny plots at the edges of the property.[10] In the middle were comfortable farmers on acreages of varying sizes. And at the bottom were the cottiers who really did live in tiny cabins, often as subtenants, or even subtenants of subtenants, usually under the 'conacre' system whereby rent was paid with labour rather than cash or crops. The scope for complicated resentments was limitless, and the Whiteboys were just one of many rural vigilante movements. These 'agrarian disturbances' of the eighteenth and early nineteenth centuries seldom attacked the overarching concept of landlordism.[11] The targets were more often the hated 'middlemen' who administered tenancy and taxation systems, as well as other members of the peasantry deemed complicit in or acquiescent to land-related social iniquities. The Whiteboys and their ilk certainly didn't represent a resurgent political Jacobitism, or indeed an incipient Irish nationalism, even if the alarmed earls and Dublin authorities sometimes misrepresented them as such.[12]

The original Whiteboy movement began in Tipperary in the 1760s and was named for the white overshirts that activists donned during their nocturnal activities. The initial complaint was a perennial one in rural Ireland: the tithe. As the official national denomination, the Anglican Church of Ireland claimed a tithe on all grain crops (and in Munster and parts of Leinster also on potatoes). This was despite its congregation coming a distant demographic third place behind Catholics and Ulster Presbyterians. The collection of tithes was typically farmed out to middlemen – often themselves local Catholics – who knew how to wring a personal profit out of the process. The other major complaint was the enclosure of common land. There were fewer commons in Ireland than in England at this stage, and any unenclosed land was ultimately owned by a landlord. But such places were traditionally used freely for turf-cutting and rough grazing by locals. In the eighteenth century, however, former commons were increasingly taken in and fenced off for commercial cattle-rearing by the largest tenant farmers. In the first instance of Whiteboy activism at Drumlummin, the offenders were a well-to-do Catholic farming family, the Rosses, who leased land belonging to the eighth Baron Cahir.[13] The Whiteboys took to gathering after dark to trample new fences on the commons and to intimidate and torture middlemen and their lackeys. They swore theatrical allegiance to the mythical Queen Sadhbh, subjected their targets to mock executions, buried them up to the neck in pits lined with gorse and did indeed slice off a few ears. At one point in 1762, a crowd of 500 Whiteboys gathered near Fermoy in Cork where they put a horse belonging to a local magistrate on trial, declared it guilty and executed it.[14]

* * *

Richard Twiss avoided any encounters with the Whiteboys and returned to Dublin in September 1775 after three months on the road. He made a few further excursions and hung around until 12 November when he boarded a packet bound for Holyhead and returned to London via 'the stinking town of Birmingham'. *A Tour in Ireland in 1775* appeared the following year – and in Ireland it raised an instant outcry worthy of a Whiteboy mob in pursuit of a particularly venal middleman.

Skimming the book today, you might wonder what all the fuss was about. Twiss is broadly positive about Ireland. He declared that the roads were 'almost universally as good as those about London' and that the lodgings were as good as any traveller 'who is not over-nice' could wish for. Contrary to popular belief in England, he reckoned that 'at present almost all the peasants understand the English language, [and] they converse with as much propriety as any persons of their class in England'. He enjoyed the scenery, and in fact, he recommended Ireland as a good place to retire for anyone of adequate means. But he also scattered some more barbed comments through his text. He mocked the shoddy spelling of shop signs and newspapers in Dublin and complained about poor-quality 'vile editions' put out by its publishers. He declared that the work of the Irish artists displayed in the capital's galleries was 'detestable'. But it was when he got on to the topic of the Irish gentry that he really hit his offensive stride. He reported that they were marked out by three peculiar customs: eating boiled eggs incessantly for breakfast; eating potatoes instead of bread, with 'even the ladies indelicately placing them on the table-cloth, on the side of their plate, after peeling them'; and, bizarrely, the universal forging of postage franks, by 'the ladies in particular'. His judgements were not restricted to the Anglo-Irish upper classes, however: everyone in Donegal, especially the children, had 'the itch'; lodging houses on the coast north of Dublin were literally indistinguishable from pigsties; and he avoided the counties of Connacht altogether 'as I was assured that they were inhabited (especially along the coast) by a kind of savages, and that there were neither roads for carriages, nor inns'.[15] As for 'the natural history of the Irish species, they are only remarkable for the thickness of their legs, especially those of the plebeian females'.[16]

Twiss also had a mischievous habit of inserting wildly provocative quotes from previous books without further comment of his own. He quoted a seventeenth-century Scottish traveller claiming to have seen Irish women carrying children on their backs and 'laying the dugges over their shoulders [to] give sucke to the babes behind their backes without taking them in their armes'.[17] And he reproduced another seventeenth-century traveller's claim to have seen young women in Cork grinding corn stark naked and 'striking off into the tub of meal, such reliques thereof, as stuck on their belly, thighs, and more unseemly parts'.[18]

The ferocity of the Irish response was astonishing. In the months following the book's publication, the columns of newspapers in Dublin, Cork and Belfast filled with furious letters and satirical counterblasts. There was a whole series of poems mocking Twiss, and various lampooning efforts presented in an impersonation of the traveller's own voice, including a confession supposedly delivered from the gallows. One of the poems took a general swipe at English travel writers, who on returning home shamelessly 'Paint Scenes they never saw, nor e'er shall see, / And Things, that never were, and ne'er shall be'. The poem declared Twiss foremost in the roll of travel writing infamy: 'A prating, forward, vain, conceited Creature, / *Twisted* by Art, and quite unknown to nature'.[19] Various caricatures were also produced, some featuring Twiss with a set of donkey ears. An anonymous contributor to *The Hibernian Magazine* provided hair-raising accusations about Twiss's behaviour during his tour, claiming that he was frequently thrown out of respectable Irish houses for 'indecency to the ladies' and that at one point 'on a visit to a noble lord, he had the impudence to draw the ladies to a window, to exhibit to them a parcel of obscene pictures'.[20]

Most of the poem-writing and letter-sending was clearly done by members of the elite, the Protestant minority who dominated Dublin's print culture at the time (indeed, one of the mocking poems accused Twiss of being a Catholic himself). But significantly, the complaints were not restricted to – or even particularly focused on – Twiss's libelling of the upper-class ladies. The claim that Connacht was inhabited by 'savages' seems to have generated particular ire. The *Hibernian Magazine* contributor suggested that if Twiss had actually visited Connacht, the locals would probably have taken *him* for a Yahoo, escaped from the pages of *Gulliver's Travels*, and declared that his book had 'justly excited the scorn of all who respect this kingdom, and its inhabitants'.[21] The reaction to Twiss subtly complicates the idea that the Anglo-Irish elite themselves regarded the Catholic masses as 'savages' and didn't principally identify with Ireland as their own nation.

The outrage, however, soon spread beyond the upper-middle-class literati. A Dublin theatre staged an anti-Twiss play titled *A Trip to Ireland; or, The Tour-writer* to 'uncommon Peals of Laughter and Applause' from the audience.[22] And it was reported that the book had been burnt by an enraged crowd of chimneysweeps in Co. Clare in August 1776[23] – though by this stage any press reports about the controversy had to be taken with a pinch of salt, and the papers were regularly attributing to Twiss quotes that had never actually featured in his book. At one point, it was reported that he had been accosted in a London coffee house by an angry gentleman from Connacht, who 'took him by the Nose, beat him round the Coffee-Room with an Oaken Saplin, and then kicked him out to the street'.[24] Twiss himself denied that this ever happened, but things were clearly getting out of hand and other travellers in Ireland were experiencing the baleful aftereffects of the controversy. Mark Elstob, who visited soon after *A Tour in Ireland in 1775* appeared, recorded that the 'number of times I was asked whether I knew Mr Twiss? would appear incredible' and that 'None here thank him for his remarks'. Three years later, the Dutch artist Gabriel Beranger had an alarming moment during a visit to Connacht, when he was briskly approached by two 'genteel dressed ladies' who had actually mistaken him for the notorious travel writer: 'As soon as they were assured of their mistake, they inveighed against Twiss for his slandering of that province'.[25] Meanwhile, a Liverpool ceramic manufacturer with a knack for turning a profit from public outrage had produced a special chamber pot for export to Dublin. At its base they printed a caricature of the traveller and the phrase, 'Let Every one Piss On lying Dick Twiss'.

You have to suspect that Twiss himself was delighted by the controversy. It certainly did wonders for book sales, and he probably knew exactly what he was doing from the start. In a handwritten note beside the anecdote about the naked corn-grinders in his own reading copy of the book, he claimed to have included it only to win 'a wager of a dozen [bottles] of Portwine'.[26] *A Tour in Ireland in 1775* had only one printing in London, but it went through three editions in quick succession in Dublin.[27]

Twiss was part of a long tradition of British travellers heaping calumny on Ireland. The pattern begins in the twelfth century with the notorious *Topographia Hibernica*, written in Latin by the Cambro-Norman Gerald de Barri, better known as Giraldus Cambrensis or Gerald of Wales. Gerald probably never travelled much beyond the Norman-influenced southeast of Ireland, but he was an eager collector of hearsay, and his book contains many of the 'wonders' that typify medieval travel writing: wolves that engaged in complex conversations with priests, hermaphrodites and bearded women, corpses on offshore islands that never decayed, and more besides. He also includes an eye-catching anecdote about a woman in Connacht who regularly had sex with a particularly handsome goat, 'having seduced it to become the instrument of her unnatural lust, rather than that the animal was the guilty actor'.[28] But the book's most striking feature is Gerald's repeated insistence on the general barbarity of the Irish people. They were barbarous in their dress, in their customs, even in their style of horse-riding and their beards, which they 'grow enormously in an uncouth manner'. All told, the Irish were 'a rude people, subsisting on the produce of their cattle only, and living themselves like beasts – a people that has not yet departed from the primitive habits of pastoral life'.[29] *Topographia Hibernica* was hugely influential and widely translated, and it was still frequently cited many centuries later. It primed whole generations of travellers heading for Ireland to expect barbarism the moment they arrived.

Among those who followed in Gerald's wake was Edmund Spenser, whose *A View of the Present State of Ireland* declared it 'the most barbarous Nation in Christendome'. The supremely well-travelled Scotsman William Lithgow (whom Twiss quoted on the topic of Irishwomen breastfeeding babies over their shoulders) visited in 1619 and declared the Irish 'the least industrious, and most sluggish Livers under the Sun'. The 'vulgar Irish' he declared, 'live more miserably in their brutish Fashion than the undaunted, or untamed *Arabian*, the Devilish Idolatrous *Turcuman*, or the Moon-worshipping *Caramines*'.[30] And so it continued, Ireland providing British readers with their most readily accessible Other, a discourse of barbarism and indolence running right through to the official response to the famine of the 1840s, the infamous *Punch* cartoons of 'wild Irishmen' and a thousand bad 'Paddy Irishman' jokes.

All this can leave a contemporary travel writer decidedly uneasy – a foreigner in Ireland and a British citizen to boot (even if you've noticed that when people grumble about 'foreigners' of late they somehow don't mean you). No one wants to end up on the bottom of a chamber pot, after all. But what can you do? Surrendering the right to write seems regressive. Travel writing has always been about encounters with difference, a landscape and a society seen with the eye of the outsider. Should you simply restrict yourself to polite platitudes? But then H. V. Morton will quickly draw you into reductive clichés about whitewashed cabins and fairy lore. All you can do, ultimately, is reflect on your own point of departure. If Gerald of Wales had done that, he might have realised that rather than being *barbarous*, twelfth-century Irish pastoralism was simply *different* from his own Norman conception of what agriculture should look like. And *you* might realise that the big newbuild houses along the rural roads of Galway appear crass to *you* because you grew up in a place dominated by crooked cottages where overt displays of expenditure were viewed askance. There's nothing *inherently* crass about them. And then you might also realise that the lack of proper, legally enshrined public access to the Irish countryside has preoccupied you for over a decade only because *you* grew up with footpaths stretching across the fields and moors in all directions. If at that point you still feel that it deserves discussion, then you might decide that you need to consider the historical context – over the course of several hundred kilometres and several hundred pages. And then that question of historical context brings something else to the fore, something you feel inexplicably uneasy about addressing. The woman at the unconference said, 'The English have always *had* their land, so maybe it doesn't matter to them if other people walk all over it; but *we* had it taken away from us.' That 'we' – a contemporary collective elided with a historical pronoun. And who exactly might that historical 'we' include and exclude?

* * *

It had been hot when I left Tullamore – the first properly hot day since my night on Moylussa. I set out, still drawn irresistibly eastwards by the Grand Canal, on the well-trodden grass of the southern bank. There were dog walkers and joggers on both sides here, and a shading line of beeches. Suddenly I was awkwardly aware of where I was: this stretch of the canal had been in the news a couple of years earlier. A young woman, a primary school teacher out for an afternoon jog, had been murdered here in a random attack. I was abruptly conscious of the weight of my own presence – on this or any other footpath. A six-foot, broad-shouldered man moving along with a stick in his hand, blithely forgetful until now of the unease that his own approach might generate for a woman walking alone. I was grateful that after the Twenty-Fifth Lock, I passed no one else on my side of the canal.

Eight kilometres out of Tullamore a secondary canal, the old Kilbeggan line, branched sharply away to the northwest. It allowed me a long overdue correction, a ten-kilometre dogleg that would get me back on track, heading properly for Burr Point at last. This secondary canal was no longer navigable, a mere ooze in a willow-tangled ditch. The route alongside it: bits of faded tarmac, bits of gravel track, the occasional stretch of grass. At one point the line ran gently uphill across a reddish bog. Oxeye daisies danced beside the path, yolk-yellow asphodels and a lemony eruption of lady's bedstraw. At the top of the rise, I looked back and saw the familiar line of Slieve Bloom falling away to southward, blue under oyster-coloured cloud. A hot breeze ran in at my back and brought with it another of those uncanny moments of transportation – to long journeys on rattletrap buses across yellow landscapes on another continent, a quarter of a century ago.

Beyond the bog, in a stretch of cool shade, I saw a red squirrel with a mustard-tinted tail looping along the path towards me. I froze. It kept coming, and I saw a strange growth at its neck. It was only when the squirrel was almost at my feet that I realised the growth was a bundled baby, clamped gently in its mother's jaws. She halted, recognising my presence at last, flicked her yellowish tail and hopped neatly aside into the brambles.

A little while later a small herd of cattle appeared in silhouette on a narrow ridge to the right. A glacial esker! Recognising one in the landscape always brings me a peculiar thrill. They seem so obviously *constructed* that they appear as relics of a vanished civilisation: the mysterious ceremonial hedges of a lost race of ice giants. I paused to take a snapshot of it with my phone, and as I did so I remembered where I was – right on the Offaly–Westmeath border. This wasn't just any esker, then; it was *the* esker: the Esker Riada, the band of glacial rubble that runs from Dublin to Galway.

There is a reference to the Esker Riada in the *Annals of the Four Masters* – an account of Irish history compiled by Franciscan monks in Donegal from myriad older texts in the early seventeenth century. According to the *Annals*, on the night of the birth of Conn of the Hundred Battles, a semi-mythical second-century king, there 'were discovered five principal roads leading to Teamhair [the Hill of Tara], which were never observed till then'. These mysteriously emergent roads were the 'Slighe Asail, Slighe Midhluachra, Slighe Cualann, Slighe Mhór, [and] Slighe Dala', of which the 'Slighe Mor is that called Eiscir Riada'. This ridge-cum-road provided 'the division line of Ireland into two parts'[31] – that in the north ruled by Conn, and that in the south controlled by his rival, Mug Nuadat.

The existence of the 'five great roads' is broadly accepted by historians, though there is some scepticism about their purported prehistoric origins and much debate about their true terminus – whether it was Dublin or Tara, the ceremonial hillock in Meath claimed as the inauguration place of the high kings.[32] But in either hypothesis, the Slighe Midhluachra ran in from the north, the Slighe Cualann from the south. The Slighe Dala began in the southwest, possibly on the Shannon estuary, and the Slighe Asail began in Roscommon. The Slighe Mhór, meanwhile, the 'Great Highway', stretched east–west from Dublin to Galway Bay. The exact route is a topic for academic arguments – and much dedicated fieldwork, with researchers agonising over which particular ridge or overgrown boreen might mark its true trajectory.[33] But it's worth remembering that early travellers were not necessarily bound to a single road on a cross-country journey. As the scholar Linda Doran notes, cross-country routes usually followed the path of least resistance. We're back to Le Corbusier's 'pack-donkey's way' here: 'Where there was a hill to climb or a difficult area to pass through, multiple tracks would develop, each traveller taking the easiest route', Doran writes.[34] Those on foot might have headed straight up the steepest slope on a narrow footpath, while those with laden beasts and carts followed a longer, leveller track. There might also have been seasonal shortcuts, only accessible when the ground was dry or clear of vegetation. And all along the way, individual travellers would have cut in or peeled off, to and from their own homeplaces along smaller side paths. Some of the tracks and footpaths running along distinct ridges of the wider Esker Riada band were still in use well into the twentieth century.[35]

The subsection of the Esker Riada I was looking at here was

part of the Rahugh Ridge. Later, I traced its line on the Google satellite image. It stretched in an almost unbroken arc for twenty kilometres, from the banks of the Clodiagh River near Rahan, past the northern suburbs of Tullamore – where it had been turned into a golf course and quarried for building aggregate – and eventually subsided at the edge of the Bord na Móna-owned Toar Bog near the M6 motorway at Tyrrellspass. In places, this esker still carries a minor local road. And in 2014, archaeologists working on the Toar Bog uncovered the remains of a *togher*, a timber and brushwood bog road running on a southwest–northeast orientation and carbon-dated to the twelfth century.[36] Perhaps the *togher* was a continuation of a route that once ran along the entire length of the ridge. But on this hot July afternoon in the twenty-first century, the section of the esker cut by the line of the Kilbeggan branch of the Grand Canal was off limits behind a double fence-line, and trafficked only by cattle.

* * *

The woman behind the bar in the visitor centre in Kilbeggan Distillery said that she'd walked the final hundred kilometres of the Camino de Santiago in Spain at the end of the COVID-19 pandemic.

'If you'd said to me a few years before that I'd go on a walking holiday one day, I'd never have believed it,' she said, 'but I absolutely loved it.'

I'd shambled into Kilbeggan past the drained and grassed-over harbour at the end of the old canal, hoping for a coffee and a slice of cake in a café. But there was a drab afternoon silence to the place and everything on the long main street was closed. The distillery was open for visitors, however. A trickle of American couples in their sixties and seventies, detouring briefly on the drive between Dublin and Galway, came through for a whiskey sampler and a visit to the giftshop. And the bar was serving coffee and plastic-wrapped muffins.

The barmaid was in her thirties, with short dark hair. She

asked every visitor who came to the bar about their trip with the specificity of genuine interest: what was the accommodation like in Kerry? How was the food in Galway? What exactly had they liked about Clare? How long were they staying in Dublin on their return? And she gave back merrily unabashed chat about her own life, her friends and family, things she did in her spare time. When I went up to pay, she offered to fill my water bottle and told me all about her Camino trip. She'd loved the social aspect, she said, meeting people from different places, different backgrounds, walking for different reasons. But she also liked the way you could move at your own pace, spend the days walking alone and then meet with a merry pilgrim crowd in the hostels at night.

'The Camino's all about the wine!' she said. 'They should do something like that in Ireland – like, a walk right across the country with places to stop every night. They really should.'

She'd grown up in Kilbeggan, lived at the edge of town beside the little Brosna River. When she was a child there was never a summer when they didn't get a few people camping in their field. 'They'd ask permission first; cyclists, usually, not walkers.' Most had been from Dublin, but there'd been a few English and Germans too, teachers, many of them, making the most of long summer holidays – 'But you just don't get that anymore.'

I said I was trying to steer clear of the roads as much as I could.

'There's a Westmeath Way here – goes through the fields!' She made it sound as if this was the wildest imaginable concept. 'But don't ask me where it is! I see the signs for it all over the place, but I don't know where it actually is!'

It was immediately behind the distillery, running up the banks of the Brosna from a little public garden with weedy gravel and desiccated lavender. There were stiles and way-markers with yellow arrows and permissive access across farmland. But no one was using the route. Someone had cut back the riverbank scrub in the spring, but the nettles had grown back high with no one to tread them down. Mallards chattered disapprovingly and a heron burst out of the channel with histrionic outrage at my passing.

Afternoon heat and a humid breeze. I passed a ruined mill with water still moving mysteriously through its hidden passageways like the esker-making streams in the ice-channels of a glacier. The way ran on through fields, some well grazed, some deep with reeds. A herd of skittish red bullocks eddied and feinted as I passed. What an exotic pleasure this was – to move over farmland in Ireland without the fear of being accused of trespass. But as far as I could tell, no one else had walked this way for months. I had to batter away at the brambles with my trekking pole to find the stiles through the hedges. Where the river ran into the shade of a big esker, an unused footbridge crossed the water. They must have intended to carry the path onwards that way, but perhaps the landowner on the far bank had pulled out, and now the route detoured west to a road. The tarmac was greasy in the low evening light. It made for joyless walking after the interlude in the fields, so when I came to a pub at a quiet crossroads I ducked gratefully into the cool of the bar. There were no other customers and the barmaid was wrestling with a vacuum cleaner. But she came behind the bar and placed her hands firmly on the pumps.

'Now, my lovely, what can I get you?'

She was thirtyish, with blonde hair and a nose stud. But she had that motherly way that barmaids in certain village pubs pick up early, part of their professionalism, their technique for deftly managing the boozy older men on the other side of the bar.

I asked if she ever saw walkers passing on the Westmeath Way.

'Never. But me and my friends did used to go down on the other side of the river with the horses when we were kids.' This would have been on the route from the closed footbridge.

'Can you get through to Kilbeggan that way?'

'Ah, you can go down a way. But then you'd be out onto land.' There was something about the inflection she gave to 'land', some specific meaning: not just any land, but *farm*land, privately owned, protectively claimed, off limits. I'd often heard people talking about 'the land' when specifically discussing their own family farms, but not this other broader categorisation without the definite article.

She said that at the pub in her own village, a few kilometres down the road, two teachers from Dublin had dropped in one afternoon a few years ago looking for a place to camp. They were walking to Galway, she recalled, sticking to the quiet roads, and one of them got a harmonica out of his backpack after a few drinks.

'Now, my village would be borderline redneck, so they all loved that and started buying them pints; and anyway, they camped in the pub garden in the end, but I don't know if they ever managed to put up the tent.'

She came back out from behind the bar to finish the cleaning.

'You've a bit of a twang,' she said as she bent over the vacuum cleaner.

'A twang?'

'A twang. Do you know what a twang is?'

'I do, of course. Where would you say I was from?'

She looked up and narrowed her brows as if I'd presented her with an enjoyable riddle. 'I'm not sure. I was wondering if maybe you were just very well educated; like, you'd been over to Oxford or something.'

I laughed. 'I was never anywhere near Oxford!'

When I went on into the evening I did so with a certain gratitude that eased the resurgent pain in my feet: at least she hadn't been sure.

I'd hoped to camp beside Lough Ennell. But when I got there an hour later, there were 'no camping' signs around the parking area. The story goes that Jonathan Swift had a moment of inspiration here, looking back from a boat on the lake and noticing how small the people on the shore appeared. The place was known as 'Nure' at the time, but they renamed it 'Lilliput' in honour of *Gulliver's Travels*. Lilliput House was an adventure centre now. There were sun-bleached sit-on kayaks stacked at the water's edge, picnic benches, customised camper vans parked up in a circle in a field and a low thud of dance music. The lake was wide, wind-cut, a single boat drifting far off, two huddled anglers in silhouette.

I could have trampled my way into the reeds, found a hidden spot to put up the tent under the nearby trees. But I'd walked a full forty kilometres from Tullamore, further than on any other day, and I couldn't summon the resilience needed to spend a night where I knew there was an interdiction. I hobbled away from the lake on a quiet lane instead and came out onto a bog. A hare raced away between stacks of footed turf. I pitched the tent on a clear patch among the heather in the dusk. I could hear big aeroplanes overhead, throttling down on the approach to Dublin. A dog barked somewhere nearby, and the thud of the dance music drifted in from Lilliput late into the night.

* * *

The bog where I slept is given no name on the modern 1:50,000 Ordnance Survey Ireland map – nor on Google Maps. But I know now that my campsite was right on the mid-bog border of two townlands, Rathnamuddagh to the north and Monaghanstown to the south. And I know that because of a 200-year-old map.

In the first half of the nineteenth century, Ireland was subjected to the most detailed mapping project the world had ever seen. The initial impetus for the project was taxation. In 1800, an Act of Union had abolished the old Irish Parliament, turned Dublin from a working capital to a mere provincial city and concentrated legislative power in London. The Westminster Parliament rapidly decided that the existing regime of taxation based on land values in Ireland was 'inaccurate, inequitable and corrupt'.[37] The smallest unit of land division, and the basis of taxation, was the townland – an old system, probably long predating the arrival of the Normans. The 'town' of the name is a translation of *baile*, anglicised as 'bally'. In its original sense, this didn't mean an urban centre but perhaps something more like 'settlement' or 'commune'.*

* Townlands have a parallel in my own home part of Cornwall where the standard settlement pattern is the *trev*, the nucleated farming hamlet. *Trev* is sometimes translated from Cornish as 'farm', but a more authentic rendering is revealed in the vernacular English-language terms attached to such a settlement: the communal area at the heart of a *trev* is the 'town-place'; the first field out of the farmyard is

Ireland is subdivided into more than 60,000 townlands. But the exact boundaries of these little units, typically no more than a few hundred acres apiece, could be hard to determine, especially in the bogs and mountains. And there were local variations – ploughland, tate, carvagh. In 1824, a Westminster select committee authorised a survey of the whole of Ireland at the unprecedented scale of six inches to the mile (1:10,000). It would fix the precise borders of the individual townlands and allow for the proper collection of dues from their owners. It would also, of course, provide an invaluable military resource: comprehensive topographic knowledge of an island that, for the British authorities, stubbornly retained the qualities of a restive colony, Act of Union notwithstanding. It was only a quarter of a century since the last large-scale conflagration in Ireland, the 1798 rebellion of the United Irishmen, backed by France and defeated by the British only after a four-month campaign.

The survey got underway in 1826 at the top-right corner, near Belfast. It was organised by Thomas Frederick Colby, the Kent-born head of the Ordnance Survey. Colby was missing his left hand (he blew it off in a shooting accident in Cornwall in 1803), but the disability hadn't prevented him becoming one of the most brilliant practical geographers of the nineteenth century – and a ferocious cross-country walker. During an 1819 surveying operation in Scotland, he covered 513 miles on foot in twenty-two days, stopping to set up equipment and take bearings at every available vantage point.[38] Under Colby's supervision, a precise baseline for Ireland was established at Lough Foyle, trig points were fixed on every prominent hilltop, and the whole of Ireland was gradually enmeshed with triangular calculations of distance and altitude. The initial fieldwork was done by officers of the Royal Engineers and the Royal

---

the 'town field', and a hamlet with a church is a 'church-town'. The lands historically attached to an individual *trev* – traditionally a mix of infield and rough moorland grazing – are usually similar in acreage to a typical Irish townland. The *trev* and the townland may, then, represent a similar and perhaps directly related old system of land division.

Artillery. Over the course of a decade, they dragged their chains and plane tables and theodolites across every acre of Ireland. Even the remotest of mountain townlands got a visit – military outsiders turning up and hanging around, clambering up ridges, squinting at far horizons, scribbling in their pocketbooks, recording every field wall, every cottage, every bend in every stream.

The survey quickly grew in scope and ambition – and in cost (the final bill was £860,000, three times the original budget).[39] The original government commission required only the boundaries of the townlands to be mapped; but Colby unilaterally decided to include all field boundaries, vastly increasing the detail recorded on the final maps.[40] He and his second-in-command, Thomas Larcom, wanted their finished work to be more than a record of mere physical geography. For Colby, it was 'scarcely necessary to remark, that a map is in its nature but a part of a Survey, and that much of the information connected with it, can only be advantageously embodied in a memoir [a book-form gazetteer], to which the map then serves as a graphical index'.[41] The aim was to capture *everything* – to corral all there was to know into a body of official documentation. This was very much an exercise of a post-Enlightenment era in which knowledge was power – and absolute knowledge was believed possible, if only you had enough time and manpower and money. By the time Colby and Larcom set their teams to work in Ireland, another epic of British imperial mapmaking had been underway for more than twenty years: the seven-decade Great Trigonometrical Survey of India. There too the aim was perfect topographical knowledge and thus supreme colonial control. The mapmakers in India soon took note of activities in Ireland and borrowed their new techniques.

There were those on the ground in Ireland who recognised what these measurers and notetakers were about, knew well that the army and the taxman follow the mapmaker. The earlier epic mapping project, William Petty's Down Survey of the 1650s, had been explicitly conducted to facilitate the Cromwellian Settlement. Perhaps some memory of that lingered in the 1820s and 1830s. There

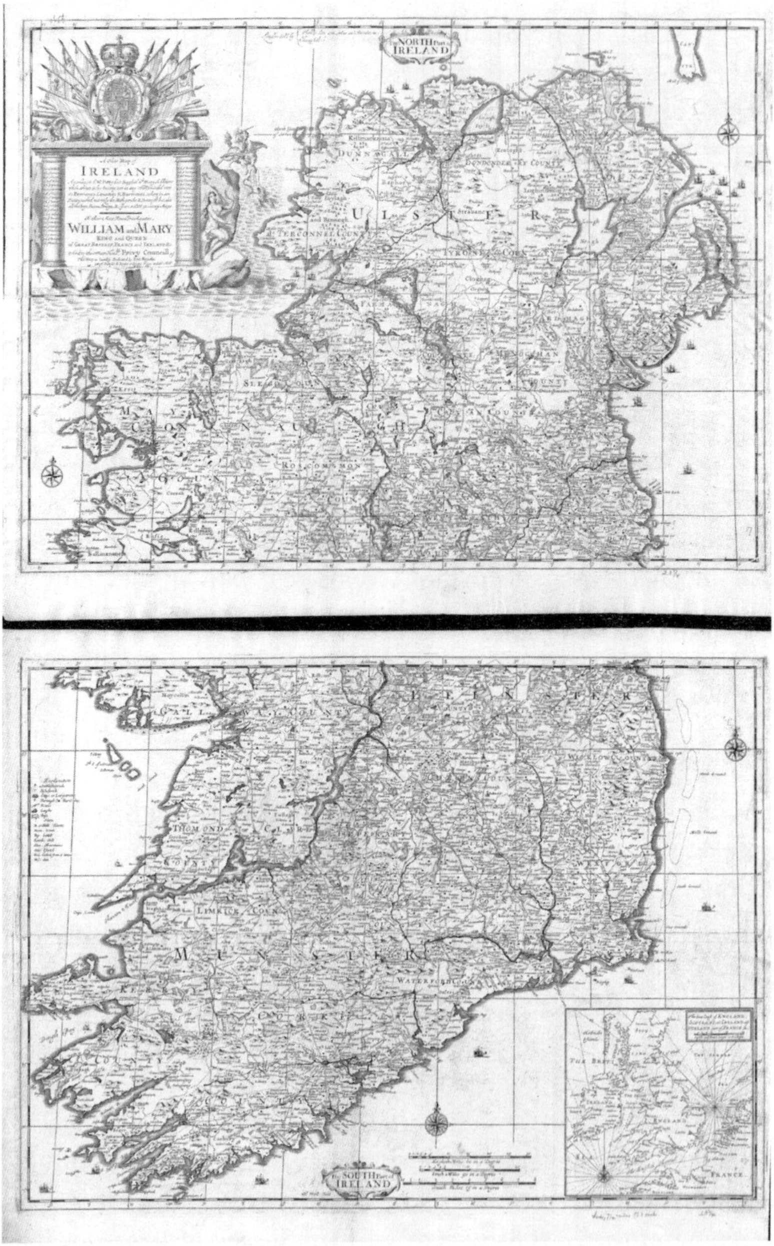

A 1695 map of Ireland, based on William Petty's original Down Survey

was passive resistance in places, occasional open hostility. In 1827, one supervisor had to demand that locals be cautioned 'against removing or changing the situation of any of the poles put up by the Surveyors'.[42] In Wexford and around Bantry in West Cork, surveyors had to work with police protection,[43] and in 1838, a trio of Royal Engineers were attacked and one of them was stabbed on their way back to the survey's base in Galway.[44] And as with any collection of folkloric material, you have to suspect that at least a few of the recorded placenames were the product of spur-of-the-moment improvisation or mischievous leg-pulling by local informants.

The idea of the Ordnance Survey as a problematic colonial endeavour is well established in Ireland today – in no small part thanks to Brian Friel's 1980 play *Translations*, set in a fictional Donegal village during a visit from the mapmakers. Among the villagers are those who quietly resist and those who abet the survey process, those who can communicate directly with the British officials and those who speak no English but are comfortable with Greek and Latin, thanks to the activities of the unofficial 'hedge school' system. The mapmakers are seen crudely translating and arbitrarily anglicising Irish placenames. The main English character is the naïve young officer, George Yolland, who has ended up in Donegal after missing the boat to Bombay and has succumbed to a wildly romantic view of the west of Ireland – though he is smart enough to recognise that 'Even if I did speak Irish I'd always be an outsider here, wouldn't I?'[45]

Translations is brilliant on the slippery issues of language and knowledge and power. But it isn't a wholly accurate representation of the Ordnance Survey in Ireland. Thomas Colby was aware of the sensitivities of sending British soldiers literally into the Irish field, and he insisted that they carry no weapons during their work.[46] He also hived off the sensitive business of identifying townlands (and in some cases partitioning or amalgamating them) and valuing the land to the Dublin-born geologist Richard Griffith, a veteran of surveying work for the Commission for Bogs at the start of the century. There was no enforced policy of converting old Irish placenames into English neologisms – not for reasons of cultural sensitivity, but because continuity would make it easier to use archive documents and older maps in future legal wrangles over land.[47] Nor was the anglicisation process as casually arbitrary as *Translations* suggests. And though locals were barred from employment in the initial mapping work, once the mission-creep into historical research began that had to change. Language scholars, historians and antiquarians were signed up – to the increasing alarm of Thomas Colby's paymasters. (Colby's plan to produce a book-form 'memoir' for every region had to be abandoned after the first edition – covering just one parish – came in at the then staggering cost of £1,700.)[48]

The greatest of the Irish scholars working on the Ordnance Survey was John O'Donovan. Born into a moderately comfortable Catholic farming family on the Kilkenny–Waterford border in 1806 and initially educated in an unofficial 'hedge school', O'Donovan had planned to join the priesthood. But he switched to scholarship of Irish history and language. In the late 1820s Colby's deputy, Thomas Larcom, decided that if he was to map a landscape overwhelmingly named in Irish, then he really ought to learn the language himself. The recommended tutor, who showed up on Larcom's doorstep in 'peasant garb',[49] was O'Donovan. He was later taken on in the survey's 'topographical department'. Thomas Colby was uncomfortably aware that 'The mode of spelling the names of places was peculiarly vague and unsettled', and that for the purpose of map-making 'it was desirable to establish a standard orthography'. He quickly realised 'that a sufficient extension of the original orthographic inquiries, to trace all the mutations of each name, would be, in fact, to pass in review the local history of the whole country'.[50] This was John O'Donovan's task. He began in the Dublin archives, but soon headed out into the field. He attempted to verify and decipher the placenames recorded in 'name books' by the military surveyors, while also gathering general history, folklore and miscellaneous landscape trivia.

Over the course of the 1830s, O'Donovan travelled thousands

of kilometres across Ireland, usually alone and on foot. By day he would traipse across fields and bogs and spend hours quizzing locals about their own landscapes. Night would find him in a village inn or lodging in a family home, scribbling long letters to Larcom by candlelight in a sharply slanted hand with flamboyant descenders. The letters contain a good few complaints about his salary and his workload, but they are also laced with humour. He could be scathing about other people's work. In 1838, he wrote to Larcom from Galway to acknowledge receipt of a copy of a 'Statistical Survey' of the county published a decade earlier, and to inform him that 'I shall send it back again as it is not worth carrying'. Its author, he declared, was 'a regular helter skelter Irish writer, who has not the organ of order very prominent in his pericranium' and 'knows more about potatoes than antiquities'.[51] At one point, Larcom had to reprimand O'Donovan for adding sarcastic marginalia to official papers: 'by this destruction of documents – by ribaldry – you really lower yourself in the opinion of everyone'. O'Donovan responded with a palpable smirk, promising 'to give up this style of writing, for the future, and to become very serious, cold and un-Irish'.[52]

O'Donovan was clearly a man of astonishing talent and stamina (during the course of his career he also walked the entire length of the Esker Riada[53] and translated the *Annals of the Four Masters*). But it was exhausting work. On 21 May 1835, he wrote to Larcom from Carrickmacross in Monaghan to explain that he had 'worked incessantly for twelve hours every day, but could not get through the County sooner [because] the [place]names are so very numerous'. He had, however, chanced upon a potential assistant from a rural townland called Greaghnaroog in the Farney barony, east of Carrickmacross:

> If you wish to let me have an assistant I have at last met a most useful person, Mr. Thomas O'Conor, a native of the Farney, and one of the best Latin, Greek and Irish scholars I have met this long time. He is about 23 years of age, single, and at liberty to do whatever he

> pleases; and as he is principally engaged in teaching Latin, Greek and Irish he would be immediately useful to us, and I think in a great measure necessary, as I fear the names would take up all my time, and prevent me from doing anything else. I asked him if he would wish to get employment in the Ordnance Survey and he said that he would provided he would receive any salary at all worth his notice (all woulds no shoulds, the Irish idiom).[54]

Larcom agreed to pay O'Conor 7s a day, and he spent the next six years crisscrossing the country as O'Donovan's assistant.[55]

For Tim Robinson, a later mapmaker and collector of language and lore, O'Donovan's work on a standard anglicised orthography of placenames was a 'systematic corruption', a 'great betrayal' and 'the second great trauma of the sense of place in Ireland' after Christianisation.[56] But this doesn't seem entirely fair. Robinson's chosen Connemara stomping ground and the Donegal setting of *Translations* were certainly overwhelmingly Irish-speaking at the time. But elsewhere, especially in the Midlands and the east, English was already the dominant community language. Thousands of placenames had *already* been thoroughly anglicised through local use, and O'Donovan was much concerned with unravelling the riddles they presented. In these places he seems to have been less about systematic corruption than earnest salvage anthropology. And it's worth remembering that subsequent official efforts to 'correct' anglicised placenames back into proper Irish in areas that have been English-speaking for generations emerge from their own centres of academic power and may enforce new systems of standardisation on centuries of fluid local tradition.

In the autumn and winter of 1837–8, John O'Donovan and Thomas O'Conor were at large in the Midlands, travelling separately, occasionally rendezvousing in one of the larger towns and sending nightly letters back to Dublin. O'Donovan noted with frustration that corroborating the etymology of already corrupted placenames was often impossible, 'as the Irish language is not spoken in any parish [in Offaly]'.[57] And O'Conor had a similar experience travelling between Mullingar and Tullamore. On 8 October 1837 he wrote to Larcom from Kilbeggan and explained that he had walked down from Mullingar the previous day, 'and endeavoured on my way to get the names in the parishes through which I passed, settled, but could not make out one man during the journey who could speak Irish, or could throw more light on the names than the varied orthography in the name books affords'. There was a glimmer of hope when he arrived in Kilbeggan, however, for there he met 'a very old man named Jack Daly, whose mind is possessed of youthful vigour, and vivid memory'. Daly – who sounds rather like a character from *Translations* – spoke very fine Irish and was 'the only person I met with here that is of any worth to me. He [has] read deep into history in general and thinks that Aristotle was the greatest man that ever lived.'[58] O'Conor decided to recruit Daly to help him iron out the original Irish meanings of the local townland names – though he astutely noted that as the old man was 'too fond of speaking of the diminutive form of words, of the accusative and vocative cases, and of how things ought to be, but seldom of how they are', he 'did not think it safe' to depend on him altogether. The following day he hired a cart and driver to take them into the surrounding countryside. O'Conor would identify the 'most intelligent' locals and get them to offer their own versions of the placenames, which were then 'elucidated very much by Jack's native Irish pronunciation'. This, O'Connor reckoned, served as a 'purgatorial' for the corrupted names of the 'un-Irish inhabitants' and 'sent forth a tail of brilliancy, as a comet does among the naturally dimmer lighted stars'. O'Conor explained to Larcom that he had been obliged to hire the cart because of Daly's great age. For himself, he much preferred to travel on foot: 'I find I can collect more information respecting the things enquired after, when I walk among the people and fall in with them in discourse, than if I had fifty conveyances about me'.[59]

The imperial hubris of the Ordnance Survey project – which was complete in its mapping component by 1834 and published in its entirety by 1842 – is obvious. Had Thomas Colby been able to secure funds for the full extent of the 'collateral objects' he had planned – the 'memoirs' and the detailed histories – he would have been well on his way to matching the 1:1 'Map of the Empire whose size was that of the Empire' described in Jorge Luis Borges's satirical short story 'On Exactitude in Science', a monstrous product of cartographic overreach rendered useless by its own minute detail.[60] But unlike Borges's map, the sheets of the first Ordnance Survey of Ireland have not been left to rot away in the 'Deserts of the West'. They are freely available in various digital archives. And at a distance of two centuries, they have surely been drained of their original controlling impetus to leave something more benign: a vast repository of placenames, many of which might otherwise have been lost, recorded in snapshot in the 1820s and 30s, and an intimately detailed record of a landscape that would change drastically in the decades to come. At the very least, they allow a transient visitor passing through any townland in Ireland to peel back the scaw of anonymity and access a little of the layered meaning beneath.

And so: the place where I camped near Lough Ennell, though I didn't know it at the time, was on the border of the Monaghanstown and Rathnamuddagh townlands – and the straight line of the boundary where it passes through the bog certainly has the look of an arbitrary surveyor's decision. Monaghanstown is obvious enough, and obviously English: a townland probably associated with a landowner named Monaghan (or perhaps Manchán, for it appears as 'Manchanstown' on the earlier Down Survey map). Rathnamuddagh, however, provides a pleasing puzzle. A modern 'correction' would make it *Ráth na mBodach*. *Ráth* is easy enough: an earth-banked ringfort. And indeed, when I scan the old maps, I see that this quarter of Westmeath is densely pocked with ringforts, dozens of them, like old acne scars on the green face of the farmland. *Bodach*, meanwhile, originally meant something like 'lowborn freeman', a member of the lower ranks of the old Gaelic peasantry, just above the actual serfs. It is often translated as 'churl'. Could Rathnamuddagh, then, be a truly ancient survival? Could it be that sometime in the first millennium CE there was a ringfort here – perhaps the one still identifiable today under a clump of trees in the northeast of the townland – which was occupied by a family of churls? Could the name of their place have somehow stuck, down through the centuries, through the Norman invasion and the Cromwellian Settlement and all the rest, to be noted in the pocketbook of a Royal Engineer and tentatively confirmed by Thomas O'Conor? Well, maybe. But ringforts in Gaelic Ireland were generally higher-status dwellings rather than the homes of churls – and in any case, there is another, more recent meaning of *bodach*. Prejudicial ideas about the uncouth nature of lowborn peasants seem in later centuries to have turned *bodach* into a sort of bogeyman, the folkloric 'old man' partnered to the hag. So perhaps a ghost story about an 'Old Man's Ringfort' is the more likely origin for the townland's name.* But there remain devilish further possibilities: perhaps an English soldier working on the shores of Lough Ennell in the late 1820s made a mistake in his name book. Perhaps Thomas O'Conor found no one to help him confirm or correct it on his walk down from Mullingar. Or perhaps he came this way with Jack Daly, and when he asked Jack Daly to provide the authentic pronunciation, *Jack Daly pulled his leg…*

* * *

I woke once or twice in the night to the pop of rain against the flysheet and came awake properly in the grey of the dawn. I cooked my breakfast noodles inside the tent, then scrambled out into a wild wet morning.

There is something that travel writers seldom discuss: toilet

---

* There's a story from Rathnamuddagh in the 1930s The Schools' Collection of folklore about a fairy-occupied ringfort called 'the Black Fort'. See The Schools' Collection, Vol.0737, p.476. Available at: www.duchas.ie/en/cbes/5009087/4985352/5122326.

matters. You could easily come away with the impression that the digestive tracts of certain long-distance walkers and cross-continental cyclists simply cease to operate when they are on the road. A six-month journey through the deserts of the Middle East or across the mountains of Central Asia and not a single mention of the bathroom! So here's my small subversion of genre norms: a bog is an excellent place for outdoor defecation. The ground is perfectly pliable and there are always bits of wood around to dig with. So, I dug myself a fine, deep latrine, squatted down in the drizzle, and afterwards backfilled it and trod down the black, crumbly peat and no one would ever have known.

Turf footed in elaborate Jenga stacks at the edge of the bog; a three-piece living room suite, upholstered with red velvet, dumped at the side of an access track; and a sign for the Westmeath Way pointing off into muddy fields. I followed it past a clutch of ruins in a grove of tall trees and saw a big hare up close, gingery, pale-eyed, frozen in a rutted gateway. The grass was deep and wet. There were more stiles and step-throughs along the line of the path here, but they were completely unused, grown over thick with nettles and brambles, their timber rotted. I'd walked plenty of abandoned paths like this in Cornwall. But a way through the fields was such a rarity here in Ireland that I'd have expected a queue of hikers waiting to experience the novelty of it. Why was no one using this path? I could see a string of houses beside a road in the distance. Why did no one who lived there make it part of their daily circuit, a jogging route or a place for a quick leg-stretch with the labrador? The woman in Kilbeggan Distillery had enthused about the Spanish Camino but couldn't locate the start of a footpath a couple of hundred metres away. Was there a kind of Stockholm syndrome at play – a popular sense that 'land' is so firmly off limits that even if it were all thrown open tomorrow, no one would dare to walk on it? An Irish colleague once told me of a visit to Cornwall to explore the prehistoric sites of Bodmin Moor. She'd spent the whole day in a state of reflexive anxiety about what felt like brazen trespass, despite the reassurances of her English husband. Or was there such a habituation to 'walks' on tidy loops of gravel, tarmac or duckboard that no one could countenance the wet grass, the brambles, the mud?*

After a couple of kilometres, the path came out onto tarmac and I was instantly consumed by the grimness of road walking on a wet morning: the unforgiving surface, the uneven camber dropping away into the litter and lumpy tussocks of the verge, the whine of oncoming cars and the bleakly expanding distance on the straight stretches. It was fourteen kilometres to Mullingar, where I'd knock at the door of the first B&B I saw and stand shivering at the threshold, hoping that they had a room. Along the way I found myself moving with a certain belligerence, scowling into the rain, flinging my trekking pole far out to my left whenever an approaching car showed no sign of slowing as it passed. I saw a placard nailed to a post: an image of a wind turbine and the bold word 'NO'.

Beyond Dysart I turned on to a side road to get away from the worst of the traffic for a few kilometres, and just beyond the junction I saw another sign nailed to a telegraph pole, this one bearing nothing but the two-letter refusal: 'NO'. The plastic was green with algae and the red paint of the letters had faded. It probably dated from the run-up to the 2018 referendum to repeal the Eighth Amendment which outlawed abortion in the Republic of Ireland. But in my own bad humour that morning it seemed like a distillation of all the signs I'd seen along the way: no wind turbines; no cycleway; no trespassing; no entry. The capital 'N' looked like a barricade of broken pallets fixed across a footpath.

---

* I suspect that the latter may be the answer. A recent one-star review of the Westmeath Way on the Sport Ireland website declares it a 'disaster' and fulminates at length about the overgrown path, 'unsanitary conditions' (cowpats) and above all the shocking experience of encountering livestock along the way.

7

Exodus: Mullingar to Kells

But sometimes it's a 'Yes', and then the initial letter appears not as a barricade of broken pallets, but as two paths diverging in a yellow wood – and there is *always* a way through the woods…

'Are you lost?'

I'd stopped to look at something on the banks of the Royal Canal, a kilometre outside Mullingar, and two men on mountain bikes had skidded to a halt alongside me, big friendly heads on them.

'Sure, how could I be lost? There's only two options – up the canal or down the canal.'

'Well, you never know!'

I had been lost yesterday, though. I'd stared at the wet maps, spread on the bed in the B&B for a long time, then gone out without a solution to slither along the rain-slicked pavements of Mullingar in flipflops (my soggy walking shoes were still airing out on the radiator and I'd abandoned the heavy hiking boots back in Portumna). I sat for a long while over a bowl of chowder in a corner of an old-fashioned hotel dining room: carvery lunches, banquette seating, floral carpets and servers who greeted the elderly diners by name – 'How you doing, Joe? The roast, is it? I'll bring it over for you so…' When I got back to the room the maps were dry, more or less, and the answer was obvious: small steps. I'd plot my onward journey day by day – hour by hour, even. There would be a lot of roads, I knew; but if I didn't look too far ahead, the prospect wouldn't seem so bad. All I needed to do was make sure that I kept heading generally towards the northeast. And there was an irresistible escape route from Mullingar itself: the Royal Canal, an intended rival to the Grand Canal which bankrupted its builders in the 1790s. It ran in the wrong direction, southeastward. But it would get me out into the countryside without having to walk the busy roads around the town. The rain had cleared overnight, and I'd set out in a cool grey morning.

The mountain bikers were both sixtyish, with thick grey hair and ruddy faces. They had the look of people committed to adventure sports but without the dry seriousness that that commitment sometimes brings. I got the sense that they'd known each other forever and had maintained a constant merriment for decades. But there was an air of sensitive intelligence behind the laddish banter. They stood astride their bikes to chat. The one on the left was shorter, stockier; the one on the right was taller than me. They were heading down the canal for a coffee in Cunningham's Pub at Riverstown. They asked about my own route, and I said I'd been on the Grand Canal and its branch lines as far as Kilbeggan.

'And then how did you get to Mullingar?'

'There's a route,' I said. 'The Westmeath Way, up the Brosna, though I'd say I was the first person to walk it this year.'

'Ah, I know it; you see the signposts,' said the taller man. 'And where did you sleep?'

I was vaguely aware of an emerging joke at my own expense. There was a decided twinkle in each of their eyes. 'By Lilliput,' I said, warily.

'You camped at Lilliput?'

'Well, not actually at Lilliput; in the bog, there – do you know it? Inland a bit from the lake...'

It seemed that I'd unwittingly delivered the punchline, for they both roared with laughter.

'That's his land!' said the shorter man, flicking a thumb at his friend. 'He owns it! You camped on his land!'

This was unexpected, and I was fearful of reprimand. 'I was keeping a low profile,' I said. 'I didn't leave any mess or anything...'

The taller man flicked his head back. 'Ah, no bother at all! Sure, why would I mind? It's not really the bog itself anyway. It's where the path goes in across the fields beyond. I own that land. That's my house beside it.'

'The path is across your fields?'

'It is,' he said, grinning.

The coincidence was outrageous. This felt like a carefully engineered encounter, designed to answer the questions that had nagged me walking over those same fields twenty-four hours earlier. I asked how the route had been developed. He said it was done years ago. They'd come to him and asked if they could run the path that way – someone from the council, he thought it was – and then put the stiles and the signs in. But there'd always been an unofficial path there anyway.*

---

* Waymarked paths across farmland in Ireland are often developed under the 'Walks Scheme', launched in 2008 by the Department of Rural and Community Development. A landowner – almost always a farmer – agrees to the development

'Why would I mind someone walking across the fields?' he said. 'What harm would they do?'

'You're a rare man in Ireland to talk like that!'

'But what harm is someone like you going to do?' He motioned to my backpack, my trekking pole. 'It's the lads with cars and all that who do the damage, and they'll go in whether they have permission or not. Now, there's people who might go onto the land with a dog, and if there's cattle there it can be dangerous, and they don't understand that. But otherwise, what's the harm?'

Instead of the unembodied hostility I'd conjured from the 'NO' sign on the telegraph pole, here was its absolute opposite, manifested on a mountain bike on the banks of the Royal Canal. I must have been staring at him because he laughed again and leant in slightly, as if to reassure me that the joke was a friendly one. 'What's the *harm*?'

But my sense that the path was little used was correct, he said. He'd never noticed anyone walking across his fields since the Westmeath Way opened.

'We're not used to the idea of it,' his friend chipped in. He meant the idea of being allowed to walk across *land*.

'Well, you see,' said the landowner, 'in England they've mass paths everywhere, all over the place, and other paths too. And we had them here! *We had them here!*'

'Did we?'

'We did, of course! But didn't they have a big movement there for walkers' rights in the 1920s and 30s? And that's why they have them still and we don't.'

'So, what you're saying,' said the shorter man with a wink at me, 'is that if we'd waited a few years for independence, we could have had all the footpaths too!'

We chatted about the greenway network. It was better than

---

of a walking route in return for a modest annual payment and an initial additional lump sum to develop path infrastructure. They commit to an initial five-year lifetime for the route – but it remains strictly permissive only.

nothing, they agreed, grand for cyclists like them though maybe the tarmac wasn't so nice for walkers like me. I mentioned the signs of opposition to the proposed cross-country greenway I'd seen coming up the Shannon from Portumna.

'Farmers!' The shorter man winked at me again and nudged his friend. 'Would they just be looking for a few bob, by any chance?'

'But what I don't understand', said the landowner, 'is why they have to fence it all off when they make a new greenway. All the building work and the compulsory purchase orders and the millions they spend on it. Why can't they just put a footpath across the land instead? What's the harm in it?'

I saw them again an hour later, coming back in the opposite direction where the canal passed under the motorway by a derelict pub. They'd made it to Cunningham's, had their coffee and were on their way back to Mullingar.

'The coffee powered you up, anyway,' I said. 'You were flying up that hill.'

'Ah, that was just a show we were putting on for you – we're wrecked! You should stop at Cunningham's yourself; they'll do you a nice hang sangwich.'

The canal, motorway and railway ran in close together here, portioning off little strips of farmland, some with their own islanded house and yard, accessed via an underpass or a level crossing. I passed a derelict one-storey cottage, side-on to the tarmacked towpath, the scrub grown in tight around it and piles of mouldering litter in what was left of the garden. The place looked abandoned, but a scraggy ginger cat sat at the threshold and a thin stream of smoke rose from a vent in the tin roof. There was someone within.

Cunningham's, when I reached it, turned out to be an old-fashioned country pub with a dark bar at the back and a little general store in front where you could buy a paint roller, an electric toaster, a can of beans – and a hang sangwich.

I sat to eat on a bench outside and when I'd finished, I took out my notebook to jot down the details of the conversation with the mountain bikers. A man passing on his way to the bar saw me writing and stopped. He was in his late seventies, I'd say, with a well-maintained belly beneath a blue jumper.

'You're writing a history.' It was more a hopeful statement than a question.

'Not really,' I said. But he was proud of his local knowledge, it seemed, and he'd impart it regardless. And so here is what he told me: there'd been a station on the Dublin line at Riverstown, but it had closed in 1963. Cunningham's was a staging post on the canal and there were still rings for tethering the heavy horses that pulled the barges out the back of the pub. On every bridge over the canal, you'd find a mark called a 'crow's foot' used by the surveyors (he meant an old Ordnance Survey benchmark, a horizontal line with three strikes below, marking an established point of altitude). Surveyors still used them today if they wanted to take a bearing. Old Man Cunningham used to sell bicycles and motorbikes; they'd be lined up out the front and if he didn't have it, he'd get it for you. It was Old Man Cunningham's daughter had the place now. He himself was from Raharney. (I was planning on walking that way, but he gave me no chance to say so). Raharney was a hurling village, while in neighbouring Kilucan they played Gaelic football, and it had always been that way. There'd been another football team here in Riverstown at one time, and an old lad who lived in a shack and it was called 'the Barber's' and people went in there for their haircuts.

There was a slight hesitation at the end of each fragment, but before I had time to plug in a response he'd remember something else and begin again. It felt more like an oral exam than a conversation. I had a peculiar sense that I was the one being examined, even though he was doing all the talking.

His mother was a Clare woman, he said, from Lisdoonvarna. His parents had met in England and his father had been conscripted into the British army – he still had his old leather army belt at home. But they'd wanted to send him to the Congo, so – *scoot!* – he did a runner, came home to Westmeath and never went back. His own family name was an English one, he said: 'But I've never looked into the history of it.' And that, it seemed, was the end of the exam.

'Now, I'll go on in for a pint.' He gave me a look that suggested a confessed naughtiness here, and vanished into the bar.

I packed away my notebook and returned to the canal, and there was more history there too, a particular history, coagulated as a narrative so grand that it generates its own gravity. What I'd been looking at when the mountain bikers stopped and asked if I was lost was a bronze cast of a pair of tiny shoes bound with a strip of cloth, part of the contemporary architecture of the 'National Famine Way'.

* * *

On 26 February 1846, the American abolitionist, author and orator Frederick Douglass sat down in his lodgings in Montrose on the east coast of Scotland to pen a letter to his friend and fellow abolitionist, the campaigning journalist William Lloyd Garrison. He had just spent four months in Ireland, mainly in Dublin and Belfast, and he wanted to tell Garrison what he had seen there.

'I had heard much of the misery and wretchedness of the Irish people, previous to leaving the United States,' he wrote, 'and was prepared to witness much on my arrival in Ireland. But I must confess, my experience has convinced me that the half has not been told.' Douglass had made a point of visiting some cabins on the outskirts of Dublin, and was rather more appalled than Richard Twiss had been, seventy years earlier: 'of all places to witness human misery, ignorance, degradation, filth and wretchedness, an Irish hut is pre-eminent', he told his friend. What makes this impression so striking is that Douglass was himself born into slavery in 1818 – probably in a basic cabin on a plantation in Maryland. He had escaped just seven years earlier and was in Ireland and Britain to promote the abolitionist cause and his autobiography, *Narrative of the Life of Frederick Douglass, an American Slave*.

Douglass gave Garrison grim details of the cabin interiors, the dirt, the smouldering turf fire, the cesspit festering just outside the door, with the 'picture representing the crucifixion of Christ, pasted on the most conspicuous place on the wall' the only ornamentation. He also described the scenes on the Dublin streets which were 'almost literally alive with beggars, displaying the greatest wretchedness'. Many were clearly severely malnourished or displaying terrible physical ailments. Douglass sometimes dreaded leaving the house where he was a guest, for he would at once be surrounded by the destitute, 'all telling a tale of wo [sic] which would move any but a heart of iron' and beseeching the American visitor 'For the love of God, leave us a few pennies'. He was particularly upset by the large numbers of children on the streets.

That a man who had grown up in slavery and who knew extremes of poverty and suffering firsthand was so shocked by his experiences in Dublin clearly indicates that something was badly wrong, here in what was notionally a constituent nation of one of the world's great powers. But rather disappointingly, Douglass offered a simple and banal explanation for the poverty in Dublin: 'The immediate, and it may be the main cause of the extreme poverty and beggary in Ireland, is intemperance. This may be seen in the fact that most beggars drink whiskey.'[1] He had presumably been swayed by the prejudices of certain middle-class informants in Dublin and by his own feelings about alcohol (he was a committed abstentionist). The real underlying reasons for the poverty were dramatic population growth coupled with changes in the agricultural economy in recent decades. But those factors had now been horribly compounded, and in late 1845 Ireland was on the brink of an appalling catastrophe.

Between the early eighteenth century and the mid-nineteenth century, the population of Ireland almost tripled. In 1718, there had been around 2.9 million people on the island of Ireland;[2] 123 years later in 1841 the census recorded a rising population of 8.2 million. At the same time, changes in commercial agriculture had pushed many of the smallest subtenants off their tiny holdings. The big farmers were converting oat- and wheatfields to pasture to raise beef cattle for export – and a cattle ranch requires far fewer labourers than an arable farm. Between 1814 and 1844, the number of livestock in Ireland increased at a faster rate than even the burgeoning human population, and most of the evictions were probably carried out not directly by Anglo-Irish landlords but by their larger tenants,[3] the 'strong farmers' who accounted for just a quarter of the farming population but rented 60 per cent of all the land[4] and wanted to open up more of it for cattle. The combination of population growth and displacement pushed ever more people on to marginal land. Empty mountain townlands were now rented for the first time and often organised on the communal 'rundale' system with a clachan, a nucleated hamlet, at the centre and the land divvied out among the resident families so that each had a garden plot here, a meadow there and a chunk of rough ground for grazing and turf-cutting. All of this was enabled by the dominance of the potato.

In the seventeenth century, potatoes had mainly been found in the kitchen gardens of the big houses, a side dish for the gentry.[5] But from around 1750 they rapidly became the staple for millions of people. Potatoes were supremely productive and thoroughly nutritious. You could get six tonnes of the high-yielding 'lumper' variety – enough to feed a family for a year – out of a single acre (around two-thirds of a football pitch). By the 1840s potatoes weren't just the staple crop; they were literally the only thing millions of people ate day to day. Smallholders sometimes also planted grain crops and usually raised a pig each year. But those things went to cover the rent while the potatoes provided their own sustenance. And potatoes grew where nothing else would, improving newly reclaimed ground by breaking up the soil. No other crop could possibly compete. This led to a strange phenomenon: the population grew most rapidly on the poorest land. There's a popular misconception that the huge numbers of people living in the wildest parts of Connemara and Mayo in the early nineteenth century were the descendants of Catholic refugees from east of the Shannon, forced into these places by the Cromwellian Settlement two centuries earlier. But it was actually a relatively new phenomenon.[6] A burgeoning population pushed people on to marginal land; and the availability of that marginal land, coupled with the fecundity of the lumper potato, meant that the population could keep on burgeoning. New clachans popped up in remote glens, producing new rents for distant landlords, and potato ridges ran up forty-five-degree mountainsides where nothing but heather had grown a century earlier. The last fragments of old-growth forest in the western mountains disappeared.

By the 1830s, potatoes made up almost the entire diet of around a third of the Irish population. Only in the northeast did oats remain the principal crop and the staple food.[7] This made for an alarming precarity. There were lean months every summer ahead of the potato harvest, and partial crop failures – and resultant hunger – due to late frosts or disease were common. And then, in early September 1845, right about the time Frederick Douglass arrived in Ireland, blight appeared in the potato fields around Dublin.[8]

There was nothing truly natural about the catastrophe that engulfed Ireland in the second half of the 1840s. Neither the potato nor the blight we now recognise as a fungus called *Phytophthora infestans* were native to Europe. Each had arrived, 250 years apart, from the Americas via emerging networks of globalisation entwined with European colonial power. The fungus destroyed around a third of the crop in 1845; the following year the destruction was near total. In 1847 – the proverbial nadir of the famine – blight attacks were actually minimal, thanks to a run of dry summer weather. But by that stage there'd been so much displacement and death, and so little seed potato stock remained uneaten, that almost nothing was planted. And what went into the ground the following spring was destroyed by yet another outbreak. There were sporadic recurrences of the blight right up to 1852. Potato crops failed all over Britain and Europe in the same period; but nowhere else had such a precarious combination of population density and potato monoculture – and nowhere else was the official response so disastrous.

From the very start, the British government reaction to what was clearly an impending famine in Ireland was typified by needless complication, a wholly unwarranted overconfidence in the competence of their own bureaucracy, a significant amount of flipflopping and a constant search for someone else to blame. There were also various individual moments of grotesque absurdity – such as a scheme to have Irish smallholders start growing yams, imported from the Caribbean, instead of potatoes[9] and the recruitment of the pompous celebrity chef Alexis Soyer to come up with a recipe for a soup made principally of water on which to sustain the starving masses. Above all, the British response was governed by an almost psychotic commitment to unsullied economic liberalism and a profound ideological horror of 'handouts' – especially to those suspected of being less than entirely deserving. Laced through all this were the nasty prejudices about Irish 'indolence' at large in the British imagination since the days of Gerald of Wales: 'if the Irish once find out that there are any circumstances in which they can get free government grants we shall have a system of mendicancy such as the world never saw',[10] wrote the Assistant Treasury Secretary, Charles Edward Trevelyan, charged with managing the crisis from London, to the Chair of the Famine Relief Commission in early 1847. Popular famine mythology has the British authorities actively forcing the export of grain from Ireland while the people starved. But this isn't really true: more food was shipped in than out over the course of the famine.[11] But there was a destructively myopic official conviction that if only the government maize stocks could remain locked in the depots and the handouts kept to a minimum, the 'market' would magically kick into action and provide for everyone. Trevelyan, who had never actually been to Ireland, seemed incapable of understanding why the existing resources plainly available within the country couldn't simply be 'drawn out' organically by demand.[12] But participation in a free-market economy requires cash, and thousands of starving people had literally *nothing* with which to buy food.

The famine has become the preeminent story from Irish history, iterated over and over in myriad retellings with certain standard narrative elements. The eviction from the tiny cabin in the glen; the fever-haunted workhouse; the pointless relief works with gangs of famished labourers building roads to nowhere for a meagre government dole; Trevelyan as the dastardly villain of the piece, possibly engineering the whole thing deliberately; and the desperate flight to New York aboard the leaky 'coffin ship' (this last sometimes provides a hint of a redemptive arc, as descendants of famine emigrants end up in the White House several generations later). One of the key tropes in nonfiction famine narratives is the eyewitness account. A visitor, often as not to Skibbereen in West Cork, peers through the door of a squalid cabin and graphically describes the dead and dying within – sometimes finding it hard to tell those two categories apart – and is later quoted by a twenty-first-century author or presenter or podcaster. But I don't want to repeat these accounts here. We need no more of them, and nor do we need to see further facsimiles of the accompanying engravings. In their own time, like a report from a BBC journalist in an Ethiopian refugee camp, they helped to rouse a popular outcry and prompt charitable donations in London and New York. But at a distance of 180 years, just like lurid accounts of medieval torture, they risk mere titillation rather than proper imaginative empathy. (I am aware that I came dangerously close to something similar with Frederick Douglass's account of the Dublin beggars; but I haven't actually quoted his most graphic descriptions: you can find them for yourself.) There's also something about the specific gaze of the eyewitnesses involved. It is always that of a morally impeccable Quaker, an appalled American missionary or a righteously indignant London journalist. The individual agency of the human bodies within the cabin is never retrievable. They are always 'creatures' or 'wretches', never named individuals. Here's the old pattern in repeat, the one that runs back to Edmund Spenser's description of crawling, beastlike flocks of famished peasants in sixteenth-century Munster: *look at the depths to which they have sunk*! Surely, this could only ever happen *here*, to *these* people. It's the same gaze, the same language, however well meaning, that would go on to be deployed so often in places like the Horn of Africa in the twentieth century.

So what, then, to do instead? We might turn to the archive in search of the recoverable voices of those directly impacted by the famine – not those dying in the Skibereen cabins; they cannot speak to us; but perhaps those departing on the emigrant ships and writing messages home (this is something that the historian Cian T. McMahon has done brilliantly in his 2021 book, *The Coffin Ship*). Or we might turn instead to fiction to generate what scholars sometimes call 'affective identification'[13] with the most marginalised and oppressed. This is what the creators of the National Famine Way – which runs from Roscommon to Dublin along the Royal Canal, and which I followed for fifteen kilometres out of Mullingar – have done. They identified the name of a real child emigrant bound along the canal for Canada, a twelve-year-old boy named Daniel Tighe. Then they commissioned Marita Conlon-McKenna, author of the hugely popular 1990 children's novel *Under the Hawthorn Tree* (which Cara, my partner, credits with providing her own most concrete images of the famine as she was growing up), to describe the emigrant journey along the canal in this boy's imagined voice. Each episode in the narrative is tied to a canal-side location marked by a bronze cast of a pair of child's shoes like the one I was looking at when the mountain bikers stopped to talk. The story is compelling and convincing and moving – all the things it should be. But such undertakings always make me uneasy. They leave me wondering what decades of discourse, of iconography and narrative, have produced the voice, who is *really* speaking here – and where the actual historical person spoken *for* might be located. Perhaps it is better simply to turn to the famine stories written into the landscape itself.

In upland areas from Connemara to the Cooley Peninsula you can still clearly see the old potato ridges, rough rectangular patches of them, angled up improbable slopes. It's easy to bracket these ridges – which give the lower mountainsides a strange corduroy texture – with the wider architecture of abandonment, the ruined cottages and overgrown field walls, the relics of those who achieved an illusion of permanency here – the same illusion that we all achieve for a while. But those ridges do not represent the decades or centuries during which the community endured; they represent a single season. One spring – probably that of 1846 or 1848 – people bent themselves over the hillside, turned the stony clay, manured it as best they could, pressed in the wizened leavings of last year's crop with all the hope they could muster, then banked up the ridges. But when autumn came there was nothing to harvest. The rotten tubers were left in the ground. And the next year there was no one there to dig the hillside anew.

* * *

On a quiet lane beyond Raharney, late in the day.

I'd come off the canal at Thomastown (where there was another pair of those bronze shoes), and made my way north past bungalows, dying ash trees, a few modest old cottages. Raharney was a small place with a big church and a shed-like shop that sold yard brushes and rolls of barbed wire as well as newspapers and groceries. I sat for a while on a bench beneath a copper beech in a little public garden beside the glass-clear River Deel and ate my way through a whole packet of Bakewell slices. Then I ambled on northeastwards, still on tarmac. The sky seemed to sag under its own cloud-weight and a faint smell of decay rose from the hedges.

A kilometre beyond the village, a large ruin appeared on the right: what looked like a stable-yard with arched entranceways, all roofless and ivy-choked, adrift in a tide of ripening wheat. I leant on a galvanised gate for a while, looking across at it. A man came striding past along the lane, a big man with a baggy blue tee-shirt and fancy earphones clamped over his head.

A few steps further on, the big house itself, Grangemore, came into view on a little hillock at the head of a broad field. It was roofless, with two wineglass-shaped plumes of ivy surging up the façade, big trees rising like thunderheads from the walled garden alongside and a hint of a ha-ha in front. Facing it directly, 350 metres away and right beside the lane, was a tiny derelict cottage. I hopped the nearest gate and ducked through its dark doorway. A solid brick-built fireplace at the centre of the building divided its small footprint into what had once been two rooms, floored now with desiccated dung and bits of baler twine. Ivy hung in green streamers from the cracks in the roof. It would be tempting to imagine this as a cottier's dwelling, its occupants evicted by the owner of the big house in the famine years. But the walls were of rough concrete. A later dwelling, then. The Grangemore ruin was perfectly framed in its window, and I wondered for a moment if the audacity of the position was deliberate, whether it had been built as small statement of triumph. But it was probably just a convenient roadside plot. And anyway, the cottage was a ruin now too.

Further on, the lane unexpectedly became an unsurfaced track in a tight tunnel of trees with a mohawk of grass running down the centreline. Here I met the man with the blue tee-shirt and the headphones, striding back in the opposite direction. He brought himself to a halt, lifted one earphone and offered a greeting. He had a greying beard and his accent was dimpled with warm Dublin diphthongs. He lived in a house I'd seen back at the edge of the village, where the lane passed through the old gates of the Grangemore demesne. He was from the city, and he'd never planned to live in rural Westmeath. But he'd been driving past one day with his wife, and they'd seen the 'for sale' sign. They'd been here five years now, were raising a family in Raharney.

Stories about the area poured out of him. His own home had originally been the church for the big house, a Protestant chapel, and then later a forge. The owner of Grangemore was the master of the local hunt – 'That building you were looking at back up the lane? That was the hunt kennels!' This landlord had been targeted by the IRA – the old IRA – in the revolutionary years. The authorities had given him a guard and moved him into the old church as it was an easier place to defend.

'So did the IRA burn the big house, then?'

'Ah!' He waggled a finger. 'I'm coming to that!'

Grangemore had survived the Revolution and the Civil War and had stayed with the same family, he said; but they fell on hard times.

He thought the house had served as a convalescence home for a while. 'And then there was a local lad who worked for the council on the roads, and he got a bad burn from hot tarmac and got a big payout. So *he* bought it. But then there was a building tax brought in on roofed buildings or number of windows or something like that, so he took the roof off and moved into a little house alongside. Now, there was this beautiful staircase inside the big house, and local kids – and I'm talking about men who'd be in their sixties now – used to play inside. But he was a grumpy bugger, and he didn't like this, and with his contacts on the roads he had access to dynamite, so he blew the place up himself!'

'Well,' I said, 'that's not the usual story!'

His wife had been pregnant when they first moved to Raharney, he said, and on the day their daughter was born they found a hurley propped against the door of the house, her sporting future already marked out by the community. I remembered now what the man outside Cunningham's had said: Raharney was the hurling village.

'Now! I'd better stay going and let you get on!' He started forcefully forward, his big torso swaying.

'That was a mighty heap of good stories you gave me there!' I called after him.

'I made them all up!' he laughed over his shoulder as he lowered the earphones back into place. 'Ah, no, I didn't…'

The track came out onto the straight line of the old Mullingar–Dublin road, and a little further on, right on the Meath–Westmeath border, the expanse of the Carranstown Bog opened to the north. I'd spotted it on the map earlier, marked it as a place to camp – and to escape the roads for a few kilometres. But the sheer vastness of the place caught me off-guard. Among the wheatfields and pasture and tree-lined hedges of the old Grangemore Estate, you'd never suspect that this enormous feral place existed nearby. The bogs in this low-lying country were always like that: you had no chance to view them from a distance and they brought an abrupt dissonance when you walked out onto them and found a sudden extended black horizon or a scrubby jungle where you might reasonably have expected more tidy fields. It was as if something had gone awry with the temporal matrix and random shards of landscape from another epoch had been left in the twenty-first-century countryside.

Carranstown Bog was another decommissioned Bord na Móna property. I walked out onto it along a rusty tramline for a kilometre, then found a place to camp among the bracken on a tree-crowned hillock. It was late and cold. The light was fading, and there were a few specks of rain in the wind. But as I was cooking a dinner of packet pasta a figure appeared a couple of hundred metres away, moving fast across the bog with a pack of six or seven longdogs – lurchers or greyhounds – racing around in a ragged orbit. I stiffened and sat very still, but they stopped for a moment and looked directly towards my little campsite. The tent was unzipped and the orange interior must have showed plainly in the gathering dusk. The figure moved forward and the dogs raced on. Then they stopped again as if considering something and turned towards me once more. It was a longer pause this time. I stayed motionless as the pasta hissed and belched on the stove. Eventually they moved on across the bog, first south towards the road, then off to the east and back north on a more distant line, the dogs racing and turning and racing and turning the whole time until they disappeared into the treeline.

It was nearly dark and I was too tired to load up and move deeper into the bog. But I ate my pasta and then wriggled into my sleeping bag with a nagging unease. It was the first time on my journey that I'd camped out aware that someone knew of my presence. Long into the night, I heard occasional cars speeding along the road to the south and dogs barking in kennels somewhere behind the trees to the north.

* * *

In popular perceptions of the famine, the people who lived in places like Grangemore are lumped together with Trevelyan and his government colleagues as 'the English', all very much on the same side. But in fact, British officialdom – and indeed, British public opinion – quickly decided that the Anglo-Irish landlords were part of the problem. They were profligate. They had managed their estates badly, allowing them to become crowded with huge numbers of tenants whom they plainly exploited. And in the two centuries since Cromwell, they'd been too busy carousing and fox hunting to make any real effort to anglicise Irish peasant culture or modernise the rural economy. Worse still, they now expected the British government to cover the costs of a famine that was probably their own fault.

In reality, there were some progressive landlords who organised and paid for local famine relief out of their own pockets – and tried to convince the London authorities to change their own disastrous approach. But there were others who had, out of mismanagement and greed, allowed their tenant lists to lengthen unsustainably. They did nothing to stop the repeated division and subdivision of existing tenancies among family members, or to restrict the development of precarious new upland settlements. More tenants, of course, meant more rent. But those rents were diced into ever smaller individual amounts for ever more precarious holdings, and when a crisis like the famine plunged the entirety of the tenantry into penury, the estate itself faced abrupt insolvency. Worse still for the landlord class, once it became clear that the famine wasn't going to end any time soon, the government decided that it was time for 'Irish property' to start paying for 'Irish poverty'.

The Irish Poor Law Extension Act, passed in mid-1847, transferred the entire cost of poor relief to Irish ratepayers. This was an appalling prospect for most landlords, who were already legally obliged by an earlier 1843 Act to cover all rates for any tenant on a holding worth under four pounds (larger tenant farmers had to pay their own land-related taxes). Most of the representatives of Irish constituencies in the London Parliament were themselves from the Anglo-Irish landlord class, and they vehemently opposed the bill until the late insertion of a clause by one of their own – a clause cunningly designed to get rid of the least lucrative tenants from their estates. William Gregory was the Harrow-educated Tory MP for Dublin and heir to the beautiful Coole estate in the low-lying country between Slieve Aughty and the Burren in the south of Co. Galway. (Half a century later, his widow, Lady Augusta, originally of the neighbouring Roxborough estate, would make herself the grande dame of the romantically nationalist Irish Literary Revival; but she was many years her husband's junior and wasn't even born at the time of the famine.) Gregory's notorious 'Quarter-Acre Clause' meant that any person holding more than a quarter of an acre of land (1,011 square metres) was ineligible for poor relief. Your family might be literally starving to death, but if you had a smallholding scarcely bigger than a modern suburban garden then there was no point showing up at the workhouse gates. The only way to get relief was to give up your tenancy. On the eve of the famine, around 45 per cent of all agricultural holdings in Ireland – and 64 per cent in western regions – were smaller than five acres, and by 1847 virtually every surviving smallholder was deep in rent arrears. The pressure of the Quarter-Acre Clause from below and the four-pound rating rule from above created an irresistible imperative for dispossession. In 1848, the *Tipperary Vindicator* declared that 'The work of undermining the population is going on stealthily, but steadily [. . .] We do not say that there exists a conspiracy to uproot the "mere Irish;" but we do aver that the fearful system of wholesale ejectment [. . .] is a mockery of the eternal laws of God – a flagrant outrage on the principles of nature.'[14] There were, the paper reported, 'vast tracts of the most fertile land in the world now thrown out of tillage'. By the end of the famine, perhaps as many as half a million people had been evicted[15] and an untold number had abandoned their holdings 'voluntarily'. The land had been effectively cleared of the poorest smallholders to make way for commercial agriculture and a whole tranche of the population had vanished.

Taking account of continued growth and likely omissions in the 1841 census, the total Irish population when Frederick Douglass arrived in 1845 probably stood at around 8.5 million. By the time of the next census in 1851, it had dropped to 6.55 million – and it was still falling rapidly. There are nuances within these national statistics: the populations of Dublin, Belfast and Cork actually increased during the famine. The same was true of many small towns around the country, as the destitute moved into urban areas in search of relief. The population of Mullingar, for example, went from 4,569 in 1841 to 4,789 (not including the 1,786 in the workhouse and the 202 in the jail) in 1851, while the wider county of Westmeath lost 30,000 people in the same period.[16] The greatest depopulation was in the rural west and south. Overall, perhaps as many as a million people had died of starvation and associated epidemics of typhus, relapsing fever and cholera. The rest had left. Crucially, emigration was only reaching its peak during the census year. Around a quarter of a million people left in 1851 alone, and the frantic famine exodus didn't really tail off until 1855.[17] Even after that, high-volume emigration continued for decades, far into the twentieth century. Co. Galway, for example, went from a population of over 440,000 on the eve of the famine, to under 183,000 at the turn of the twentieth century[18] – rising to around 278,000 today. The overall population only began consistently to climb again in the 1970s, and well into the twenty-first century, Ireland remained the only country on earth with a smaller population than it had had in the 1840s.

In the modern iconography of the famine, it is the departure to America aboard the proverbial 'coffin ship' that dominates.* In some cases, landlords did their sums and concluded that it was cheaper to pay for unwanted tenants to cross the Atlantic than to add their numbers to the local poor rate role. One of the most notorious instances of this was at Strokestown in Roscommon, where the National Famine Way begins today. The Strokestown landlord was a British army veteran, Denis Mahon, who had inherited the

* The term 'coffin ship' was little used during the 1840s and was only popularised in nationalist retellings of the famine story towards the end of the century (see McMahon, *The Coffin Ship*, p.2). Similarly, the widely favoured term for the famine itself, 'The Great Hunger' (*An Górta Mor* in Irish) really only gained traction after the 1962 publication of Cecil Woodham-Smith's hugely popular narrative history of that title.

estate from an insane uncle, along with some £30,000 of debt and a huge tenantry in deep rent arrears. His land agent cousin, John Mahon, calculated that it would cost him twice as much to allow the unwanted tenants into the local workhouse as it would to arrange their passage to Canada. Under considerable duress, 1,490 of them departed Strokestown for Dublin on foot along the Royal Canal in May 1847 to embark for Liverpool and onwards to Quebec. While poor conditions and high mortality on the so-called coffin ships can be overstated, the vessels that Mahon's agents had chartered were entirely worthy of the name: 158 of the 476 passengers on the first ship were dead before they reached Canada[19] and almost half of the original 1,490 died, either en route or during quarantine on arrival.[20] Mahon also evicted a further 3,006 tenants, including 84 widows. It's not entirely surprising, then, that he was assassinated while travelling in an open carriage near his estate later that same year, and that according to a local engineer, celebratory bonfires 'were to be seen on the hills for many miles in extent the next evening'.[21]

Landlord-assisted emigration was relatively unusual, however, and the vast majority of those who left for the Americas paid for their own passage – or were sent the fare by relatives who had gone on ahead and found work. The cost of the journey across the Atlantic – which often required transit through Liverpool or Glasgow – was beyond the reach of the poorest. But the short hop across the channel to Britain was very cheap – and sometimes even free. It was quicker for ships returning empty to Welsh ports from Ireland to take on a human cargo gratis than to load up with ballast.[22] And there were also persistent reports of 'strange gentlemen' handing out free tickets to England to the destitute on the docksides of Dublin and Cork as a simple way to make them someone else's problem.[23]

The famine had left thousands of people on the move in the Irish landscape. They travelled by mountain passes and bog roads, and surely by many forgotten footpaths, towards distant workhouses or outdoor relief stations. And many drifted inexorably towards the ports. Those with a little money to spare might take the train or a passenger barge along a canal, but many had no other option but to walk along canal towpaths or public roads. In 1847, 'thousands of men, women and children' were reported 'upon the high roads, moving towards the sea side for the purpose of embarking for England, most of them begging their way and all apparently in a state of great destitution'.[24] Even four years later in 1851 it was still recorded in the Irish press that 'Every day – every hour – the inhabitants of this once populous country may be seen thronging the public roads on their way to England'.[25] Some were following the old, pre-famine seasonal migration routes of the *spailpíni*, the itinerant labourers who crossed from Ireland each year to work in the fields, especially in Scotland. Some probably hoped to travel onwards to the Americas but ran out of money, or were cheated on arrival in Britain. Others may have heard rumours of better conditions in English workhouses. But still others simply went because onward movement to *somewhere* was the only form of agency they retained.

Some of the most destitute emigrants were eventually rounded up and shipped back to Ireland by city authorities in Liverpool and Glasgow. But many, many others survived, settled, endured – and in time found that their own children and grandchildren were growing up with the accents of the antagonists.

* * *

There were fresh boot prints in the bank of bare peat just below my campsite in the morning. They were small – perhaps those of a woman or an older child. They climbed the slope towards the place where I had slept, then bent away to the right. Had someone come out at first light to investigate? Or had they walked happily unaware then felt a lurch of shock at the sight of the little tent in the bracken and turned hurriedly away, unnerved by the unexpected human presence? I stopped and looked out across the bog. But it was perfectly empty in the thin rain.

I got back onto the line of the old tramway and headed north, where Carranstown merged seamlessly with Bracklin and Lisclogher – further expanses of decommissioned commercial bog.

The rain eased and a low and watery sunlight came through the fast-moving cloud in the east, but my shoes were soon wet through. A covey of pheasants took flight at my approach – a hen and four half-grown chicks. One was left behind, a biscuit-coloured bundle of feathers, quivering in the wet grass. Willows, birches with papery trunks, young rowans; and in the barer places, sundews, sphagnum moss and the livid scarlet caps and treefrog-coloured limbs of red soldier lichen. A scraggy landscape, a place in recovery. Was this what Ireland had looked like in the first centuries after the retreat of the ice? Was this the kind of landscape that the first path-makers, the first bear-hunters, had moved across? The bog certainly felt primordial – or post-apocalyptic. I don't suppose there's much distinction between those states, except for the occasional glimpse of the rusting rails through the wet grass, the odd shredded tractor tire or piece of half-buried plastic sacking.

This was a place that you could actually 'roam' across without a proper path to follow. The arrow-straight drainage ditches hadn't been plugged here. They ran like white roads through the asphodel-starred heath, just narrow enough to jump across. But the willow and birch were advancing rapidly, and drain-blocking and rewetting are on the agenda here as part of Bord na Móna's rehabilitation plan for Lisclogher, as is 'restricting access' to prevent 'illegal and unsocial activities'.[26] Soon enough crossing the bog on foot will be impossible – unless they cut a way through the scrub and build a new duckboard path.

Eventually, I came down from the raised core of the bog into the private cutaways with their stacks of footed turf and rubble-strewn access tracks. A treacle-coloured, cat-sized creature appeared at the edge of a track fifty metres ahead, paused, lowered its head and then pottered across with the unmistakable clownish gait of a mustelid – a pine marten! A little while later two boys shrieked past on a speeding quad bike, bound for the open bog. And then I was out onto the roads – the quiet country roads, kilometre upon kilometre of them. The vast and lawless space of the bog vanished behind a façade of trees and fields.

Ramshackle farms, weedy yards crowded with disembowelled cars; a steady susurration from the big roadside trees; and gateways opening to wide fields. I spoke to no one, saw no one who was not behind the wheel of a passing car. The heat came up as morning swung to afternoon and I knocked on the door of a white bungalow at a crossroads, hoping to fill my empty water bottle. There was no one in, but there was an outside tap beside the door. I used it, feeling absurdly ashamed of the tiny trespass. Further on, the road ran alongside a modern demesne wall. The mature trees within made the invisible presence of the big house palpable. A sign by the gateway indicated that the place was now the Triermore Stud Farm. A little further on, another big house: Drewstown, a big grey place, viewed from the rear. Something about the awkward angularities, the downpipes and the narrow windows made me think of lukewarm custard, voices echoing down long halls and old radiators layered with yellowish paint. It was a 'Christian retreat and adventure centre'. A Pentecostal 'family conference' was underway and the parking area was full of cars with UK plates.

Beyond the house, a six-kilometre 'eco walk' ran along staple-studded boards through the Coillte-owned Girley Bog. I lay down for a while in a quiet place away from the path, eating the ripe bilberries that grew among the heather. Then I pushed on to the busy road than ran into Kells. Cars streaked past without slowing. At one point, feeling horribly vulnerable on a long bend, I clambered up onto the top of the roadside bank and laboured along that as best I could. A car, passing below at a hundred kilometres per hour, sounded its horn in salute. I was glad to reach the first stretch of pavement on the edge of Kells.

I ate a bowl of greyish vegetable soup in a dim bar, then went onwards. A tenth-century market cross knotted with time-blunted carvings beneath a Perspex shelter; men speaking Slavic languages into mobile phones as they dangled fishing lines from a bridge; and the gates to yet another big house, Headfort, this one converted to a boarding school with a golf course in its grounds. The light softened and dimmed and the sound of bleating sheep drifted in from far off.

I sat for a while at the edge of a small conifer plantation, eating the wild raspberries that grew there and trying to muster the energy for the last few kilometres along a quiet lane. Finally, I veered off the tarmac, crashed across an overgrown ditch and came out onto a little triangle of long-abandoned bog, securely shielded by deep banks of trees. I pitched the tent in a patch of heather and was fast asleep long before it was properly dark. I'd walked forty kilometres, thirty of them on tarmac.

* * *

Stud farm, Christian retreat, boarding school: some of the alternatives to abandonment and ruination for the former seats of the Anglo-Irish gentry in modern Ireland. Luxury hotel would be another prominent possibility.*

It would be easy to imagine the famine as the ultimate triumph of the landlord class; but it was really the beginning of the end for the 200-year-old Anglo-Irish Ascendancy. They had lost the sympathy of the London government and the British public (the arrival of thousands of penniless Irish emigrants heightened popular hostility in Britain to both the bottom and the top ranks of Irish society). And many of them were in dire financial straits. In contrast to the Penal Law which enforced gavelkind inheritance on Catholic estates in the eighteenth century, the Protestant gentry were bound to primogeniture not just by custom, but sometimes also by legal 'entailment'. The occupier of an entailed estate essentially held it in trust for his heirs, which made it virtually impossible to sell or break up, even in the face of huge mortgage arrears. Effectively bankrupt estates passed from generation to generation along with their enormous debts. Some owners did attempt to take

* Triermore belonged to the Rotherhams; Drewstown was the ancestral home of the McVeaghs; and Headfort was the seat of the Taylour marquesses, the fourth of whom, Lord Geoffrey, a man with a naughty moustache and a roguish twinkle in his eye, converted to Catholicism in 1901 to marry Rosie Boote, a glamorous singer from the Gaity Theatre in Dublin.

advantage of the famine to radically restructure their tenantry on modern commercial lines – risking assassination in the process, as Denis Mahon found out. But others found themselves mired in even more debt. The Poor Law Extension Act was followed up in 1849 by the Encumbered Estates Act, which established a special court to enforce and oversee the breakup of indebted estates on the application of either the owner or their creditors, regardless of entailment.

Charles Edward Trevelyan hoped that the released land would be snapped up by professional, modernising agricultural investors from Britain. But just as with virtually every plantation scheme right back to the sixteenth century, things didn't work out as planned, and 85 per cent of the land that was sold via the Encumbered Estates Court went to buyers already in Ireland. Some of these were surviving landlords of old who took the opportunity to expand their own estates yet again. But others were members of the emerging urban Catholic bourgeoisie, the businessmen, the property developers, the lawyers and doctors who had sailed unscathed through the famine years and were now eager to join the landowning class.[27] In practical terms, the 'strong farmers' also became unintended beneficiaries of the famine turmoil, even if they had yet to trade their tenancy agreements for title deeds: some 200,000 smallholdings and all their occupants had simply vanished from the landscape, leaving empty space to rear cattle for the export trade.[28]

You can clearly trace the impact of the famine and the further churn of the late nineteenth century on the old maps. Thomas Colby's original six-inch Ordnance Survey work was completed a decade before the famine. A fresh survey at the supremely detailed scale of twenty-five inches to the mile (1:2,500) began in the late 1880s. And a final six-inch update was completed in the 1930s and published the following decade.* If you flip between the first and second surveys, the transformation is astonishing.

* The only available current maps covering the whole of Ireland are at 1:50,000 – a scale frustratingly lacking in detail for walkers.

* * *

Somewhere in the west of Ireland there is a low hill, rising just above the sixty-metre contour line. It could be anywhere, but it happens to be in Co. Galway – not the part that people from outside the county always imagine, not the tawny mountains or fractal shoreline of Connemara, but the low green farming country that stretches inland for sixty kilometres from the head of Galway Bay to the banks of the Shannon.

A lane runs up the southern flank of the hill. At the top there is a small farm: a house with whitewashed walls and a lean-to at the back; a scrubbed concrete yard; a small Dutch barn with a humpback roof; and a stand of thinning conifers that sigh sadly in the slightest breeze. The lane is known locally by the name of the family who own the farm. This is the sort of placename that mapmakers often miss. Not an abstraction or a piece of mythic lore in a language no longer routinely spoken hereabouts; just a prosaic but thoroughly meaningful piece of local usage: a name tied to a place tied to a person – though the specific person in question has changed with each generation, for the same family have held the farm for well over a century. They were recorded here in the 1901 census as tenants, and then a decade later as freeholders. Urbanisation is creeping towards the hill, new housing estates lapping in from the south and west. Fifty years from now the farm may have vanished, and the name of the lane will have been altogether lost. Or perhaps it will be preserved for a cul-de-sac lined with boxy houses. But for now, this still feels like an assuredly rural place.

If you look at the last six-inch map in the digital archives – the one from the 1930s – the modern housing estates are missing, naturally enough, as are the nearby bungalows. But the field boundaries are just the same, and there's the farmhouse and the yard (the conifers and the Dutch barn have yet to appear). Scroll back to the twenty-five-inch map, surveyed in the early 1890s, and again, there are the same familiar field walls, the same farmhouse on its breezy rise. But now turn to the original map, the one surveyed in the decade before the famine. You might think for a moment that you are looking at a map of an entirely different place. Gone are all the familiar walls and the five- and ten-acre fields. In their place is a far denser mesh of enclosure, the fields just one or two acres apiece with unfamiliar laneways running between. And at the top of the hill, something so unexpected that it takes a moment to process what it is: thirty small buildings surrounded by a grid of quarter-acre garden plots. It is a clachan, a tightly huddled farming hamlet, something entirely alien in this same landscape today. How many people lived here in 1840? A hundred? Maybe more? And what happened to them? Did they die – or did they go? This is just one place; but like I say, it could be anywhere – anywhere at all.

The ruins of a community in Co. Galway in the immediate aftermath of the famine

You might walk up the lane to the top of the hill a hundred times and never know of the vanished clachan. But once you've seen the old map, you'll pay more attention. And if you walk that way late on a cold clear winter's afternoon when the smallest tussock casts a long shadow, you might notice the faintest unevenness in the fields immediately around the farmyard, a turbulence beneath the placid green surface.

* * *

I find I have reached the point at which I intended to finish this chapter – with the traces of a vanished community showing in the winter sunlight and myself asleep in a bog beyond Kells. But I realise that there is one more obscure famine-related story that I need to include. I should have told it back on the Royal Canal, or during my uneasy night on the Carranstown Bog – or maybe even right back at the start of this book. But for reasons I cannot properly fathom it feels like an embarrassing admission. I have been putting it off. But now I've run out of road, and so here it is.

In 1817 a girl was born and named Ann McBride, somewhere in Ireland (I have no idea where; it's a common sort of name and there are only fragments of Irish census records available from the nineteenth century). She turned thirty at the height of the famine, but by that time she was in Glasgow. There, in late 1847 – the 'Black 47' of popular memory – she had a child of her own, a little boy called John.

It's possible, of course, that Ann had left Ireland ahead of the famine. Irish immigrants had been moving into the Clydeside region for decades. But 1847 was the year the major exodus got underway, and that John's birth was recorded in the city and not in some outlying industrial town suggests a recent arrival – perhaps even a thwarted intention to continue to the Americas. Little John's father was another Irish immigrant, Peter, and if the scanty records are correct, he was twelve years Ann's junior, still a teenager when his son was born. Had they known each other in Ireland, married there, travelled together? Or were they thrown together during the passage or in some crowded boarding house in the unfamiliar city? Were they even married at all? It's the sort of detail that can easily be glossed over in the journey from one place to another, after all. But whatever the origins of their relationship, sometime after John's birth they moved a few miles east along the Clyde to Rutherglen, a place of cramped cottages surrounded by coalmines and chemical works. Wherever they came from in Ireland, it would have looked nothing like this. But Rutherglen was full of Irish immigrants, and there was a new Catholic church, St Columbkille's, to serve their community. Peter found work as a coalminer. Ten doors down from them on Rutherglen's main street lived another Irish immigrant couple, Michael Carroll and Margaret McBride (I've no idea if Margaret and Ann were related; as I say, it's a common sort of name).

Where did these people come from? 'Ireland' is all the Scottish records can tell us. That they ended up in the Glasgow area might suggest a departure from Belfast or Derry and thus an Ulster provenance – Donegal, perhaps. McBride is a common name in Ulster, and especially in Donegal – as are many of the other names in this story. But they could have come from anywhere, really. Were they Irish speakers? Probably, if they really were from Donegal. Had they been evicted? Had they begged their way across Ireland and scrambled gratefully onto the first available ship? Or had they come on the recommendation of a friend or relative with the intention of finding work in the Rutherglen mines? Did they, perhaps, have private reasons for leaving other than poverty or homelessness? Who knows! But in 1848 the Carrolls had a baby of their own, a girl called Margaret. (It's unclear whether she was born before or after they left Ireland: she gave 'Rutherglen' as her birthplace in later censuses, but there's no official record of her birth in Scotland.) Twenty-two years later she and John married. They stayed in Rutherglen; John worked as a coalminer like his father and father-in-law before him, and they had their own children, including a boy called Michael Thomas, born in 1874.

At some point in these same decades – during or soon after the famine – yet another Irish immigrant arrived in another colliery region, far away in the English Midlands. His name was written down as 'Heeley' (though there were several other ways they could have spelt it). His descendants would later claim that when he first saw his granddaughter (or was it his great-granddaughter?) he said, 'Ah! The blue-eyed Irish are coming back!' This is as much as I can tell you about the man named Heeley.

Meanwhile, back in Scotland, on the other side of the Clyde in Airdrie, another burgeoning industrial town that would eventually be subsumed by Greater Glasgow, another immigrant family had settled and found work in the mines: the Halleys, James and Mary and their daughter Bridget. These were people who had lived through the famine in Ireland and arrived later (I don't know exactly when, but they were certainly in Airdrie by the late 1870s). In this case, a specific provenance missing elsewhere has somehow survived the passage from Ireland: they came from Roscommon; Bridget was born there in 1860. In Airdrie, she found surface work at one of the coal mines, and when she was seventeen she had a daughter out of wedlock. Bridget was illiterate and could only sign the birth certificate with an 'X'; but she gave the child's name as 'Catherine McGhee Halley' – which probably tells us the father's family name (and McGhee, again, is a common name in Ulster, and especially Donegal). Six years later, she married another young Irish immigrant, James Connolly. The child took his surname and he was recorded as her father on later documents, though he almost certainly wasn't. (This secret was kept well from later generations until someone thought to crosscheck a handwritten family tree against the official records a century and a half later.)

In early adulthood the young woman now known as Catherine Connolly took a job as a domestic servant in Cambuslang, yet another industrial town on the edge of Glasgow. There she met Michael Thomas from Rutherglen. Some upward mobility was clearly underway, for his occupation was recorded in this period as 'coal merchant and newspaper reporter'. After their marriage, the couple moved away east to Dundee, where Michael Thomas – known professionally as 'M. T.' – became manager of the local edition of *The Catholic Herald* and publisher of the *Dundee and District Catholic Yearbook*.

M. T. and Catherine had eight children, the seventh of whom, born in 1915, was called Desmond. As an adult, Desmond had thick glasses and a round, bald head. His legions of nieces and nephews called him 'Uncle Elephant', which might have had something to do with a prodigious memory. He once walked out of a job interview because the interviewer gave him the Freemason's handshake. He married a small woman called Eileen Johnston, whose own recent ancestors – Clarkes and Mulhollands and Grahams – had also all arrived from Ireland. They had two sons, the second of whom, born in 1943, was named after his father and known as Des. As a teenager, Des strained against the snobbery and grimly judgemental Catholicism of mid-twentieth-century Dundee, and when he was twenty-one, he fled. He went to Cornwall – as far as he could go without a passport. There he met and married a local woman called Pauline, whose own mother had blue eyes and the maiden name Heeley and was originally from somewhere near Wolverhampton. In time they had a son who inherited nothing from any of those people above, no religious affiliation, no hand-me-down identity or careworn legend of the auld sod, nothing at all, really – except the recessive gene for blue eyes, fortuitously paired with the Heeley heritage. That and the name, of course: the surname of Ann McBride's husband, Peter, and their son, John; the name of the first paternal ancestor born outside of Ireland at the very height of the famine; the name which I have now carried back and passed to my own blue-eyed, Irish-born children after a five-generation absence.

The reason this all feels like an awkward confession, I think, is because for most of my life it has meant so little to me. I have always known exactly where I am from: a little clachan-sized hamlet in the far west of Cornwall, the land around which I have walked and walked and walked until its very contours are charted in my neural pathways. For the longest time, nothing else mattered – and certainly not the fact that a shade over half of my ancestry was

Irish. I was aware of it, of course; but it was an abstract concept – as, indeed, it must have been for my own great-grandparents in Scotland.

The summer holiday at the Irish homeplace was an experience for later emigrant generations. The people who left Ireland for Britain during and immediately after the famine had no homeplace to go back to – and certainly no neat little farmhouse with the grandparents waiting at the door. If they carried the language out with them, they did not pass it on. And how could their own children, growing up amid pitheads and factory chimneys and long dark lines of workers' cottages, imagine Ireland as a place, a personal landscape with a concrete particularity? Soon enough they forgot where exactly their people had come from – which townland and parish, which county, even. And by the end of the nineteenth century, 'Irish' in Scotland was often little more than a synonym for 'Catholic'. That, in obscure fragments, is all I have to go on: stories from my father about gangs of identically accented little boys shouting 'Scots or Irish?' across a Dundee street as a prelude to either camaraderie or sectarian brawling. The stern parental interrogation at any mention of a new playmate: 'Which *school* does he go to?' An anecdote about Granny Catherine – illegitimate daughter of Bridget Halley from Roscommon – throwing unripe pears from her shopping bag at a passing Orange Order parade from a Glasgow bus stop. An account of a teenage struggle of the soul ahead of eventual flight to Cornwall which made James Joyce's *A Portrait of the Artist as a Young Man* seem oddly familiar the first time I read it. And the hologrammatic image of the Crucifixion at the top of the stairs in my uncle's house. There is also an apocryphal story about M. T. Hannigan ordering an electioneering Winston Churchill off his Dundee doorstep in 1922 with an earful about the deployment of the Black and Tans in Ireland two years earlier (it's certainly true that M. T.'s newspaper described Churchill as 'a dangerous, double-dealing, oily-tongued adventurer' around this time).[29]

Other people in other places have constructed an entire ethnic identity out of just as little, I suppose; but I had no such need. I've seldom thought about any of this at all until recently, and it would be grotesque for me to claim any kind of famine-related generational trauma. It was only as I was preparing for the journey described in this book that I looked idly at the family tree, sent to me by an elderly cousin, and noticed the date of John Hannigan's Glasgow birth: 1847. And only now – *right* now – does it occur to me that the Halleys, James and Mary and Bridget from Roscommon, might conceivably have left along the towpath of the Royal Canal. But these people are not my ghosts. They were *not* with me as I walked across Ireland, and they are not at my shoulder now. I *cannot* conjure a fictive simulation of their voices: that could only ever be made from all the books and movies and poems and songs I've consumed. But from time to time, whenever someone deploys that historical 'we' – Cromwell stole *our* land; *we* were oppressed and starved and evicted for eight long centuries; *we* were forced into exile aboard a coffin ship – I hear the faintest whisper, like the sound of a high summer wind running through roadside trees.

8

Road Frontage: Kells to Knockbridge

Three objects from the road to Dundalk – and it's all road now, sixty unrelenting kilometres of it, from the bog beyond Kells to the slopes of the Cooley Mountains:

A bungalow, built dead-centre on a plot clipped from the corner of a silage field; a big house ruin like a broken skull on a small hill; and a thatched cottage at a quiet T-junction, long and low, with a polished granite plaque against the wall commemorating an eviction here in 1881, 'a turning point in land reform'. All three, somehow, are connected.

* * *

It was cold at first light, colder than any morning yet, a thin gauze of mist over the bog and the first transatlantic flights descending towards Dublin. I sat shivering in the doorway of the tent with my sleeping bag around my shoulders while the water boiled on the camping stove for coffee and noodles. A lone swan flew overhead, labouring hard in the windless air with a sound like a leaky foot-pump. I packed up and scrambled back out onto the road. I'd looked closely at the maps and the satellite images and I knew I could expect nothing but tarmac for the next two days – no more bogs, no forestry, no rough tracks. But the landscape hereabouts was veined with minor roads, and I reckoned I'd be able to steer clear of heavy traffic. I planned for shorter days too, aimed to keep my daily distance below thirty kilometres until I reached the mountains.

New sunlight slanting through oak, willow and birch, falling on the road in bright patches with glimpses of the open bog beyond. This was a busy working place, the bog almost entirely cut away. I'd heard heavy machinery clanking and grinding out in its deeper reaches late into the dusk. But now there was only birdsong, a first bee-buzz from the bracken at the verges and a cow bellowing somewhere far off. A red-and-white 'no trespassing' sign was nailed to a tree.

The road unspooled ahead and low cloud ran in with a cooling breeze and a low hum of distant milking parlours. Rabbits scattered in cropped paddocks and a hooded horse turned blindly at the sound of my passing. I crossed the line of a new greenway, another stripe of fresh black tarmac on the route of the old Navan–Kingscourt Railway. Low hills rose to the right – the first hills I'd seen for days – and the road climbed gently towards Lobinstown. And here was the bungalow: an ornate gateway, half-drawn curtains, lobelias spilling from concrete urns between concrete doric columns. It was one of two dozen houses on the approach to the village. The older buildings – the ones from the 1980s – were long and low with pantile roofs; the more recent ones were enormous two-storey mansions. No two were the same in style, but each sat dead-centre on its roadside plot.

* * *

It was my second abiding impression on first arrival in Ireland, after the hi-vis striders on the ring-road: the pale, starkly modern houses, strung along the roadsides. They gave rural Ireland a weirdly suburban feel. For someone from a place where the dominant rural settlement pattern is still the tightly huddled farming hamlet, where the bungalows are confined to the village fringes and where even forty years ago planning officers demanded concessions to traditional building styles, it was genuinely shocking and weirdly dissonant. In places, you could drive for kilometre upon kilometre through corridors of displaced suburbia, the fields and bogs and woods glimpsed only in snatches behind the laurel hedges and back-garden goalposts. The pattern showed even at 30,000 feet on a flight out of Knock or Shannon: a vast green canvas crisscrossed by meandering double lines of pointillist white dots. My initial reaction was blimpish bafflement: 'Are there *no* planning regulations here?' And at first, I lazily assumed that the whole phenomenon was a product of Celtic Tiger-era excess. Some of the newest houses were certainly ostentatious – buildings that would pass for stockbrokers' mansions in Surrey, here just the homes of people with ordinary jobs and enormous mortgages. Others had never been completed at all, weeds sprouting in defaulted driveways and scaffolding rusting against foreclosed walls. But the origins of this striking feature of the human landscape go back much further than any transient, turn-of-the-century boom.

Much of the traditional credit – or blame, depending on your perspective – for modern Ireland's distinctive pattern of rural ribbon development goes to an architect with a social conscience named Jack Fitzsimons. I didn't realise at the time, but I'd spent the night just a couple of kilometres from Fitzsimons' childhood home in Gravelstown, north of Kells. Perhaps his family had cut turf on the bog where I slept. He was born in 1930, and he spent the first four years of his life in a two-room cottage with cracked mud walls and a thatched roof, built into a hillside; 'if you can imagine such a situation,' he later wrote, 'it blended into the landscape'.[1] The family then moved into a slightly larger council cottage nearby. But it was still miserably cold and damp. In 1940, when Fitzsimons was ten, his baby sister Annie died. He came to blame her death on their living conditions and later wrote that she 'had a more profound influence on my life than any other human being'.[2] He grew up to become a draughtsman for Meath County Council and the Office of Public Works; and in 1971, he self-published a guidebook to the technical and legal aspects of modern housebuilding, complete with a selection of twenty basic architectural plans. It was called *Bungalow Bliss*.

The Irish countryside of the early 1970s was a place of patchy public services and significant deprivation. But there were signs of coming prosperity. The population was finally rising again after a century of decline and stagnation; and crucially, grants were available for housebuilding. Fitzsimons saw his book as a fast-track way for people of modest means to escape from poor housing without having to pay for the services of an architect. *Bungalow Bliss* was a bestseller, and soon small farmers across the country were moving out of old cottages and building Fitzsimons-designed, grant-aided dwellings nearby. Adult children no longer needed to leave the parish; they could build a bungalow in a field instead and settle into a working life of fifty-kilometre commutes to Navan or Mullingar. By the mid-1970s, 5,500 bungalows were being built each year. By the early 1980s, that figure had doubled, and one-off rural bungalows accounted for 40 per cent of all the new houses built in Ireland.[3]

Bungalow Bliss went through twelve editions, growing thicker with each reprint. The original plain rectangular outlines were supplemented by bold bay windows and pillared porches as the 1970s gave way to the 1980s. It sold a quarter of a million copies in all.[4] No one knows exactly how many houses were built using its plans – certainly many thousands, all over Ireland.

The *Bungalow Bliss* phenomenon was quickly punned as 'bungalow blitz' by detractors. Frank McDonald, environment correspondent of *The Irish Times* in the late 1980s, condemned the 'blight of bungalows' with their 'pervasive vulgarity' spreading across the land.[5] Fitzsimons himself always hit back at the obvious snobbery of such attacks. But the criticisms were about more than aesthetics, and on any journey through the Irish countryside the bigger problem is plain to see. Instead of growing organically in broadening rings, villages and small towns seem to have *burst*. It's like one of those eerie exhibitions of plasticised human bodies: epidermises unfolded like bats' wings; muscles peeled back; vascular systems extended in a mushroom cloud of scarlet tendrils. In the frenzy of one-off rural housebuilding, urban viscera have shot out to great distances along the surrounding road networks, leaving voids of bankrupt pubs and atrophying schools at the old centres.

What struck me most forcefully, as I walked along the roads through Westmeath and Meath and onwards into Louth, was how isolated, how *lonely* even, the houses of the ribbon development seemed. Any view of neighbouring properties, or even of the surrounding fields and woods, was often blocked by towering laurels or leylandii. It wasn't simply that anyone living here would need to drive to get to the shop and the post office and the school – or to go for a walk that wasn't on tarmac. Growing up in rural Cornwall in the 1980s, we also had to drive to get to shop, post office and school. But we had a dozen neighbours in hailing distance. The hamlet was set back from the main road and there was an easy fraternisation between the properties; you didn't need to get in a *car* to pop in for a cup of tea or to borrow a ladder. I find myself thinking again here of that vanished clachan on its Galway hilltop – and of what replaced it: a sense of 'rural community' gradually detaching from its tangible physicality. But we can hardly blame Jack Fitzsimons for that. To build a bungalow – or, indeed, an angular twenty-first-century mansion with floor-to-ceiling windows – you need more than an architectural drawing and a relaxed planning officer:* you need *land*. And that's a much longer story.

* * *

It changed things, knowing that I'd be on tarmac all day long. Until now, I realised, I'd always treated the roads as an unavoidable preliminary to the *real* walk – even if the real walk only amounted to a couple of kilometres across a small bog. I'd lower my head, look inwards on the tarmac, then look up and out, *notice* more, when I broke away onto stone or turf. But now I was firmly hemmed in on the hard surface. The grim rhythm of the early stages returned: *dull ache at heel, sharp sting at toes*. But I found that I walked with my head up now, paid attention, paused in gateways ('WARNING: NO TRESPASSING, NO HUNTING, NO DOGS, VIOLATORS WILL BE PROSECUTED'). And the contours helped. I was moving into a rumpled landscape here, the alternating ascents and descents varying the metre of the journey.

Lobinstown was a hilltop place. There was a pub, closed at this early hour, and two vacant shop units with scabby paintwork and a faded sign promising an upcoming opening date already nine years in the past. There was no one about, no passing cars, even. I rested for a while in a weedy little garden shrine in the ruins of an old chapel. Feathers and last autumn's leaves gathered under the benches, moss on the stones and a mouldering pint glass with an inch of stale lager under a crust of drowned insects on the ledge beneath the crucifix. At the edge of the village a long view opened to the north: green country, thick hedges, a low ridge of hills on the horizon. It brought an abrupt release from a claustrophobia I hadn't

* In recent years, planners have belatedly attempted to restrict further one-off housing and ribbon development, generating much understandable grievance in places where it's been around long enough to have become a traditional settlement pattern, especially in the Gaeltacht regions of the far west.

realised had beset me. It was the first time in four days that I'd been able to see objects more than a couple of kilometres away.

Forty minutes later, at the summit of the next rise, I came to another place of worship: a church with dark stonework and a sharp spire; simple country gothic, a shaggy yew tree overspilling the graveyard wall; a Church of Ireland place. The door was locked, but a sign outside promised a weekly Sunday service. This was fat farming country, grazed by sheep and small herds of Friesians, the hills swelling like green buttocks. How good it would be to walk away from the road here – but not to 'roam'. I knew well that any attempt to wander freely across a landscape like this would unravel in a sweaty, spiky scramble at the very first hedge, followed by a limping, bramble-scratched retreat to the road. It was a stile and a signpost I longed for, a chance to trace a way along the field edges trodden out in advance by other feet, from a village to a hilltop church, perhaps – and then onwards, to those dark hills on the horizon and beyond. But there was only the road, dropping again past a derelict Catholic church and a primary school, shuttered for the summer, then rising once more. And at the top of the next hill an unexpected vista: the Cooley Mountains were suddenly in view. I shucked off my backpack, leant on a gate for a while. Yellowing wheat in the middle distance; a red tractor patterning a thumbprint of cut grass in the next field; a swarm of swallows above. Fifty kilometres away to the northeast, a clutch of still higher mountains showed faintly behind the Cooley ridge: the Mournes, beyond the border, rising out of another jurisdiction. I had a sudden sense of dizzying distance spilling out behind. The journey's end was abruptly palpable.

* * *

In the summer of 1887, a young American journalist named George Pellew made his way around Ireland to report on the 'land question' which seemed to lie at the heart of everything. Pellew's mother came from an old-established East Coast family; but his father was English, and he'd been born there, on the Isle of Wight, in 1859. The family returned to the US soon afterwards. Young George went to the best schools and graduated from Harvard with a law degree. But journalism was his real calling. He moved to New York and took up a post as the local correspondent for *The Boston Journal*, then joined the staff of *The New York Sun* as an editorial writer. Decades of immigration had created a large 'Irish' constituency in the city, and the local press gave much attention to Irish political affairs. It was with this in mind that Pellew embarked in 1887 for Ireland, where, he wrote, 'The system of "landlordism" is to be superseded, we are told, by "peasant proprietorship," [and] the government of Great Britain by Home Rule.'

Change had come in fits and starts in the decades after the famine. The Encumbered Estates Act had broken up some of the worst-managed of the old estates. This did lead to a fresh wave of evictions as new, commercially minded buyers took over. In 1851, a total of 1,223 tenants were evicted in the space of ten months in East Galway alone.[6] But in the following decades, evictions were relatively rare.[7] Living standards crept upwards (aided, of course, by the fact that two million of the very poorest people had vanished from the equation due to the famine). The one-room cabin, long the dominant dwelling type, accounted for just 10 per cent of homes by 1861 (and would all but vanish by 1901).[8] The Church of Ireland had been formally disestablished in 1869, ending the absurd situation in which everyone was liable to pay tithes to a church which represented only a small minority of the population. Disestablishment also saw the Church of Ireland stripped of its substantial estates, with 6,000 of its former tenants gaining full title to their land.[9] Meanwhile, Catholic emancipation and the end of the Penal Laws at the close of the eighteenth century, coupled to the gradual expansion of the franchise, meant that Ireland's elected representatives were increasingly likely to be middle-class Catholics with a nationalist agenda, rather than Anglo-Irish Protestant gentry loyal to the Crown. The political impetus for 'Home Rule' – a proposed broad devolution of domestic powers to a restored Dublin Parliament – was growing insistently.

But if you were a small tenant farmer in the deep countryside – or worse still, a landless labourer – little had changed. In the 1870s, around half of all Irish land was still in the hands of just a thousand wealthy owners.[10] A run of bad harvests, a resurgence of potato blight and a general agricultural recession at the end of the decade saw farm incomes fall while rents rose. The countryside was primed for a fresh bout of agrarian unrest, led by the newly formed Land League.

The League's founder, Michael Davitt, was a one-armed socialist raised in industrial England after his family's eviction from their Mayo smallholding at the end of the famine. He believed that all Irish land should be nationalised. The League's president, meanwhile, was Charles Stewart Parnell, a parliamentarian from a family of Anglo-Irish landowners with no particular personal interest in land reform but a very clear understanding that the political drive for Home Rule needed to be fused with the popular concerns of the countryside. And the bulk of the League's active membership were not the landless poor, but farmers eager for permanent title to their own holdings. It was an awkward coalition, but it worked.

From 1879, the League fought a 'Land War' against high rents, evictions and insecure tenure. Some of the old intimidatory tactics of the Whiteboys were revived, along with the occasional summary killing. Large-scale rent strikes were a key tactic: if a landlord refused to fix new and lower rents in line with Land League stipulations, their entire tenantry were expected to stop paying rent altogether. The League would then organise active resistance to any attempted evictions that resulted. Another favoured Land War tactic was 'stopping the hunt'. Compared to rent strikes and interference with evictions, this was a mere symbolic gesture; but it had a particular psychological impact for the old landowning class. Unlike in Victorian England, organised pheasant shooting never really developed in Ireland, and riding to hounds remained *the* upper-class leisure activity. Mounted fox hunting required unfettered access to large areas of land, for a fleeing fox paid no heed to property boundaries or rights of way. Through the long centuries of the Anglo-Irish Ascendancy this had never been an issue. But now, suddenly, emboldened tenant farmers were ready to resist the nuisance of dozens of riders thundering across their fields, knocking down walls, churning up grass and trampling winter crops. One 1887 account describes a large group of peasants rearing up from behind a wall just as the cross-country chase is about to begin, wielding sticks and flinging stones to drive the hounds off the scent. The dejected master of the hunt retreats from the field muttering, 'I have had enough of it; I have seen Irishmen stone my hounds. Well, I thought there was more sport in Irishmen than that. I believe in the country no more.'[11]

But the most effective – and most notorious – technique of the Land War was the 'boycott', the practice of total ostracisation named for one of its first targets, the Mayo land agent Charles Cunningham Boycott. Boycotting was used against agents, landlords and most importantly anyone accused of 'land grabbing' – that is, taking over the holding of an unjustly evicted tenant.*

The first Land War ended in 1881 following government concessions in the form of a new Land Law Act, which secured various tenant rights. But another campaign got underway in 1886, and it was during this second Land War that George Pellew arrived in Ireland. He knew that there were already many books about Irish affairs on the market; but these were generally 'the controversial statements of professed partisans'. He was interested instead in impartial reportage – in simply listening to the opinions of as many people as possible. He travelled widely across each province, sometimes in a hired carriage, sometimes alone and on foot (he walked the whole southern coast of Connemara, from Galway

* The term 'land grabbing' has a resonant afterlife in contemporary access conflicts. It shows up reliably on the placards of those protesting new greenways: 'Stop land grab for greenways'. But on the other side of the argument, I spoke to a veteran campaigner for one of Ireland's first greenways who also described the farmers who had opposed the project and tried to claim old state-owned railways through adverse possession as 'land grabbers'.

city to Clifden, for example). And he sought out a wide range of informants: landlords, agents, activists, Home Rulers, Unionists, rich and poor. He was an excellent journalist and an assiduous note-taker, and he gave over great swathes of his published book, *In Castle and Cabin: Or, Talks in Ireland in 1887*, to the direct speech of his interlocutors. He even managed to gather a firsthand account of what it felt like to be boycotted – and in doing so revealed the way that ugly personal vendettas could play out under the cover of a righteous cause.

On a bright summer morning, Pellew rented a carriage to drive him thirty kilometres northwest from Cork to the townland of Barrahaurin on the slopes of the Boggeragh Mountains. There, in a low wooden house at the end of a muddy lane 'surrounded by a mass of sodden manure', he met John McCarthy, a man with a 'goatee and lean cheeks like a typical Yankee', who greeted him 'with the enthusiastic warmth of one who seldom sees a friendly face'. McCarthy and his wife were more than happy to tell the visiting journalist of their recent ordeal. They had taken on the farm four years earlier, and insisted that there had been no violation of Land League rules. There'd been a long legal dispute over the tenancy in the past: the original long-term tenant had apparently sold her lease to a local man named Callaghan, but her son insisted part of the farm was his and took the case to court. The rival claimants were removed by the landowner, a Mrs Longfield, only when they had reached an impasse in the courts and run out of money for further litigation. The place had lain empty for years, and when it was eventually put up for rent again, several locals bid for it – including Callaghan himself. But the McCarthys won. At the outset, everything went well. But then Callaghan – who ran a pub in the nearby village of Donoughmore – began to complain that he would have got the place if McCarthy hadn't joined the bidding. This still shouldn't have resulted in a boycott. But as Mrs McCarthy told it to Pellew, chief among the local activists were 'some young men belonging to a wrangling family named B—':

> Their father had a lawsuit with a neighbor sixteen or seventeen years ago, and, when the suit went against him, hung himself. A friendly farmer told us that one of the B—boys said we had called them the hangman's sons. We would never have said such a thing, and we wouldn't say so now. But there was a boy in our house who might have said something of the sort. Then, when Callaghan said he would have got the land if we hadn't taken it, the B—s were glad to turn his talk against us, and boycotted us out of spite.

A meeting had been called in Donoughmore village, with the nationalist members of Parliament James Christopher Flynn and Charles Kearns Deane Tanner whipping up the crowd. An effigy of John McCarthy was paraded through the village on a donkey then battered to pieces. After that, the McCarthys found that no local tradesmen would take work from them, no one would shoe their horses, no nearby shops would serve them and no one would buy their produce. Boycotts were enforced through intimidation, and even when they took livestock further afield to sell in Macroom or Kanturk, as soon as the buyers found out a boycott was in place, they returned the animals. 'I cannot get a tailor, carpenter, or blacksmith nearer than Cork,' McCarthy told Pellew, 'and even in Cork tradespeople who used to give us credit now refuse it. Our letters have to be left at the police barracks, for no one dared bring us letters from the place the post-boy leaves them.' They found that they could no longer hire labourers to work on the farm. Their last hire was a boy from a neighbouring family, but within a couple of weeks of his arrival, shots had been fired into the house to warn him off. The young McCarthy sons had been badly beaten on their way to mass, and the whole family were ritually humiliated whenever they attended church: 'I was hooted at mass, and stones were fired at me as I left the chapel,' McCarthy said. 'The Sunday after my wife was bedaubed with rotten eggs in the chapelyard.'

They insisted that they still had many friends locally. All privately agreed that the boycott was illegitimate; but none dared to say so publicly, and they would only visit the farm in disguise and under cover of darkness. The authorities had offered them protection: a pair of policemen came to the farm each evening and stayed through the night – 'and we feel uneasy if they are late'.

McCarthy himself had joined the Land League some years earlier, under the coercion of a man who falsely promised to sell him a threshing machine if he did so. He agreed that the League's work had been necessary to break the grip of landlordism and enforce fairer tenure. But he felt that recent legal changes had made it redundant. As Pellew was leaving the farm, McCarthy called him back to clarify a point: 'I don't even condemn boycotting absolutely. A man who goes behind another's back and takes his farm, might be fairly boycotted; but then the people ought to make sure of the facts.'

Keen to get the other side of the story, Pellew went on to Donoughmore village, where the Catholic curate claimed to know nothing about the case, but did acknowledge that the boycott principle began with tenants merely pledging never to take a farm from which a predecessor had been unjustly evicted, but it was later extended to cover all evictions, unjust or otherwise – which might have been the start of the McCarthys' trouble. The curate was happy to talk openly about his political beliefs, however: 'Home Rule we all want, because the Irish are a nation, and a nation ought to govern itself.'

Pellew then found the pub of John McCarthy's antagonist, Callaghan, who said that the McCarthys' higher bid for the land had scuppered his plan to take it on – by his own admission, with no intention of ever actually paying the rent – and to install a cousin to farm it in his name. He, his wife and daughter seemed to be enjoying their rivals' predicament. 'They are boycotted!' Mrs Callaghan said. 'When they went to mass they were pelted with stones and eggs. No one will speak to them or sit in the same gallery with them. Oh, they are boycotted! As for us, we are as much after the old farm as we were the day we left.'[12]

How the conflict eventually played out is unclear: there are both McCarthys and Callaghans listed in later records for the Barrahaurin townland. George Pellew's journalistic career, however, came to a sad end just five years after his Irish journey. On the evening of 18 February 1892, he was making his way home to his New York apartment. He was suffering from a severe eye infection which had affected his sight, and he seems to have stumbled off the pavement into a sunken garden area, striking his head as he fell. His body was found the following morning. He'd been due to start a new job as staff writer on *The Cosmopolitan*. He was just thirty-two.

Police and soldiers keep watch during an eviction in Galway in 1888

* * *

The British response to the Land League campaigns intersected with a broader desire to dampen the calls for Home Rule – after two failed attempts by Liberal governments to bring it into law – and an undercurrent of official antipathy to the old landlord class dating back to the famine years. The idea of Conservative governments towards the turn of the century was to 'kill Home Rule with kindness'. A series of Land Acts were passed, culminating in the sweeping provisions of the 1903 Wyndham Land Purchase Act. These Acts fixed rents, ensured secure tenure, and allowed for the transfer of ownership to tenants, with the process overseen by a

Land Commission and the purchase cost covered by favourable government loans. Some 316,000 individual holdings, amounting to around 11 million acres, were transferred to erstwhile tenants.[13]

Meanwhile, a separate Act in 1891 had established the Congested Districts Board (CDB), tasked with improving life for those in the chronically impoverished and densely populated regions of the west. The CDB built new harbours and brought in new fishing techniques, created local cottage industries, introduced new breeds of livestock and new methods of animal husbandry, reorganised the rural road networks and built 6,000 new houses. They also bought out several large estates and issued compulsory purchase orders on land held by large-scale cattle ranchers on short leases, then redistributed it as family farms. Half a century on from the famine, the tightly huddled clachan was still prominent in the west of Ireland, a hugger-mugger community of smallholders living close together with their own shared public spaces and network of routes through the surrounding fields. But in the interest of orderliness and 'hygiene', the CDB broke up clachans and established isolated individual farms. The land was reapportioned in ladder-like strips with the newly built farmhouses strung along the upgraded roads.[14] A new pattern was emerging, an abiding connection forged between the rural homeplace and the 'road frontage'.

The changes wrought by the CDB and the combined Land Acts were genuinely remarkable. In 1884, shortly after the first Land War, just 3 per cent of Irish land was tenant-owned.[15] Thirty years later, on the eve of the First World War, two-thirds of it had been transferred to former tenants.[16] In a bizarre twist, after all the centuries of profound iniquity, rural Irish tenants had ended up with stronger protections and greater access to direct ownership that their counterparts in Britain.

But imagine the fine human detail. Imagine how many small injustices and petty conflicts must have lain beneath the grand statistics, how many intractable conflicts like that of the McCarthys and Callaghans in Barrahaurin. How many festering resentments were baked into the new arrangements? How many people ended up feeling that *those lads* got more than they deserved while *we* were left short? Because there could never be enough land for everyone to get all that they wanted.

As for the British authorities, the idea that they would ever really be able to kill the drive towards Irish independence with paternalistic kindness was pathetically naïve. A few frantic decades of redistribution were never going to erase a narrative inscribed across the centuries. All you needed to do to give demands for further land reform an irresistible moral imperative was to invoke Cromwell. Throughout the second half of the nineteenth century, it was customary to blame evictions on ruthless new 'English' landlords who had done well out of the Encumbered Estates Act – despite the fact that many of those ruthless new landlords were actually middle-class Irish Catholics.[17] And the Land Wars – both in the moment and in subsequent popular memory – managed to override the complex tensions between the strong and middling farmers and the struggling labourers they employed. A year after George Pellew's visit, another American journalist, William Henry Hurlbert, travelled to Ireland to examine the 'land question'. A farm labourer Hurlbert met in Laois told him that 'The farmers will work a man just as long as they can't help it, and then they throw him away', and that they'd sooner 'let a labourer die in the ditch' than provide them with proper housing. But a nearby smallholder neatly unravelled the apparent conundrum of the labourers' political convictions: 'They hate the farmers,' he said, 'but they love Ireland, and they all stand together for the counthry!'[18]

* * *

Five kilometres out of Ardee on a long straight road: a gateway opening to the east; elaborate cast-iron railings with the rust coming through; heavy fluted columns bearded with ivy. A rutted track bends away beyond between unkempt ash trees and horse chestnuts; a castellated gate lodge stands behind the bushes to the right. A sign is fixed to the railings with an arrow pointing on up the road: 'Yard traffic next entrance'. This used to be the grand entrance to the Lisrenny demesne.

I'd walked into Ardee in the grey of early afternoon, pottered around the place, sat scribbling in my diary over coffee and cake. Having walked in – and knowing that I would be walking out too – gave me a pleasurable feeling of deviance among the shoppers and café-goers. There was a busy working bustle to the town and a blocky fifteenth-century castle dominating the main street like a cuckoo in a dunnock's nest. The UK reg cars waiting at the traffic lights and the Ulster twang in some of the voices in the shops made the presence of the border palpable. It was only a day's walk away now.

I pottered around in the similarly grey morning too, drank more coffee, wrote up more notes, then set out at midday. Within half an hour the grey had cleared. Blueish oat fields rolled away from the roadside and the air was fierce with skimming swallows. The plum-coloured bank of the Cooley Mountains surfaced in the distance from time to time. I knew I'd be on tarmac all day again today, but I didn't mind. A curious lightness had entered the journey with the view of the mountains, a sense of ancient pilgrimage. The sky above was streaked with high cirrus.

I passed the shabby gateway to the Lisrenny demesne, and a little further on I found the mausoleum of its former owners, the Filgates, in a cemetery on a hillock by the roadside. Crooked, lichen-blotched gravestones with a mass of mouse-ear hawkweed growing in between, the usual lemon-yellow of the flowers tinted here with the colour of a ripe blood-orange. A few hundred metres away on the far side of the road, the ruin of Louth Hall was in view, skull-like on its own low hill. This part of the country was densely stamped with the footprints of lost demesnes. Red House, Rahanna House, Lisrenny House, Louth Hall, Glyde Court, Corbollis House, Corderry House, Stephenstown House, Clermont Park. Some stood almost in hailing distance of one another. A congested district of the gentry – how had they all fitted in here? But they were almost all gone now, the houses in ruins or vanished entirely. It's the same all across Ireland. You see a mouldering ceremonial gateway, incongruous among the working fields, and find that it leads only to a scruffy farmyard or comes to a dead end in a conifer plantation. And the ruins: hundreds of them, in every county; sometimes a relatively modest two-storey manor house, roofless and jackdaw-mobbed; sometimes a vast gothic or Palladian extravaganza reduced to gaping window sockets and crumbling gables. What hypothesis would a team of alien archaeologists descending on this landscape produce? They'd surely propose some kind of extinction, the abrupt collapse of a culture. And as they began to excavate individual sites, they'd surely find indications of catastrophic fires.

It's sometimes claimed that the 1903 Wyndham Act meant that the festering 'land question' which had haunted Ireland for centuries had 'virtually disappeared' by the start of the First World War.[19] It's a useful idea if you want to cast everything that happened from 1916 onwards in the glow of pure ideological nationalism. But the fact that the Land Commission was still divvying up and handing out new smallholdings half a century later makes it obviously untrue. The Act did, though, accelerate the departure of the old landowning gentry from the countryside. Those who gave up their estates entirely had the option to lease back their houses and the immediate untenanted surrounds. And the Act included a provision for former landlords to retain 'sporting rights' – which included 'any right of hunting, shooting, fishing and taking game or fish on any land' – on their former estates.[20] This allowed some old Anglo-Irish families to get rid of their enormous mortgages, retreat behind their demesne walls, have the hunt still meet on their lawn and pretend that nothing had changed. But if there wasn't a significant alternative source of income besides the land itself, the gradual slide into insolvency was inevitable.

Some of the grandest estates had already been broken up and their owners had vanished by the time Ireland was partitioned into the six Protestant-majority Ulster counties that would be kept in the UK and the twenty-six-county Free State which in time became the Republic. But not every landowner sold up, and the big house would become an obvious target during the revolutionary years. Between 1920 and 1923 – the period spanning the second half of the Irish War of Independence and the subsequent Civil War – at least 275 big houses were deliberately set on fire.[21] Just in the area I was now walking through, Annaskeagh, Ballygassan, Cavananore, Knockabbey, Milestown, Ravensdale and Clermont all went up in flames in this period. There was often a curious formality about the attacks: a letter would arrive giving advance notice, or there'd be a polite knock on the door. Sometimes the occupants were permitted to remove the contents – all that dark oak furniture, all those ancestral portraits – and stack them on the lawn before the windows were knocked in and the flames lit. On other occasions, they'd be briskly woken in their beds, told that the place had already been doused with petrol and given just minutes to clear out.

In the simplified revolutionary fable, these big houses were all righteously destroyed as bastions of English oppression or to prevent their takeover as barracks by the hated counterrevolutionary forces. But modern historians – Terence Dooley in particular – have increasingly emphasised the significance of ongoing 'land hunger' to the violence of the revolutionary years.[22] What better way to get rid of a stubborn landlord and free up their estate than an arson attack? The relatively modest Ballydugan House, which sat on a 1,500-acre estate in East Galway, was burnt down in 1922 during the period of uneasy quiet between the end of the War of Independence and the start of the Civil War (the earlier Land Wars had been particularly violent in East Galway, and 'agrarian unrest' had never really gone away there). The owner, Michael Henry Burke, was descended from the original twelfth-century Anglo-Norman incomers and the family had been in the area for centuries. He was, by all accounts, a difficult man. He'd been subjected to a long campaign of boycotting and general harassment, led by a similarly hard-headed tenant named Michael Dempsey who was determined to enlarge his own holding. The house was set alight by three men in the early hours of 15 June, when Burke himself was away in Dublin lobbying for official protection. In the aftermath,

Burke insisted that he would not be 'smoked out'. He pursued compensation, rebuilt the house and passed it on to his son, who ran it as a dairy farm. Burke's granddaughter inherited it in turn in the 1960s. Into the 1970s and beyond she experienced occasional low-level intimidation – walls knocked down, cattle driven off the land, stones left in the milking machines. Even more recently, the researcher Ann O'Riordan found that some locals still responded evasively or gave vague answers about the IRA and the Black and Tans when asked about the burning.[23]

Other old Anglo-Irish families in other big houses lingered for a surprisingly long time. Sometimes, you'll spot a ruined mansion, a mere shell with all trace of surrounding gardens utterly obliterated, and assume it has been this way since the days of the Encumbered Estates Act, or at very least since the early 1920s. But then you'll look it up online and find that it was inhabited well within living memory, maybe even within your own lifetime, that it went rapidly to pieces only after a final auction in the 1960s or 70s or 80s. Big houses were sometimes deliberately demolished by new owners. Coole House in Galway – seat of William Gregory of Quarter-Acre Clause infamy and later playground for Yeats, Synge and the other literary associates of his widow Augusta – was broken up for its stone by a local building contractor in 1941. But here and there – usually in the smaller houses, places rivalled in scale by the grander roadside newbuilds – a family like the Burkes is still in place. The hunt probably *still* meets on the lawn a couple of times each winter. But there are no gardeners now to keep the flowerbeds in order; the sash windows badly need replacing, and the old demesne is just a working farm.

* * *

A few kilometres further on, beyond the tidy little village of Tallanstown with its flowerbeds and redbrick window reveals, there was yet another ruined big house. It was 300 metres south of the road; but there was no one about, so I hopped the galvanised gate and followed the track along the edge of a wheatfield. The

ground was hard and dry and my feet raised a smoulder of pale dust. The big trees of what must once have been the park lay to the right, a skittish herd of half-grown yellow bullocks rumbling in and out of their shade. Behind the house, a morass of crusty slurry, a stack of black-wrapped silage bales, a botheration of Lucozade-coloured dung flies. Sheds and old stables with the doors and windows gone, a carpet of desiccated droppings within; a sickly scent of elderflowers. Trees were welling up from inside the house itself. I could see a coat of arms carved into the end wall, two gothic arches leading into shadow. But there was an electric fence in the way and the bullocks were mustering excitedly at my presence, so I went no closer. This was Glyde Court, seat of the Foster family. It had only fallen empty in the 1980s, but already it looked less substantial, more decayed than the medieval towerhouses I'd passed earlier on the journey – and less robustly secure in the landscape than the ancient oratories and churches back on the Dingle Peninsula.

It was properly hot now, with a high summer hum to the afternoon. The Cooleys came back into view, and away to their left the warty bulk of Slieve Gullion, across the border in Armagh. I'd seen it yesterday from a greater distance and it had looked like a Javanese volcano on a rainy season afternoon. But it was close enough now for the detail of its slopes to show: houses, fields, forestry, heath, its apparent scale diminishing as the distance narrowed.

A stripe of grass down the middle of the lane; a man spot-spraying ragwort in a yellowing field; a stag-headed pine tree on a silvery skyline; and Proverbs 22:6 chiselled into a weathered plaque on the wall outside an old schoolhouse: 'Train up a Child in the way he should go and when he is old, he will not depart from it.' And at a quiet junction, a long low thatched cottage. Blue frames on the tiny windows, reptilian stonework showing through scabby limewash and the ivy forging a forking path up the gable end. There was a scruffy yard behind the cottage with low outbuildings, red flowering crocosmias and unpruned yellow roses. And by the roadside, a plaque, 'Erected by Louth Farmers' in 1998, 'in memory of Lawrence Crawley whose eviction from this house by Lord Louth on 11th June 1881 was a turning point in land reform.' The countryside here seemed to be dense with land history, all the vague theory thickening in a sense of place.

* * *

Dramatic resistance to attempted evictions was a particular Land League tactic during the 1880s, and they were adept at turning such events into prime pieces of political theatre. Huge crowds would gather to jeer at the police and the 'emergency men' who worked for the Property Defence Association formed by landlords to resist the League and enforce evictions. Journalists and sympathetic members of Parliament would be on hand; and elaborate strategies were put in place to make the evictors' task comically difficult. Sometimes a high-profile eviction would descend into real violence, as in the notorious evictions at Bodyke in Co. Clare on the southern edge of the Slieve Aughty hills in 1886.[24] But Laurence Crawley's case was a veritable circus (quite what made it a 'turning point' is unclear, but it certainly generated some good press for the Land League's campaign).

Crawley's ancestors had held the farm here as hereditary tenants of the barons of Louth for two centuries. He was an active member of the Land League, and by 1881 he had paid no rent for four years while attempting to negotiate a reduced rate. When the negotiations ground to a halt, an eviction notice was served for 11 June. The authorities were clearly expecting trouble, for they sent two troops of the 19th Hussars and 200 policemen to accompany the 'emergency man' acting as bailiff and the four labourers he'd recruited to help with the eviction. When they arrived at Crawley's cottage, they found a huge crowd of Land League supporters jeering and blowing horns to herald their arrival, several hostile local priests and a correspondent from the *Daily Express*. The emergency man and his helpers first had to break down the firmly chained gate to the farmyard. They were then faced with an 'immense pyramid of stones' built up against the cottage door and 'plentifully coated over with farmyard manure and other offensive matter'. They had to remove this to a constant chorus of hooting from the crowd outside the yard. Crawley and several others inside the house would periodically stick their heads out of the little windows to join in with the laughter. When the stones were finally removed, the bailiffs found that the door still could not be battered in (it turned out later that an internal porch had been deliberately collapsed behind it). So they then turned their attention to the contents of the outbuildings, for all Crawley's possessions were to be removed as part of the eviction. 'Here, too,' according to the newspaper reports, 'a ludicrous obstruction had been provided for.' The wheels had been removed from the carts and 'an immense quantity of turf and three or four tons of small potatoes' had been piled up in the main barn, and Crawley 'had not left a single vessel about the place in which the potatoes could be carried out'. The carter who had driven the eviction team out to the cottage had reportedly been 'got at' by the assembled Land Leaguers and refused to help, so the emergency man resorted to using two small zinc buckets from his own picnic hamper to remove the potatoes – which took nearly four hours in the heat of the afternoon, with Crawley inside the cottage and the crowd outside jeering the whole time. After this, they had a second go at smashing in the cottage door with a battering ram, to no avail. But then someone discovered a back entrance through the barn, and they were finally able to get inside and remove the occupants and the household goods. Laurence Crawley simply walked straight across the road to another timber house, newly built by his supporters on a neighbouring property. In a final gesture of defiance, he lifted the cottage door off its hinges and took it with him.[25] By the end of 1881, he was back in the original cottage, presumably on satisfactory terms determined by the new Land Law Act.

It all seems like a classic instance of an Irish tenant facing off against a dastardly 'English' landlord. But there are certain nuances. For a start, by the 1880s, the Louth Hall estate's rent roll was managed by the Dublin-based Stewart and Kincaid agency, so Crawley's immediate conflict was with them, rather than with Lord Louth himself.[26] And the pedigree of the Plunkett family, ancient heirs to the Louth baronetcy, wasn't exactly that of the archetypal Anglo-Irish oppressor. They were Old English. Their earliest Norman ancestors had arrived in the twelfth century – though living just inside the Pale they had never really become 'more Irish than the Irish'. In the sixteenth century, the Plunketts stayed loyal, more or less, to the Elizabethan Crown. But they joined the Gaelic chiefs of Ulster in the 1641 rebellion, and in consequence had their lands confiscated – stolen by Cromwell, we might say – during the mid-seventeenth-century settlement. They managed to get most of the estate back during the reign of James II. But Thomas, second son of the seventh Baron Louth, joined the Jacobite cause at the century's end. He was among the Catholic besiegers of Derry and fought on the losing Irish side in the battles of the Boyne and Aughrim. He was joined by his older brother Oliver, the new eighth baron, in the final engagement of the Jacobite conflict at Limerick. Thomas went into exile and Oliver was formally outlawed. Somehow, the family kept going – and remained Catholic even as the Penal Laws began to bite, though the tenth baron pragmatically converted to Protestantism and thus kept the estate intact. The family stuck with the Church of Ireland for a century, but it seems to have been a grudging affiliation (the celebrated seventeenth-century martyr, Oliver Plunkett, gruesomely executed by the English state 'for promoting the Roman faith', was a close kinsman). In 1867, Randal Percy Otway – the thirteenth Baron Louth and Laurence Crawley's notional adversary – was received back into the Catholic Church. Most of the Louth Hall estate was sold to its tenants in the aftermath of the 1903 Wyndham Act. The family held on to the house and demesne for a while, but that too was passed to the Land Commission and broken up among local farmers when the fourteenth baron died in 1941. The surviving family ended up in Jersey. And of course, Louth Hall itself is now a skeletal ruin in the middle of a field, while Laurence Crawley's cottage has a new thatched roof and a fresh coat of blue paint on the window frames.

* * *

And then there are the bungalows.

All the way to Knockbridge, where I'd booked a room in an old-fashioned B&B with heavy floral carpets and a century-old palimpsest of high-gloss paint on the skirting boards: bungalows, face-on to the road. And between the bungalows, bigger things of more recent vintage: *huge* houses, each boldly centred on its roadside plot, armed with a battery of dormer windows and surrounded by a prairie of sheeny grass.

Tim Robinson, defending the particularly intense late-twentieth-century blitz of bungalow-building in southern Connemara from its snobbish detractors, pointed out that the enduring sense of place and higgledy-piggledy community was lost on those simply driving through.[27] And it was true. Walking along these and other roads, I discovered something surprising: the ribbon development didn't seem so intrusive when viewed on foot. It was only seventy-five metres deep and the strip was by no means continuous. There were still unkempt hedges flanking the road for much of its length, with cattle and trees and thickening silage grass beyond. It was much easier to see past the modern houses at five kilometres per hour than at fifty, to recognise that you were still in the countryside. But there was always a faint echo, passing a line of modern roadside housing: something about the elaborate gateways, the fluted cast-concrete pillars, the bold exclusion of the surrounding block wall, the way the houses seemed intentionally sited to be *seen*. I always tried to ignore it, told myself I was forcing a phantom connection out of a random aesthetic. But those gateways, those columns…

Jack Fitzsimons himself wrote that he had always believed when he was growing up 'that people who live in big houses and look out through big windows must have a superior outlook, a desirable dimension to their character, that is denied to those who are brought up in poky rooms with puny windows'.[28] And in the Co. Meath of his 1930s childhood, the term 'big house' still came with implicit capitalisation.

* * *

In 1923, the old Congested Districts Board and the commission that had administered the various Land Acts were dissolved and their functions rolled into a new Land Commission for the independent Irish state. There were plenty of departing gentry with estates still to be divided up, and a few stick-in-the-muds refusing to see the writing on the demesne wall and in need of compulsion. There were also the large cattle ranches that had developed since the famine, especially in Connacht. Some were directly owned; others were leased from old landlords on eleven-month arrangements (which made the ranches technically 'untenanted' in law). There'd been a period of agitation against the ranchers in the early 1900s under the slogan 'the bullock for the road and the land for the people', and there was an enduring sense of moral opprobrium against large holdings, regardless of who owned them. Some strong farmers who'd only gained full title to their holdings after 1881 actually had the land taken away from them again through compulsory purchase by the Land Commission.[29]

Over the course of its existence, the Land Commission transferred 2.34 million acres to new owners.[30] It only stopped acquiring land in the mid-1980s, and it was still signing off on the last transfers into the 1990s. In the west of Connacht, it took up the incomplete task of the CDB, and continued to replace traditional clustered communities with isolated individual farms. The Commission also made an attempt at a kind of reverse plantation. Around 14,500 families from Connacht were given new holdings in Leinster and Munster,[31] most provocatively in three 'Gaeltacht colonies' in Co. Meath. In the late 1930s, Irish-speaking families from the far west were relocated to the townlands of Rathcairn, Gibbstown and Allenstown where their presence was expected to help the re-Gaelicisation of rural Ireland. Unsurprisingly, the move went down badly with locals hoping to get land for themselves. Two local election candidates took out an advert in the *Meath Chronicle* declaring that 'Meath wants no more migrants'. Characterisations were bandied about of the Connacht people as indolent poitín swillers, straight out of the English travel writers' discourse about Irish natives. There was a full-blown anti-migrant riot in Athboy; and the newcomers were subjected to some of the old intimidatory tactics of the Land Wars – threatening graffiti, shots fired through windows and boycotts by local pubs.[32] But they held on, and two of the three settlements retain their official Irish-speaking status even today. I'd skirted the edge of the Baile Ghib Gaeltacht on my way out of the bog beyond Kells the previous morning.

The most significant thing about the Land Commission is the size of the new family farms it created. They were *very* small, typically around twenty or thirty acres apiece and often much smaller again (Jack Fitzsimons' family was awarded a five-acre smallholding by the Commission in the 1930s).[33] This was partly down to the sheer number of people clamouring for land. By the 1940s, the Commission secretariat was receiving around 400,000 letters a year,[34] many of them from people asking for a grant of land – or, perhaps, complaining about someone *else* getting a grant of land. As one former Commission official put it at the end of his career in the early 1990s, 'An inspector must select those who are to benefit and must reject those who are to be excluded and for every one pleased several must be disappointed.'[35] Think again of the McCarthys and the Callaghans in Barrahaunin in the 1880s; think of the volume of bad blood that must have been generated. It's little wonder that the Land Commission records are still kept firmly locked away from the public domain in a warehouse in Portlaoise.*

The official preference for small farms didn't do much to ease the economic stagnation of the mid-twentieth century. In many assessments, the Land Commission's approach actually entrenched rural poverty. It 'succeeded in retarding the modernisation of Irish agriculture', as the historian and broadcaster Myles Dungan puts it.[36] Elsewhere in Europe, agriculture was mechanising, farms were consolidating and food production was becoming an increasingly globalised industry. In my own part of western Cornwall, the size of a typical family dairy farm gradually grew from around 40 acres towards 200 acres across the twentieth century as older farmers on smaller holdings sold the land to the neighbours instead of passing it on to the next generation. But in Ireland, the Land Commission was still setting up new freeholders on tiny smallholdings. Between 1917 and 1975, the number of Irish farms over 200 acres actually declined by 25 per cent – and by around 70 per cent in the former cattle-ranching regions of Connacht.[37]

Forty acres really wasn't enough to provide a viable income for a large family in the second half of the twentieth century, even after the first European farm subsidies arrived. But then people started building bungalows, and suddenly farmland acquired a new worth

* Generally, archives over thirty years old are available to the public in Ireland. But there's a special exemption for those still deemed 'working records' – as is the case for the Land Commission – and those which might cause 'distress or danger to living persons'. Recently, tentative moves have finally begun to make the Land Commission archives publicly accessible.

that had nothing to do with cattle or potatoes. If you were lucky enough to have a public road running along the edge of your property you could divide the adjoining strip of 'road frontage' into building plots and sell them off without losing too much of your overall acreage. And better yet, there was a special capital gains tax-break for farmers selling plots of between a half and three-quarters of an acre.[38] The very regular size of the roadside bungalow gardens is not an accident.

And so here they are, all along the road frontage, hundreds upon hundreds of them. The original Jack Fitzsimons bungalows have been overshadowed by the huge dormered constructions of later decades. But each still stands squarely on its regular four-cornered plot – a plot of the very size that a starving family might have been forced to give up by the Quarter-Acre Clause during the famine.

A DETOUR: THE SECRET ON THE MAP

I need to get away from the desk.

The journey on the ground is long finished now, and I'm deep into its second iteration. There are books bristling with sticky notes stacked on the floor and a daily rhythm of interlibrary loan renewal reminders in my inbox. I haven't shut down my computer properly for weeks – too many PDFs, too many browser windows to close. Between the keyboard and the screen sits the textual residue of the journey: the small notebook I kept in my pocket as I walked, and the larger one in which I tried to take down a proper record each evening. Both have brown covers and densely pencilled pages: 'Blueish oat-fields, Cooley Mountains beyond, graveyard with blood-orange-coloured dandelions, Louth Hall on a hilltop'. And beside them, a stack of tattered maps, their folded edges like the strata of an oystershell midden. I have been drinking far too much coffee.

But I'm nearing the end of this echo-journey; I can afford to leave the writing for one morning. So I drop Róise at preschool (she's grown enormously since we cycled the Listowel–Rathkeale Greenway, and she has a new baby sister called Merryn now). And then instead of heading straight back to my desk, I drive up to the far end of town. I park near the GAA pitch, dash across the busy main road and walk north on a meandering lane.

I've never been this way before, and the sudden elevation is unexpected. This is esker country, rumpled by the vanished glaciers. An ascent of just a few metres can throw an astonishing distance into view. It's a grey morning, with a fine gauze of mizzle in the air. But I can see the big wind turbines beyond Moycullen and the dark crenelations of the Maamturks and the Twelve Bens, ninety kilometres away in

Connemara. It's like looking into another continent. The blackberries are already ripening – ridiculously early this year.

A big ringfort comes into view beside the road, a double rampart with a deep fosse between. I stop here, look out uneasily across the land to the east. One of the lines I want to follow runs that way. But there are two men digging foundations for a new house in the road frontage right next to the ringfort. So I stay going, stick to the road, turn right and then right again.

Knapweed, purple vetch, a bright road-hem of ragwort. Two white dogs rush out from an enormous roadside newbuild to proclaim my passing. A green lane strikes off southward here. It's blocked by a rusty gate, but there's no sign forbidding trespass, so I squeeze past. The green lane ends at the head of a big field. There's another big ringfort 700 metres away across country with a small block of forestry behind it. But all the roadside bungalows look onto the land here. I'd be in view the whole way.

I suck my teeth, frustrated by my own lack of boldness. But this is the point: I don't *want* to trespass, don't *want* to stride out with haughty entitlement, firmly convinced that I should have the right to 'roam' across all of this. I just want a way through – a narrow way, an old way, a way that countless others have walked before me. I go back towards the road and flinch at the sight of a figure watching me from a huge floor-to-ceiling window in the house with the dogs.

The lane brings me back around to the main road, a kilometre and a half from where I started. Morning traffic streaks along it at 120 kilometres an hour. But there's a wide shoulder on either side and it's safe enough to walk here; people stride this way in their hi-vis vests every evening. I'm almost back at the car now, and it looks like the morning will be a disappointment. But there's one last chance – a lane striking back inland from the main road, hemmed with blackthorns. There are sloes, already ripening. Ripe sloes! In July! Another small reminder that things aren't right with the world, that nothing is as it should be. A new farm track cuts away to the right. I steel myself, climb the gate and hurry along it to a ruined cottage nestled in a little hollow. I'm committed now, out onto land, and I'll keep going until I find what I'm looking for. I follow a wall north from the ruin, cross a low ridge – *and there it is, right where it should be!* Jutting from the wall where it approaches the corner of the little conifer plantation I spotted from the end of the green lane half an hour earlier: a simple step-across stile; a long slab of limestone set crossways through the wall to allow a walker to pass easily into the next field. I give a little whoop of triumph, stamp down the nettles and step onto the stile myself – the first person to do so in how many decades?

I have never been here before. But I *knew* I would find this smallest and simplest piece of infrastructure *right* here – because I am following a footpath marked on a six-inch map published in 1920.

The problematic colonial context of the nineteenth-century mapping of Ireland emphasised by *Translations* and by Tim Robinson's commentary on John O'Donovan is all well and good. But a map is a many-layered thing, and as it moves from current document to archival matter – which happens inevitably even before it is complete – it quickly escapes the intentions of its makers. It carries secrets and subversions for future generations. Surely there is no better example than the huge network of footpaths, first recorded on the second Ordnance Survey of the 1880s, and confirmed in later updates, well into the twentieth century: a record of persistent human movement across the Irish landscape, regardless of the iniquities of its ownership. Once you know to look, you can find this archival record confirmed in the field-scape all over Ireland.

If people know of these old Irish paths at all, they usually refer to them as 'mass paths'. The two mountain bikers I met by the Royal Canal used that term, as does even the limited academic literature about them.[39] But these were not exclusively routes connecting outlying settlements with places of worship. Some run across fields to the former site of a shop or pub or post office. Others are simply general-purpose lines of least resistance for those travelling across country on foot.

What happened to these paths is no great mystery. They were there in the 1880s and they were there into the 1940s, and there are still fading memories of their use in some rural communities today.[40] But as emigration emptied the countryside in the mid-twentieth century, and as those who remained got bicycles and cars, the ways through the fields fell out of use. The stile I found this morning lay on a path that led towards a former schoolhouse. It was surely heavily used each morning and afternoon by local children. But once that school closed in the mid-twentieth century, fewer and fewer people walked it. In the same period the exact same thing was happening to the old customary footpaths in Wales and England. But the 1949 National Parks and Access to the Countryside Act arrived there before the atrophy was complete and ensured that the surviving path network was recorded and protected. In Ireland that never happened. This is a peculiarity – a perversity, even – in the long story of Irish land reform. In its radical redistributions, the Land Commission at times allowed the old landlord class to retain *their* rights of access to hunt and shoot and fish on land that had been handed over to their former tenants. But it apparently had no interest in formalising and protecting a far more important and democratic right:[41] the right of *all* people to move along the time-honoured ways through the countryside – whether they led to a mass rock or a holy well or some other site of small resistance in the preceding centuries, or simply to the local pub.

But the presence of these lost paths is still fossilised in their simple stiles. The little rectangle of road-bounded East Galway countryside I circuited this morning covers just 2.5 square kilometres. But when I measure up all the footpaths recorded on the old map – the cross-country route running towards the school, an arcing shortcut from the main road at the eastern edge of the rectangle, two dead-end doglegs leading to springs in the boggy centre and a short line in the northwest corner giving access to a *cillín* – they add up to five kilometres. Five kilometres of forgotten footpaths, just in this one tiny postage stamp of land. Now zoom out – zoom out to parish level, county level, zoom out to take in the whole island of Ireland. Imagine the thousands upon thousands of kilometres of paths, clearly recorded on the old maps and still just about tangible in the landscape.

PART THREE

From the Plough to the Stars

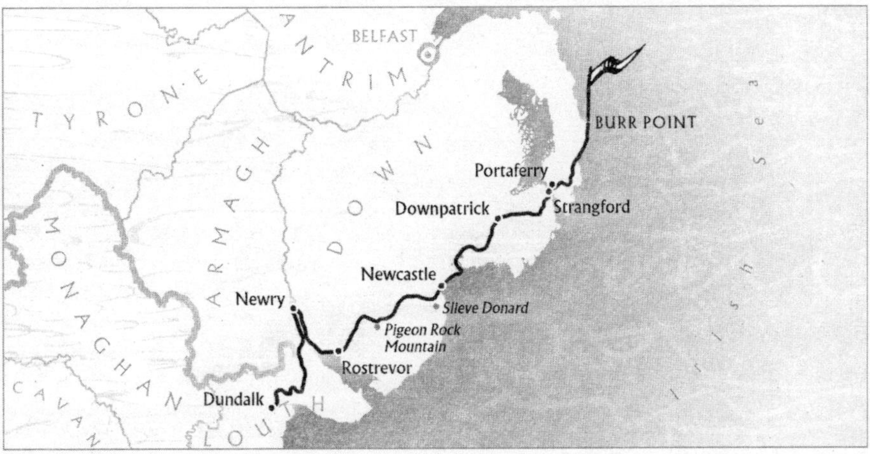

9

Partitions: Knockbridge to Newcastle

Midday at the mountain gate with seventeen kilometres covered already, mostly on tarmac.

Along the way from Knockbridge, a Bronze Age standing stone in a roadside field: the Clochafarmore menhir, a tilted three-metre slab of greyish stone with a blaze of turmeric-coloured lichen at the tip and a chiselled early twentieth-century graffito at the base ('Jim McKenna 1912'). Through Dundalk just as the shops were opening; red-brick terraces and once-proud townhouses named for long-ago holidays: Kinvara, St Ives. At the edge of town, a flush of windy sunlight and a low-tide smell of salt and mud; whickering terns. A big curlew stalked below the road bridge, prodding the air ahead as it went. I was across the breadth of Ireland now, had made it from the Atlantic littoral to the upper limit of the east coast tide.

I stopped for a coffee from a petrol station just off the N1 roundabout. The unfamiliar accent of the young woman behind the counter, the diphthong of the 'now' strained to breaking point, was a reminder that I was on the marches of Ulster. Crossing the forecourt I caught a snatch of aggrieved conversation from two women at the pumps: 'If they say yes to a greenway' – she motioned someplace to the east – 'it'll go through all those places and it'll be all those people caught up in it…'

A little further on I broke off the road onto a short track, marked on the map. There was a memorial plaque set into the field wall here. I'd passed many similar plaques at the roadside in the past weeks: a polished slab of granite or marble among the nettles and brambles; a name – always a man's – with dates of birth and death, the span of years invariably a short one. Sometimes there'd be a fresh bunch of flowers left among the hedge plants. But this plaque, for once, didn't commemorate a fatal car crash. It was dedicated to a local man 'cruelly murdered by UDR and Red Hand Commando links' in 1976 – another reminder of where I was, what I was approaching.

The track became a path, winding beneath mature sycamores to the edge of a golf course. It was less than a kilometre long, but it was lovely walking and the first real respite from tarmac since the Girley Bog three days earlier. The path led to the Proleek Dolmen, a Neolithic portal tomb, fenced off at the edge of the greens. The lumpen capstone was crusted with small rocks thrown up for luck by passers-by. A big white sign instructed visitors to beware of golf balls and warned that this was not a right of way, that the management reserved the right to refuse entry.

Back to the road, a steep uphill pull with the sweat dripping from the tip of my nose and clouding my sunglasses, and then to the mountain gate. Another sign here forbade dogs – but not walkers. The upper reaches of the Cooley Mountains were open ahead: sheep-cropped hillsides, low patches of bell heather, 500-metre summits; country that you really could 'roam' across – even if not by right. It was the first time I'd been in such a place since the Dingle Peninsula. The seventeen kilometres of the morning fell off me like a shed skin as I struck up the mountainside and realised that I'd walked myself into fitness over the previous weeks. The ascent of Mount Eagle on the very first day had been a leg-searing, lung-straining ordeal, but now I was climbing lightly, despite the laden pack.

I stopped and cooked noodles for lunch in a patch of tormentil by a busy stream then lay back for a while, looking up at a mackerel sky, listening to the sheep-blether, the fly-buzz. When I sat up, I saw two other walkers with packs and poles, descending a ridge to the south. I raised a hand in greeting, and one of the poles went up in response. The shallow valley below was corduroyed with old potato ridges.

I headed for the gap between the Black Mountain and Carnavaddy. The expectation of the approach to a mountain pass; the sense of another, wilder country about to reveal itself: the Mournes in dark profile, dropping steeply to the sea at Kilkeel; the silvery slug of Carlingford Lough, creeping in towards the quays and car parks of Warrenpoint with the invisible water-border halfway between the northern and southern shores.

* * *

This was all storied country. The mountainous Cooley Peninsula, jutting out to the southeast for twenty kilometres between Carlingford Lough and Dundalk Bay, and the low country stretching back towards Ardee, is the main theatre of the *Táin Bó Cuailnge*, 'The Cattle Raid of Cooley', the central text of the Ulster Cycle and the major epic of Irish mythology.

The earliest written version of the *Táin* is incomplete, contained within the *Lebor na hUidre*, the 'Book of the Dun Cow', probably compiled at the turn of the twelfth century in the great monastery of Clonmacnoise where the Esker Riada intersects with the Shannon. The oldest surviving complete version was pulled together from multiple sources later that century in the 'Book of Leinster', and there are further fragments matching those of the Clonmacnoise version in the fourteenth-century 'Yellow Book of Lecan'. But none of these is the work of a single author, nor even a single era. There are verse sections within the main prose body of the epic, the language of which was archaic even in the twelfth century and which must have been drawn from much older manuscripts.

The anonymous compiler of the Book of Leinster version – who may have been the abbot of a monastery in Tipperary – added a note in Latin to the end of the Irish-language manuscript:

> I who have copied down this story, or more accurately fantasy, do not credit the details of the story, or fantasy. Some things in it are devilish lies, and some poetical figments; some seem possible and others not; some are for the enjoyment of idiots.[1]

But the *Táin* was generally treated as actual history by its medieval scribes, and they dated the action to the first century CE.

The *Táin* is spectacularly violent – and its violence retains a visceral impact in modern English-language translations of a sort that seldom survives the distancing exoticism of other epics. One of the specific fields of action – the area I'd passed through on the long straight road from Knockbridge to Dundalk – was known as *An Breisleach Mór*, 'The Great Carnage', which could easily be a subtitle for the *Táin* itself. Among the central players are two towering embodiments of bloody machismo: Cúchulainn, the Ulster hero and Übermensch of Irish mythology; and Donn Cuailnge, the supernaturally endowed 'Brown Bull of Cooley' himself. Somehow I can never disentangle the image of Donn Cuailnge from that of the unlicensed stud bull of Seamus Heaney's early poem, 'The Outlaw' – though it seems generally to be death, rather than life, that Donn Cuailnge slams home like a tank.

The story begins with a bout of postcoital bickering between Queen Medb and King Ailill of Connacht. As they lie abed in their fort at Rathcroghan in Roscommon, each insists that they possess greater independent wealth than the other, and they fall to itemising their possessions. To Medb's great annoyance, she discovers that she and her husband are perfectly matched in riches except for a single item: Ailill's great white bull, Finnbennach. So she sends messengers across country to the Cooley Peninsula to ask for a loan of the most famous bull in Ireland, Donn Cuailnge. At first, his keeper, Dáire, agrees. But the messengers are overheard saying that the bull would have been taken by force anyway if their request had been refused. The offended Dáire sends them home to Connacht without Donn Cuailnge – possibly a fortunate outcome, for imagine trying to lead that beast 170 kilometres across Ireland! In response, Medb and Ailill raise a huge army and head for Cooley to seize the bull. The initial defence of Ulster – of which Cooley and the plains immediately south of Dundalk were then a part – is conducted single-handed by Cúchulainn, who appears as a sort of first-century Terminator. Towards the end of the campaign, horribly wounded and unable to stand, he straps himself upright to a standing stone and continues to slaughter every Connacht soldier who approaches. The stone in question is reputedly the one I passed in the morning – Clochafarmore, *Cloch an Fhir Mhóir*, the 'Stone of the Great Man'. The bull itself also takes to the battlefield and generates much graphic blood-splatter.

Eventually, Medb and Ailill's decimated army limps back to Connacht. They appear defeated, but somehow they manage to take Donn Cuailnge with them. The narrative ends with its most gruesomely disturbing episode. Donn Cuailnge attacks Ailill's original bovine trump card, the white bull Finnbennach, and they embark on a terrible death-struggle, roaring and bellowing across the land. Donn Cuailnge triumphs, but is mortally wounded. He staggers home towards Cooley with the mangled white carcass of his rival hanging from his horns, scattering body parts and placenames behind him as he goes. Then he collapses and dies.

Medb and Ailill agree a truce with Cúchulainn. Nothing seems to have been achieved except the deaths of two bulls and thousands of people – though I suppose the minor wealth imbalance that started the whole business has been evened out.

If the medieval inscribers of the surviving *Táin* manuscripts – cynical compiler of the Book of Leinster excepted – took the story as actual history, later scholars of folklore and myth also believed that meaningful knowledge of pre-Christian Ireland could be parsed from the text. But modern historians are more likely to see written epics as reflections of the norms and preoccupations of the era in which they were compiled rather than of that in which they are notionally set. In the early stages of the *Táin* a detailed itinerary of the Connacht army's outward journey is laid out. This must have been a route that made sense to a monk, hunched over a sheet of vellum in a twelfth-century monastery. The itinerary has a poetry of its own, a sense of people and horses moving across a landscape:

> The Monday after Samain they set out. This is the way they went, southeast from Cruachan Ai:
> through Muicc Cruinb
> through Terloch Teóra Crích, the marshy lake bed where three territories meet,
> by Tuaim Móna, the peat ridge,
> through Cúil Silinne, where Carrcin Lake is now – it was named after Silenn, daughter of Madchar,
> by Fid and Bolga, woods and hills,
> through Coltain, and across the Sinann river,
> through Glúne Gabair,
> over Trego Plain, of the spears [...][2]

And on and on through dozens of named places and at last to 'the river Cronn in Cuailnge'. Only a handful of specific spots on the itinerary can be definitively identified today – Kells, Navan, Ardagh, a few rivers.[3] But it has a certain discernible pack-donkey's quality, bending this way and that so that Medb demands of their guide, 'What kind of road is this we're taking? / – straying to the south or north, / crossing every kind of land'.[4] The army has chariots, and so the route was probably one largely traced by *slige*, the largest category of road in medieval Ireland. But at one point the army encounters a symbolic 'no trespassing' sign placed by Cúchulainn, a spancel hoop (a twist of rope for hobbling horses) marked with a simple ogham text. They decide to bypass it by making their own road. The soldiers cut the forest ahead of the chariots and thus the place 'is now called Slechta, the Hewn Place'.[5]

This is not the only instance of path-making in the *Táin*. In the early stages of the campaign, when Medb and Ailill appear ascendent and have effectively occupied the Cooley Peninsula, Medb takes her forces up the valley of the Cronn, the river which rises under the Windy Gap between the Foxes Rock and Carnavaddy. The men are heading for the main pass where the road runs today. But Medb calls them back: 'She chose to cross the summit itself and mark their track forever as a mark of dishonour to Ulster. It took them three days and three nights, tearing up the earth before them, to form the gap Bernas Bó Cuailnge'.[6] Those studying the text long assumed that this 'Gap of the Cattle of Cooley' was the Windy Gap itself. But the narrative was plainly written into the naming of the landscape at an outlying peak six kilometres to the southeast: Barnavave, 'Medb's Gap'.[7] Looking back as I made my way up the slopes of the Black Mountain towards Clermont Cairn, I could just make out the natural U-shaped cleft at its summit.

* * *

A view from the heights: Clermont Cairn in louring afternoon light, a Neolithic burial mound at the summit of the Black Mountain, named for the viscounts Clermont whose local seat, Clermont Park, was burnt out in 1923.

There is a common trope in narratives of imperial exploration in which the explorer (usually British or French and always a man) reaches a high summit or pass (sometimes forgetting to mention the local guides and porters who have shepherded him through the ascent) and gazes out over the newly 'discovered' land below, taking rhetorical possession of it as he does so. The postcolonial scholar Mary Louise Pratt calls this the 'monarch-of-all-I-survey scene' – 'a brand of verbal painting whose highest calling was to produce for the home audience the peak moments at which geographical "discoveries" were "won"'. These imperial travellers needed the monarch-of-all-I-survey scene as a heroic device in their books, Pratt says, because 'the act of discovery itself consisted of what in European culture counts as a purely passive experience – that of seeing'.[8]

The monarchical mountaintop gaze certainly didn't vanish with the end of empire, and once you know of it, you can spot it everywhere, even in contemporary books of travel and nature and place. This can leave someone who writes about this sort of thing – writes about walking, writes about landscape – in a nervous bind. An elevated summit is always a climactic point in the journey, an emotional experience worth sharing. And it's a handy practical device too, a good way to give readers a proper sense of where you are – at the top of Mount Eagle, Moylussa, Clermont Cairn. It's a way to make a sort of textual map. But now the bind of postcolonial anxiety tightens, for we know all about maps: you map a landscape both to *show* that you know it and to *enable* you to know it. And once you *know* a landscape, you control it – or so the theory goes. Pratt reckons that three elements characterise the monarch-of-all-I-survey scene: aestheticisation, 'density of meaning' – and domination.[9]

But sometimes at a mountaintop we don't look *forward* to a new field of discovery, but *back*, reflectively, on the way we've come, glad to have escaped those claustrophobic flatlands, exhausted by the journey, but hopefully a little better informed than when we started out. And seeing isn't *always* a passive experience – certainly not when it's paired to bodily movement, not when the visual stimuli are braided with the rhythm of feet in motion: *dull ache at heel, sharp sting at toes, dull ache at heel, sharp sting at toes…*

And so here I am, standing at a Neolithic cairn named for an Anglo-Irish aristocrat, feeling decidedly self-conscious and looking back into Ireland. The muddy foreshore of Dundalk fades into a yellowish sea and the coast sweeps south towards Skerries and Dublin. To the southwest is all the country I've crossed in recent weeks. I can make out the low hills I passed on the way into Ardee, but everything else recedes into blue indeterminacy. I couldn't begin to chart my own route and I certainly don't want to *dominate* the land I look out across. I make no entitled demand to *roam* triumphantly across it at will; just a tentative wish that one day we might recover the small capillaries of off-road movement trodden into place by pilgrims and well-worshippers and chapel-goers and schoolchildren, by courting couples, by the landless, the dispossessed and the hungry, and by all manner of other people.

It's easy enough to see what happened down there. Colonialism always does lasting damage, always produces myriad partitions. Someone exercises power to dispossess someone else (even if they never actually stop them moving across the land, because access and ownership aren't necessarily aggregated at the time). The dispossession is reinforced and codified with discourses of ethnic difference; and in the process colonialism inadvertently produces its own nemesis: a potent, morally cleansing narrative of dispossession rising from below. And so, in time, the heirs to the dispossessors (and perhaps others besides) are themselves dispossessed. The land is reapportioned through a bureaucratic process in which some get lucky, and some lose out. In itself, that process may have little to do with the abstract ideals of nationhood or revolutionary sacrifice; it may, indeed, have a certain grubbiness in its individual small victories and defeats. But for narrative purposes it is subsumed within the apparent climax of liberation, and the credits roll (certain loose ends notwithstanding). Meanwhile, in another aspect of lasting colonial damage, the whole place is less urban, less industrialised than its neighbours, poorer than it should be. And so no great impetus to guarantee public access to the land arises in the middle decades of the twentieth century – certainly not as a matter of social justice and certainly without any authentic working-class component. The well paths and mass paths and school paths are still in use, just about. But the only people obviously accessing the countryside for leisure are ghostly revenants from decaying big houses, still exercising their hunting rights across fields for which their grandparents claimed rent. And by the time conditions are finally ripe for an impetus for better access to emerge, by the time people are buying trekking poles and signing up for hillwalking groups on Facebook, there's an almighty barricade of broken pallets in place, declaring the narrative closed.

* * *

Below the cairn a track descended past a stubby telecommunications tower to a narrow lane with thistles on either side and another rough track striking northwards. A dumped fridge lay on its back in the purple moor grass. A big white cargo ship was in view below, moored at Warrenpoint. The afternoon was suddenly very still.

I'd spent longer peering at this particular portion of the map than at any other, wondering what exactly I'd find here, whether it would be passable, whether I'd find anything at all. The track bent around the hillside, and suddenly there it was up ahead. The black line on the map existed on the ground as a waist-high fence. Posts and sheep wire running down from the left along the line of an old drystone wall then climbing across boggy ground towards another low summit: the border; the great contention, the first of the crude partition lines left by an atrophying empire, and now, absurdly, the outer limit of the European Union. It was a simple sheep fence on an empty moor.

The track petered out in a reedy sump fifty metres short of the fence-line. But it was easy going through the tussocks. And right there, at the very point towards which I'd instinctively moved, there was a simple stile, a weathered plank set through the fence to allow for easy passage between the Republic of Ireland and the United Kingdom. Its presence made crossing the border less daunting than it would have been to hop any of the gates with 'no trespassing' signs between here and the Dingle Peninsula.

I stood on the stile for a moment, one foot in each jurisdiction. Then I headed onwards across squelchy heath and hit a good path which brought me down past lines of conifers towards the busy bowl of farmland between the Cooleys and Slieve Gullion. Ruined farmhouses at the moor-edge, slotted neatly side-on to the slope, rooftiles flaking like fish scales; two horses in a reedy field, one piebald, one appaloosa; a friendly collie tied to a fencepost while a farmer pottered at something in the field below. I came lower and there were fuchsias, a few montbretias and a sudden unexpected familiarity, a homeliness, even. It took a minute to make sense of it: the field boundaries here were made of granite, just like those in West Cornwall. Watery sunlight came through the uneven wash of cloud above, and with it a certain late heat. I reached a narrow, tarmacked lane, then turned east onto a track. The map showed the track running all the way to another road; but after a kilometre it faded into fields. Bullocks grazed in a patch of dandelions nearby and when they lowed, the sound bounced back off the hillside on the other side of the border.

Earlier in the journey, I'd have halted nervously here, fumbled indecisively with the map, and then retreated to find a longer way around on the road. But now I passed blithely into the fields, surprised at my own readiness to walk onto land where there was no known right of way. What had happened here? Was it just that the good walking earlier in the day had put me in confident mood? Did the familiarity of the granite, the fuchsias, produce a comfortable certainty? Or had something unexpected arisen now that I was over the border? It was a puzzle, and a faintly disturbing one. But in any case, it carried me downhill past the bullocks, around a ruined farmstead, over a wall and through a patch of brambles to the road, and then on to a zigzag trail through a bank of forestry and down to the water's edge, where I was suddenly very tired and aware of how late in the day it was. I'd half-expected to camp somewhere back on the heights, but now I turned on my phone and booked the cheapest room I could find in Newry. Then I got onto the greenway that followed the line of the old Newry Ship Canal towpath.

After an hour's walk, the greenway ran into an angular jigsaw of old docks where a group of Travellers had made an encampment behind a rusty fence. Caravans parked up at odd angles; small wooden kennels ranged around on the cracked tarmac with a fluffy white dog of the same breed tethered to each; white vans and men hosing down after a hot day's work. Something about the structure of the camp made me think they hadn't been here long.

Three boys came across from the nearest caravan to throw a big stone into the canal, just for the fun of it, I think. There was an older lad, maybe thirteen, blondish, in a hoody and skinny jeans, and two younger boys of nine or ten. One had black hair, dark eyes, fluorescent green shorts and a bright blue tee-shirt. The other had ginger hair, freckles and a mouthful of terrible teeth. He was dressed for a barn dance in a smart checked shirt and Levi's. They met me with a welcome welter of wisecrackery.

'Are you hiking?' asked the black-haired lad.

'Ah!' The ginger boy jabbed him in the ribs before I had a chance to answer. 'He's not hiking! You need mountains for hiking. He's walking! You're walking, aren't you?'

'I am.'

'Where you walking from? How long you been walking? Go-way! How many hours you been walking? Go-way!'

'Have you ever walked in England?' asked the older boy.

'I have.'

The ginger lad – the boldest of the three – nodded authoritatively. 'England's long,' he said. 'They've miles there and miles are longer than kilometres so it takes longer to get places.'

I asked where they were from and they all looked at me like I was stupid and pointed to the caravans.

'Sure, I know ye're from there,' I said, 'but where's the homeplace?' The caravans all had southern plates and there wasn't a hint of the North in their accents. Two of them said Dublin, and the black-haired boy said Offaly – Tullamore. I told them I'd walked here from Tullamore.

'Go-way! How long'd it take you?'

I counted backwards on my fingers. 'Seven days.'

'Go-way!'

I said I'd started out still further off, in Kerry, that I lived in Galway, worked in Sligo. The older boy said he'd been in Kerry, the Ring of Kerry; the black-haired boy said he'd been in Sligo working with his dad. They'd just come up to Newry yesterday.

'Where you going now?' asked the ginger lad. I motioned towards the town. 'No, I mean where you going *next*?'

'Is there any country you haven't walked in?' said the dark-haired boy.

'Are you not cold?' said the older lad, with what sounded like real concern for my wellbeing.

'He's a jacket in his bag – you've a jacket in your bag, haven't you?' the ginger boy asked with a decided confidence in my answer. 'He does, see! How long more are you walking? You look strong; the walking makes you strong – do this!' He mimed a bodybuilder's bicep pose.

It was the first proper conversation I'd had during a day's walk since meeting the man with the headphones near Raharney: the road walking hadn't been conducive to human encounters. I'd have happily stayed bantering with them all evening. But my feet had started to throb the moment I stopped moving. So I said goodbye and hobbled onwards into Newry, primed for redbrick terraces and a sense of difference, primed for the visceral shock at the sight of a different flag – and primed too, as on every visit to the North, for a sudden uncertainty about my own point of departure.

* * *

The last time I'd crossed the border I'd been asked to chair a daytime literary discussion at an arts centre. It was a long way to go, and the organisers had booked me a room in a B&B for the preceding night. I drove up from Galway on the backroads, through Cavan and Monaghan. It was winter. Dusk was falling by the time my phone started hysterically proclaiming changes of service provider, welcoming me to the UK, and then telling me I was back in the

Republic of Ireland; and it was long after dark when I reached my destination. The B&B owner came to the door as I was pulling into the parking space at the back of the house.

'How're you getting on? Tim, is it? How was the drive?'

'Grand,' I said, as I stepped into the warmth of the hall. 'Not too bad at all, really.' I held out my hand to shake and saw a sudden inexplicable quizzicality in his face.

He showed me to the room, and there was something there, all the way up the stairs – nothing at all unfriendly, just a faint puzzlement, as if he was trying to work something out.

'Ah, this is perfect, thanks.' I put my bag down on the bed, and he lingered in the doorway, still quizzical.

'That's the switch for the shower,' he said. Then he made a small quip, tentatively, at a venture. He pointed to a press in the corner (and I'm calling it a 'press' instead of a 'cupboard' because that's the easiest bit of the code-shift) and said, 'And there's the confessional, if you're needing it.' And I grinned and said, 'Ah, I'm probably overdue for it at this stage!' and suddenly he was no longer quizzical at all, and he left me to unpack with an easy smile. I still had no idea what was going on.

When I went downstairs twenty minutes later, thinking to head out for food, he caught me at the door, very friendly.

'Going for dinner, is it?'

'Probably just a bag of chips, or something,' I said, and he nodded. Then a trace of the quizzicality returned.

'Would you drink a Guinness?'

I hesitated. 'I would…'

'Grand,' he said, apparently reassured. 'Now, there's really only two places in town for a Guinness' – and he gave me directions.

I knew that things were complicated up here, but this was all getting too much. I called Cara as soon as I was out on the pavement.

'How was the drive?'

'Grand. Is Guinness a sectarian drink in the North?'

'I don't know…' And now someone else was taking a quizzical tone with me! 'What's happened? Why do you need to know?'

'I'll tell you later.'

I couldn't find a chipper, so I got a pizza instead and ate it at a metal table in the corner of the takeaway. The women behind the counter were from Greece, I think. And then I went to one of the pubs he'd mentioned. I didn't really want a pint, but I had to find out. It was a warm place, busy enough on a Saturday night. A gang of young women in sparkly dresses were roaring at the far end of the bar. One had a 'bride to be' sash across her shoulder. An older couple sat at a table by the stairs, picking at a bowl of chicken wings. I got my Guinness, found a quiet place to sit, and looked around. How were you supposed to tell? I couldn't exactly *ask*, could I? Maybe the whole thing was going to remain a mystery. But then I saw the TV, a big flatscreen, mounted up on the wall. It was tuned to TG4 and it was showing an intercounty hurling match.

Now I understood what had been going on. If I'd turned up at the B&B in different circumstances, had asked on the doorstep with *my* voice if they had a room available, I'm certain that I would have been exempted entirely from any quizzicality. But they'd taken a booking for a man named Hannigan from Co. Galway who'd pulled into the parking space in a small white car with southern plates.

They need to know what you are, the barmaid at the pub in Shannon Harbour had said, and *if you're from the Republic they just assume*. The B&B owner had assumed. But then I'd opened my mouth, and suddenly he wasn't quite so sure – until, apparently, I laughed at his quip about the confessional in just the right way. And so he'd sent me to the sort of pub where you might find the TV showing a GAA match on an Irish-language channel, and not to the *other* sort of pub.

I was still thinking about the whole thing during the event the next day, thought about it on the four-hour drive southwards that evening. The B&B owner had been wrong in one sense. Raised in Cornwall by a terminally lapsed Catholic father and a mother supremely indifferent to the half-hearted Methodism of her childhood, I am nothing at all. My resting place would be out in the fields, in the discreetly accepting clay of the *cillín*. But what sat with me gladly at the start of the long drive back to Galway, and then more and more queasily the further I went, was this: I was *grateful* that he'd categorised me as he did – and then disturbed to find out that I felt that way. Maybe I'd inherited more than a name and a pair of blue eyes after all; perhaps, like an Irish hare turned magically white one uncommonly cold winter, certain unused genetic machinery endured.

* * *

Four kilometres out of Newry in a cool grey morning, the traffic streaking along the main Warrenpoint road. I could see the route I'd walked along the old canal the previous evening, 500 metres away on the other side of the river, and the hillsides beyond climbing steeply towards the mountains, the border.

There'd been a pavement the whole way out of town, past chapels, petrol stations, builders' merchants. But there was a deep weariness on me that hadn't shifted with the night in a bed in a cramped terraced house with a smell of damp and sadness, a microwaved chicken korma for dinner, a chance to write up my notes in comfort and a strong morning coffee in a café by a bridge. I was almost out of time, and I knew I wouldn't make it all the way to Burr Point on this run. Cara and Róise were back from their Spanish holiday now and had gone straight on to Cornwall for the rest of the summer ahead of me. I needed to be there with them by the end of the week. Tomorrow would be the last day's walking for now. I'd be able to come back later for the final stretch; but I was eager to achieve some kind of completion. The Mourne Mountains lay ahead, a rough ring of granite rising well above 700 metres at their highest tops and set hard against the coast in the southeast of Co. Down. I wanted to get across them by day's end tomorrow, to reach the sea at Newcastle. But right now the thought of any kind of ascent was a dispiriting prospect. I had a weird sensation of being behind my own body, trying to push it forward with its laden pack but finding a constant resistance.

Beyond a pale house with a monkey puzzle tree in the garden,

I got off the road into a narrow wood; a few mature pines, some big broadleaves. The leaflitter underfoot improved matters and the trails were well trodden. There were a few morning dog walkers out and about. At the far end of the wood, a track ran out into fields. There was no forbidding sign on the gate, and I found that yesterday's unexpected confidence was still with me despite the weariness. So I climbed over, followed the line of an electric fence, skirted the garden of an elaborately gothic big house, and came back to the main road by a sixteenth-century towerhouse guarding the narrowest point of the river.

* * *

I'd expected no change at the border – at least not for a traveller crossing the land on foot. Though Northern Ireland is still a part of the UK, its arrangements for public access to the countryside are very different to those in Britain. It was covered by neither the 1949 National Parks and Access to the Countryside Act, which properly began the process of recording and legally protecting the footpaths of Wales and England, nor the 2000 Countryside and Rights of Way Act, which gave the public a statutory right of access to almost all open country there. And it had never followed Scotland's lead to make use of devolved powers and open up the countryside still further. There is an 'Access to the Countryside (Northern Ireland) Order', created in 1983 in general emulation of the 1949 Welsh and English Act. But Northern Ireland's local authorities have made little use of the powers it gave them. By the second decade of this century, there were just 245 kilometres of designated public rights of way in the whole of Northern Ireland – and just *five* hectares of designated open access land (about seven football pitches).[10] In Wales and England, meanwhile, there were some 230,000 kilometres of public footpaths and around 1.4 million hectares of 'mountain, moor, heath or down', plus all registered common land and coastal margin, on which there is an effective 'right to roam'.[11]

It makes sense that limited countryside access would be an

all-Ireland phenomenon. The Ulster Plantation might have made the northeasternmost 'Six Counties' a demographic place apart from the seventeenth century; but until partition and the creation of the Free State south of the border, the whole island was a single jurisdiction. And it all went through the same processes of land reform in the late nineteenth and early twentieth centuries – the Encumbered Estates Act, the run of post-1880 Land Acts, the original Land Commission. Just because the Six Counties had a Protestant majority didn't mean that its gentry got to stay secure behind their demesne walls. Here too, most of the big estates were broken up and transferred to former tenants – a process which only wound up in the mid-1930s. And the pathologies of a contemporary paucity of access are surely much the same on both sides of the border.

When the academics Linda Price and Mark Simpson investigated 'the trouble with accessing the countryside in Northern Ireland', they concluded that 'Attitudes to the primacy of landowners to control their land, a weak tradition of countryside recreation and ongoing impacts of conflict shape the debate and become embedded in policy approaches'. They interviewed various stakeholders – farmers, tourism and government officials, representatives of outdoor sports groups. The attitudes they recorded were the familiar ones: the fear of lads getting sued if people went onto their land; the misconception that Irish farms are uniquely small and thus likely to be impacted by walkers crossing the land in ways inconceivable amid the mythically enormous holdings of England (there are certainly some very large agricultural properties in parts of England; but a short walk along a field path somewhere like Cornwall will often take you across multiple small family farms). One local government officer Price and Simpson interviewed told them that 'land ownership was hard won' here, and so 'people are very protective of their rights and privacy'. And a tourism official they spoke to said something *very* familiar: that perhaps in Britain 'there's more confidence and they feel they can be a bit more relaxed about letting other people come onto their land'.[12]

So not a place apart at all then – or so I'd assumed. But since stepping across the sheep fence on the high moor the previous day, I'd begun to pick up on a subtle difference. At the top of the zigzag path through the woods that led me down to the water's edge the previous evening, there'd been a *signpost* telling me that the Victoria Locks at the end of the Newry Ship Canal were 1,700 metres away. This wasn't a long-distance waymarked trail; it was just a short path through the woods. The sign had a look of officialdom about it – plastic-coated aluminium fixed to a metal pole. I'd never seen such a thing on such a path south of the border. And the following evening, after the walk was over for the time being, lolling in a window seat on a bus heading back towards Newry, I would spot another signpost, pointing out into fields and marked with a yellow walker icon and the magical formula: 'public footpath'. And though I didn't notice any such sign in the little roadside wood on the way out of Newry, I didn't notice any signs of the other sort either. In fact, across the whole 120-odd kilometres I'd eventually walk in Northern Ireland, I passed only two 'no entry' signs: one a sensible warning to stay out of a disused quarry, and the other a polite request to both walkers and graziers to leave a hillside fenced off for reafforestation undisturbed. Maybe you wouldn't notice the change if you hadn't walked three weeks and 550 kilometres to get here; but the Northern countryside felt ever so slightly less hostile to a walker.

* * *

It was as if I'd received a sudden shot of a powerful stimulant, right at the point where the path angled steeply uphill.

The whole day until now had been a struggle. The weather was perfect for walking: overcast, with a cooling breeze. But I just couldn't shake the sluggishness. I'd stopped at a busy café near the harbour in Warrenpoint for a late breakfast fry and a slice of apple pie. It helped a little; but just five kilometres further on at Rostrevor – pretty houses, a Presbyterian church with missile-shaped windows, a faintly alpine feel with the pine-swaddled slopes of the Mournes rising steeply behind – I could feel myself slowing again. Another coffee; another slice of cake; then wearily on to the Mourne Way. A solid track this, running between full-grown pines, gradually climbing the narrow valley between the lower western hills and the main massif. Mercifully, it wasn't tarmacked. I walked for an hour, then lay for a while beside a stack of logs, lacking the energy even to brush away the gathering midges. Mountain bikers came past, dog walkers, a family pushing a toddler in a buggy.

When I finally hauled myself to my feet I regretted the stop. All my leg muscles had tightened and the straps of my pack dug sharply into my shoulders. But a couple of kilometres further on the trees fell back and suddenly I was on a beetling path fringed with bracken and awkwardly studded with granite boulders. My limbs felt instantly looser. Each step required attention now, its own unique calibration. There were stark Scots pines on the slope to the right; but the crunch of quartz fragments beneath my feet was familiar. I could have been on the Cornish coast path.

The path turned sharply east and steeply upwards, between Rocky Mountain and Tornamrock, and it was as if my body had belatedly located the store of calories provided by the rashers and the apple pie earlier in the day. A run of wild country opened from the top of the pass under a clearing sky. The big peaks at the core of the range showed beyond the nearer ridges, with broken cloud shadow moving fast over fawn hillsides. A fingerpost marked the line of the descending path with a yellow arrow and signs for the Mourne Way, the Ulster Way and the St Patrick's Way. I filled my water bottle at a spring under a boulder, then slipped on my arse on the muddy patch below and briefly regretted having ditched my proper hiking boots back in Portumna. But damp feet and a few slips and slides were a small price to pay, and I surged on down towards the valley bottom. I saw two young women heading downhill on another trail across a stream. I waited until they were well past, then hopped across and followed the same trail in the opposite direction. With the unexpected burst of new energy, I'd abandoned any planned route, was happy to test side valleys, try for passable lines at a venture. The trail became a much-braided path running towards a cleft between Slievemoughanmore and Pigeon Rock Mountain. There were recent footprints here and there – not the alarming sight they might have been near a camping spot in a Midlands bog, but a warming reassurance. And the big wooden cross-stile overleaping the two-metre drystone wall at the top of the rise brought further confidence.

The wall struck boldly up the slope to the left, and I followed it, giddy with the sudden sense of lightness, giggling to myself, cheerily saluting the bemused sheep, powering upwards with all the earlier exhaustion forgotten. I'd never experienced a second wind like it. It was produced, I think, by a sudden release from the slowly mounting oppression of the previous weeks, hemmed in and then eventually confined entirely to the roads.

There is no statutory *right* of access in the Mournes. But much of the land here is owned by the National Trust and the Northern Ireland water board, which both have open access policies. The rest is largely held by trusts, created after the breakup of the big estates in the early twentieth century to manage common grazing rights in the mountains.[13] This, surely, mitigates the risk of an individual private owner unilaterally deciding to forbid entry. The access here is still, ultimately, permissive, granted entirely at the whim of the organisations which hold the deeds. But the Mournes felt different from any block of Coillte-owned forestry I'd visited. The stiles, the signposts, the footprints, the glimpses of others like me, out and about, and above all the *paths*: this was permissive access of a higher order; walkers felt positively encouraged here.

I could have easily stayed walking on into the dusk, pushed on across the next ridge. But the crown of Pigeon Rock Mountain, 534 metres above sea level, was a perfect camping spot. Two drystone walls met at the summit in a neat right angle – crossed, conveniently, by a stile. Their intersection provided shelter from the wind and a soft, grassy patch on which to pitch a tent. I sat in the lee of the wall to cook my dinner. Once the pasta was simmering I stood to stretch my legs, and saw, without shock or alarm, a young man with a moustache, earphones and backpack, standing a few metres away, peering at his phone. He'd walked up on a different route and was struggling to navigate with a mapping app. I think he'd planned to camp at the summit too, and I said he was welcome to join me. But he said he'd stay going for a while and leave me to it. Later in the night it made me happy to think that there was someone else, sleeping alone in a small tent, somewhere on this same mountain.

By nine o'clock the day was beginning to fray away. I climbed up onto the top of the stile for a final view out across the land. A kilometre to the north and 200 metres closer to sea level, the reservoir of the Spelga Dam was a steel-grey blank amid the tawny contours. A few blotches of dark forestry stood at its head where the road ran across the moor, occasional headlights angled south towards Kilkeel. Further north: low country beyond Newcastle, the pale stripe of Strangford Lough. Then turning west, the sweep of the northern countryside, late sun on Lough Neagh with other hills beyond and a band of molten copper light marking the westernmost horizon. Turning to the south, I could see the hulking mass of Slieve Gullion and the dark bank of the Cooleys, the red warning lights blinking on the mast below Clermont Cairn – was it really only yesterday that I was up there? Closer at hand, the Mournes themselves were swelling into the dusk, and the huge cliffs under Eagle Mountain were black. Behind them, the low coast swept towards Dublin. I could make out Lambay Island and the Great Sugar Loaf in the Wicklow Mountains, well over a hundred kilometres away. Turning eastwards, the porcine ridgeback of Slieve Muck rose immediately across the valley, then Slieve Bearnagh, monstrously tall and crowned with bare granite, attended left and right by Slieve Meelbeg and Slieve Commedagh (I needed the map for all these names). And then back around to the headlights on the road across the moor and the reservoir, ever paler in the darkling landscape.

I stood there on the stile, turning slowly and turning again; not exactly a monarch-of-all-I-surveyed, but royally heartened by the knowledge that in the morning I could break camp and walk away from this place in any direction I chose.

* * *

The wind fell away to nothing in the night. I woke once and scrambled out of the tent to piss. A faint reddish smear showed far off to the south over Dublin, and another, nearer and in the north, over Belfast. To the northeast, the low country was a bright starscape of villages, small towns, lone homeplaces. Up above, the real firmament was dulled by haze. But the Plough hung high and clear to the north. I went back to sleep, and when I woke again the sun was already up over Slieve Bearnagh.

The midges were gathering in livid clouds, so I breakfasted quickly, packed and headed downhill towards the road, already busy with Newcastle-bound traffic, then struck straight up the flank of Slieve Muck. From across the valley this had looked like a daunting ascent; but now I found myself climbing smoothly, strongly. All day I'd power along without fatigue – the combined walking fitness built up over the weeks and the psychological release of the open country propelling me towards the provisional end of the journey. The obscure familiarity of the ground helped too. These mountains, like the moors and cliffs of West Cornwall, are formed of an ancient granite intrusion, an upwelling of igneous matter pushed through the crust of the earth into the now vanished layers of old sediment. The paths here had the same fine gravel underfoot and demanded the same boulder-hopping. They had the same braiding on the heavily trafficked sections, the same occasional patches of black wetness, the same rain-scoured gullies on the steeper slopes. I *knew* how to move across this terrain, how to sidestep, how to put in one long stride and one short, understood the no-one-step-the-same gait that fires a walker's synapses and is so very different from the metrical slog of the tarmacked road. And there were paths *everywhere* – following the drystone walls, scratched along the mountain flanks, palely striping the far ridges, far more of them than the map recorded.

At the top of Slieve Muck I came to the grandest drystone wall of all – the Mourne Wall itself, built between 1904 and 1922 to enclose the catchment of the planned Silent Valley Reservoir which would eventually supply most of Belfast with drinking water. The idea of the wall was to stop sheep and cattle from fouling the supply. Following it north towards Slieve Bearnagh, I started to meet other walkers: two men with a collie dog; a trio with double trekking poles and hydration packs, heading up towards Meelbeg; a young couple a hundred metres ahead of me on the same path, who eventually branched off, down into the belly of the range. There were others too – small figures descending ridges; a father and son, each with identical floppy blond hair; a group of Germans admiring the grey stacks at Diamond Rocks; and at the narrow pass between Meelbeg and Slieve Bearnagh a dozen shirtless young men with northern English accents and a distinctly military air despite their skimpy civilian gear. All of this cheered me too: it was good to feel that that I was sharing this landscape with others.

I skirted Slieve Bearnagh to the north, and in the steep and stony valley the wind fell away and the heat radiated from the stone (another flash of a distant youthful journey here – of goat-calls and junipers and woodsmoke). At Hare's Gap, five teenage girls sat in the shade of the spanning wall, each silently thumbing a mobile phone – on a digital break from their Duke of Edinburgh Award hike, perhaps. I picked up the Mourne Wall again at the pass east of Slieve Donard, the highest point of the Mournes at 849 metres, and suddenly there were dozens of people – some side-stepping down out of the cloud on the summit, others labouring up the trail from Newcastle. One deeply tanned young man came *running* up at a ferocious pace.

There'd be no monarch-of-all-I-survey scene up there in the cloud today, so I went on downwards into the valley, pausing to cook my final lunch of noodles by a clear stream on the way. The military lads I'd met earlier overtook me here with a stiff greeting, sweat-slicked and galloping towards the end of their circuit. There were dozens of other people too, couples, family groups, protesting children, teenagers swaying in heavy black, young men with white running shoes and reflective sunglasses, and all manner of voices, accents, languages. Again, I was glad to be among them, to find this supremely well-beaten path to bring me down from the climactic high point of the journey, down a glacier-carved valley, past a wind-damaged conifer plantation with a sweet smell of freshly broken timber, into shady woods, then out across a playing field and on to the beach at Newcastle.

Guesthouses, pubs and cafés strung along the seafront with the mountains rearing darkly behind, the cloud streaming off the Slieve Donard summit. A mechanical clatter from the amusement arcades; children pattering over wet sand and a warm breeze off the greenish water. I took my shoes off, tied the laces together and slung them around my neck. Then I walked out into the low-tide shallows. The rippled sand was hard, and below the sharp tan-line at my ankles my bare feet were unfamiliar, like bony white fish, encountered here for the very first time.

10

The Bull and the Field

Robert Dowds, the chair of Keep Ireland Open, has a story to tell me.

A former schoolteacher and county councillor, he was elected as a Labour TD for the Dublin Mid-West constituency in 2011 and served a single term during Labour's junior coalition partnership with Fine Gael. In 2013 he brought forward a private member's bill on 'Access to the Countryside', building on an earlier draft bill by Ruairi Quinn.

Reading the text today, it seems eminently sensible – and modest in its ambition. It was intended to 'provide for the public an orderly method of legal access to recreational lands that are held in various forms of private ownership'; to ensure that landowners were 'fully indemnified from any legal action that a member of the public may take against them arising from an accident occurring on the land'; and to 'provide for legal clarity between the rights of landowners and the general public in the use of land for recreational purposes'.[1] The bill's main focus was what it called 'access land' – the sort of open country on which there is a 'right to roam' in Wales and England under the terms of the Countryside and Rights of Way Act 2000. Dowds' bill made access land 'any open and uncultivated land, including moors, heaths and downs', anything over 200 metres above sea level and a narrow strip along the coast and the shores of lakes and rivers – as well as all disused railways still owned by Córas Iompair Éireann.[2] But crucially, there was no automatic designation. It would have been up to individual county councils to identify and declare areas of access land, with laborious procedures and much scope for objection. Cultivated farmland and the immediate curtilage of any dwelling place was explicitly excluded. The bill also provided scope for county councils to make byelaws to create strictly regulated access routes to the open country.

The story he wants to tell me is about the lobbying he endured when the bill was live.

'I was lobbied by the IFA, the Irish Farmers' Association, and all the other farming organisations, and I knew that would be difficult. It was just face to face, like I'm talking to you. And the arrogance of this one fellow! He came in and his opening remark to me was, "My wife and I have just come back from a lovely walking holiday in Austria!" And I said, "That's great; wouldn't it be nice if you could do the same in Ireland?" But he then said, "We will do everything we can to prevent your bill from being passed!"'

The bill failed, of course, and there has been no subsequent attempt at access legislation.

* * *

I've come up to Dublin on the train to meet Robert Dowds because I want to get a sense of what, if anything, could be done to give the public more access to the countryside in Ireland.

A gusty wind outside Heuston Station with brittle clouds scudding low from the west; gulls littering the air over the Liffey like scattered pages, the metallic shriek of the Luas and the liquid movement of hundreds of pedestrians. We meet in a noisy hotel bar. He's a merry man in his early seventies with a smile that slews across his face at the slightest thing. He has the kind of South Dublin voice that can sound faintly sardonic to an outsider, urbane and urban. But as usual in Ireland, the generational distance from the working countryside is short.

'My grandfather's family, they were tenant farmers between Moynalty and Bailieborough – I don't know if you know where Moynalty is?'

I do, as it happens: it's a few kilometres north of Kells and not too far from the last bog I slept in.

'It's Meath but it's more like Cavan,' he says; 'the land is like Cavan, drumlin country. I don't know how my grandfather managed to buy the farm, but he bought it in the late nineteenth century, I think. But, I mean, he, like so many others, started off as a tenant farmer.

'I told that farming organisation lobbyist that my auntie was secretary of her local branch of the IFA, which she *was*, and that got me about *that* far!' He pinches an inch of the stuffy hotel bar air between forefinger and thumb and a grin slides across his face.

But Robert is the one doing the lobbying now. It's a decade since he left the Dáil, but he still makes use of his political contacts in the interests of the Keep Ireland Open campaign. He gives me an overview of where things stand, the emails sent, the promises of meetings, the ears bent at the edges of book launches, commemorative events for late politicians. It all sounds decidedly thankless, but he has a certain doggedness, as if the alternative – doing nothing – would be unconscionable. He counts off the TDs he knows to be well disposed – almost all from the smaller progressive parties – and those he knows to be hostile, invariably from rural constituencies. He also mentions those he thinks might be swayed on the basis of specific access conflicts in their own constituencies. He struggles to think of anyone from the bigger parties who might support another attempt at access legislation – no one in Fianna Fáil, and perhaps one Fine Gael TD, Emer Currie, who has a particular local interest in improving access to the Strawberry Beds area on the banks of the Liffey in her own Dublin West constituency.

'But what I would really like', he says, 'is to get a Sinn Féin commitment. But the problem is that because it's such a centrally organised party, from what I can see at the moment, they are either likely to give full support or no support – and my feeling is it'll be the latter, unfortunately.'

'Why do you think that is?' I ask. 'Would they consider it a vote loser, or just something not worth bothering with?'

'It's not sufficiently high in people's agendas. It's as simple as that.' Ultimately, he reckons that the best prospect would be a commitment from a smaller party – Labour or the Social Democrats or the Greens – that might end up in a future coalition government.

'If Labour were in government with Sinn Féin, or with Fianna Fáil again, they would probably agree to something if we insisted on it.' But then he pauses and smiles ruefully. 'But you see, the hassle is that the farming organisations would react very badly. And a lot of other organisations are very compliant.' Even outdoor sports organisations and Failte Ireland, the national tourism development authority, have been wary of Keep Ireland Open's campaign, he says.

'It really annoys me that Failte Ireland is so unwilling to push this issue. I mean, they *have* to know that there's great tourist potential, even if only from an economic point of view.'

'There's always people walking up mountains in Failte Ireland adverts,' I say.

'I know! So, you know, I would expect them to be a bit more proactive.'

We ordered a pot of tea when we arrived, but the bar is busy and the staff seem to have forgotten us. Robert goes to remind them, and when he comes back, I ask about something I've picked up from other conversations: a sense that the situation has *worsened*, that access to the Irish countryside has become harder in the last few decades.

'Well, you see,' he says, 'if you talk to old people in the countryside, it was different in the past. On my grandparents' farm on the Cavan border, there was a path across the farm there. Any people coming on to the farm, they walked that path; they didn't go anywhere else.

'And when I was a teenager, I spent two summers in the Gaeltacht near Cape Clear Island and there were loads of tracks all over the place. I went back there maybe twenty years ago with my wife and most of those tracks were closed; you just had to walk on the road.'

I say that even in my own time in Ireland I've noticed more and more 'no entry' signs in places like the Burren.

'Well, that's something that has really ballooned in the last few years. One of our committee members says that if you go into any rural hardware shop you'll see these stacks of 'no entry' signs that you can just buy. I mean, it's just *such* an unfriendly sight for visitors, whether they're from other parts of Ireland or from abroad. For foreigners it must be really shocking.'

'Maybe that was where it all began – someone started a sign-writing business!' I say.

'Maybe! But really, I suppose it's a mixture of things. Farmers are probably more isolated now than they used to be. There used to be more local people around farms. But there's also this thing, you know, of "This is my land, and, boy, am I going to hang on to it!" It goes back into the nineteenth century. You've probably seen John B. Keane's play *The Field*? I mean, a lot of that is true!'

Robert is by no means the first person to mention *The Field* to me in conversations about land in Ireland. As a play, it was first performed in 1965; but most people know the story from the 1990 film with Richard Harris as the main character, Thady 'The Bull' McCabe, with his ferocious determination to own a single rented field on which he has long laboured. A colleague once told me that her English husband simply couldn't understand the premise of the film. But it made sense to me. The Bull was almost – *almost* – recognisable in some of the farming and fishing people I grew up around in Cornwall. And the message seemed clear: The Bull's sense of passionate entitlement to his field is perfectly legitimate; but the lengths to which that entitlement drives him go beyond all reason.

The last person before Robert Dowds to mention *The Field* to me was a woman who had done postgraduate research on farm succession. She'd grown up on a farm herself, knew the tensions, the complexities.

'Whenever I hear on the news about a murder in rural Ireland, I think, *that'll be about land*,' she said. I laughed, but she looked at me hard: 'I'm not joking.'

* * *

Twenty years ago, Tim Robinson – celebrated chronicler of the landscapes of Aran and Connemara, and, as it happens, an English transplant in the west of Ireland – noted that until recently 'there was in general no difficulty about crossing farmland'. The problem, he felt, had come with the 'enormous increase' in the numbers of ramblers out and about in the countryside. It's a curious line – one you see repeated from time to time on Irish Facebook pages dedicated to hillwalking: if only *we*, the small, time-served elite, could have this landscape to ourselves again, all would be well. But in mid-twentieth-century Wales and England, it was the *enormous increase* in the numbers of ramblers – many of them working-class city folk – that provided the impetus for legislation to enshrine the rights of countryside access. In any case, what was needed in Ireland now, Robinson wrote, was 'dialogue, mutual understanding, sensible legislation, etc. – rare panaceas – and, much deeper, a shared sense of the Earth's surface as a palimpsest, the compiled and over-written testaments of all previous generations, which it is our right and duty to read'.[3] More recently, another late, beloved chronicler of Irish landscapes, Manchán Magan, spoke and wrote passionately about the need to reconnect with the earth, to 'listen to the land speak'. But there seems little imminent prospect of rare panaceas.

In the months after my cross-Ireland journey ended, I noticed ever more stories about access conflicts in the newspapers. These stories were invariably about greenway developments – proposed greenways in South Kerry, Galway, Sligo, the Cooley Peninsula, all mired in controversy. With each new proposal, the hostile response from local landowners came swifter and louder. Anti-greenway 'action groups' popped up on Facebook. There was a protest outside Leinster House.[4] Some of the rhetoric was decidedly hyperbolic: hoary old stories about criminals using greenways as corridors for house-breaking;* baseless claims that Transport Infrastructure Ireland would issue compulsory purchase orders on *homes* to make space for greenways. But I felt flashes of conflicted sympathy at some of the complaints – those about costs spiralling into millions, fees paid to consultants and surveyors and above all the insistence on the *purchase* of land to provide access.

The most dispiriting story came from Tim Robinson's old terrain in Connemara, where a greenway along the former Galway–Clifden Railway had been progressing in fits and starts for years. In the summer of 2025, a farmer with land in the reedy, pool-dappled country just north of Roundstone Bog was granted court permission to challenge a compulsory purchase. He claimed that when Galway County Council first approached him, he had agreed to the greenway project on the basis that the land would remain his own and the route would be a permissive one, an 'informal track of a type that one would see in the countryside', 2.5 metres wide and open on either side so that his sheep could wander freely across. It sounded like the sort of bridleway you find all over Europe. It

* This particular scare story seems to have had its earliest outing as part of the opposition to the original proposal for the Great Southern Trail in Limerick and Kerry in the late 1980s. Those opposed to the plan tapped into anti-Traveller prejudice and warned residents of small towns along the route that criminals from Rathkeale would use it to target their homes.

sounded like the stretch of the Camino de Santiago west of Burgos that Cara and I walked one autumn before the children were born. But now, the farmer said, the council were seeking outright ownership for a tarmacked track, 3.5 metres across and fully fenced on either side.[5] When I read the story, I thought immediately of the friendly landowner on the mountain bike I met on the Royal Canal: 'Why can't they just put a footpath across the land instead? What's the harm in it?'

In November 2025, landowners' representatives opposed to greenway developments spoke before the Oireachtas Joint Committee on Transport. In her statement to the Committee, the spokesperson for the 'National Greenway Action Association' invoked the ultimate historical bogeyman when discussing the supposed threat of compulsory purchase orders:

> This entire process is Cromwellian in nature, rooted in a colonial system that was never on the side of the Irish people. It is a mechanism of dispossession, a relic of a past when land was taken from those who worked it and handed to those who ruled over it. Generations fought and died for the right to own and protect their property. That right must never again be undermined by the State. No forced project will succeed. The resentment will outlast the Tarmac.[6]

It seems an astonishing thing to say about an attempt to give the Irish public a little more access to a landscape from which they are overwhelmingly excluded. But there it is: lasting damage, history souring the discourse of the twenty-first century.

* * *

Back in the hotel bar in Dublin, they've finally brought the tea, and Robert Dowds is ordering a slice of chocolate cake.

'Are you sure you won't have something?'

I wave my hand. 'I'm grand. That's the thing when there are no footpaths – I don't do enough walking, so I have to watch what I eat!' I ask him about greenways, and he too has mixed feelings.

'In some ways they're good; but I think they're over-sanitised. I would prefer, in a way, if they were rough tracks rather than tarmac, and if they are tarmacked I'd like them to be divided between the walkers and the cyclists with the cyclists having a paved track and the walkers just walking on, you know, a rough surface.'

The cake arrives, and I turn briefly towards the window. Evening is coming on outside. The gulls are still battling the wind over the Liffey and the pavements are thicker than ever with pedestrians. It strikes me again, as it did in Limerick, that the cities here are infinitely more welcoming to a walker than the countryside: the strip of dedicated space on either side of the roads, the pedestrianised streets in the city centre. Just a couple of minutes' walk from where we sit is the Phoenix Park – 1,700 acres of accessible green space. I turn back to the busy room and mention this idea to Robert. He agrees.

'Being in the city *is* easier. My wife is more of a walker than I am; I'm more inclined to cycle. And where we live, she can walk to the canal easily, and walk along it. We have a big park of 250 acres; you can walk there. So that's a lot easier than for people who live in rural areas.

'When I'm talking to TDs about improving access, I say actually the people who will benefit the most are people *living* in rural areas. I mean, one of the things is the number of pedestrians killed on the roads – and it mainly seems to be women. I regularly meet women out in hi-vis jackets, walking along and hoping they won't be mowed down by a car. And they shouldn't *have* to do that!'

I mention the strange irony – the irony that I can never quite make sense of – in the contrast between access in Ireland and Britain, the robust legislation there, the pronounced disaggregation of access rights and ownership rights despite the old aristocrats still ensconced in the sort of houses that are gaping ruins or golf resorts here. And I mention how strange the rhetoric of current English – and really I do mean *English* – access debates seems, the claims of 'no access to 92 per cent of England'. No compulsory purchase orders are required to develop ambitious new walking routes in Wales and England.

'Well actually,' says Robert, 'maybe one of the advantages of there being so few landowners in England is the fact that it makes access easier and more straightforward.' Then the smile spreads across his face again, particularly wry this time. 'Of course, it used to be like that here too. So, if you like, you can blame all our problems of access on the British Tories who tried to kill home rule with kindness and gave the land to the tenants!'

It's a joke, of course – an outrageous one. But it will take a certain weight in my memory of the conversation, settle and solidify on the train ride home later that evening; a sense, again, of damage done, of something gone awry. Because what did the colonial power do everywhere, over and over, as its own extinguishment became inevitable? It divided, even as it relinquished its conquests. It drew new partition lines on the very maps it had commissioned, carried its own intractable neuroses home and left the erstwhile subjects to deal with the consequences.

During the Dáil debate on the doomed Access to the Countryside Bill in 2013, one of Robert Dowds' opponents had invoked the memory of Michael Davitt and the Land League campaigns of the late nineteenth century, 'when the lands were given back to the native Irish'.[7] But Michael Davitt did *not* believe in tenant proprietorship. His politics were forged amid the cotton mills and Chartist meetings of industrial Lancashire after his family's eviction from their Mayo smallholding, and he came to argue forcefully for working-class solidarity and the *nationalisation of Irish land*. He was only convinced to set aside this ideal by Charles Stewart Parnell during a meeting at the grand Parnell family seat, Avondale House, in its 500-acre parkland in County Wicklow.[8] Likewise the famous line, attributed to James Connolly, martyr of the 1916 Rising, about true Irish freedom depending on its people's ownership of everything 'from the plough to the stars'. The avowedly socialist Connolly – Scottish-born and Scottish-accented, a product of that familiar wave of migration from Ulster into urban Scotland in the second half of the nineteenth century – surely didn't mean individual *private* ownership.

But the idea of nationalised land would have been a hard sell in late nineteenth- and early twentieth-century Ireland – and harder still today, for its tangible benefits are difficult to conceive. Nationalisation cannot, practically, confer the usual individual rights associated with proprietorship: to build a house, graze livestock, grow vegetables. But there is one right that *can* be conferred on everyone *without* undermining the principle of individual ownership: the right of access. I'm back to Tim Robinson here, asking 'Where do we turn, to find a way of looking at the land, inhabiting it, loving it, other than that of ownership?' – to which I might whisper: *we turn and we start walking*. And now, finally, I'm back to The Bull McCabe. Let him have his field. Let him hold it close. A public footpath along the boundary wall does nothing to prevent that. In fact, if The Bull McCabe had ever looked at an old Ordnance Survey map, he might have found that there was a footpath there already.

* * *

It's nearly dark outside and a waiter comes to clear away the teacups. Robert Dowds needs to be heading off: there's a new grandchild in the family, just home from hospital. And if I catch the next train, I might make it back to Co. Galway in time to read Róise a bedtime story. I like to think that these Irish children will grow up to find themselves less excluded from the landscape than their parents and grandparents.

I ask Robert one final question: what, from an official Keep Ireland Open position, would the ideal future look like?

'There would be paths and places for people to walk all over the place,' he says. 'And, you know, we would very much be of the view that access should be responsible and people with dogs shouldn't abuse it. I mean, that's basically it – to be able to walk as *you* could walk in Cornwall!'

And then, as we're gathering jackets, putting away notes, he says something else: 'One thing I have against you – and a couple of our committee members, actually…'

The smile is very broad now, so I'm not too alarmed. 'What's that?' I say.

'You're *English*!'

I grimace. 'I know. The optics are terrible…'

'It's a pity. I mean, it's understandable in one sense, because you know what we're being deprived of. But we need to just spread that across to Irish people.'

I nod and grimace again.

He shrugs his jacket up onto his shoulders. 'You don't have a very strong English accent though, so that's one thing.'

'I'll take that,' I say, gratefully. And then I offer the usual feeble alibi – the Cornishness, the paternal ancestry.

'Well,' he says, and I'm not sure if he actually winks, but he definitely arches his eyebrows; 'you can play up those things…'

11

A Sense of an Ending: Newcastle to Burr Point

Where does a journey end?

The cross-Ireland diagonal, the desire line from Dunmore Head to Burr Point, was always arbitrary. It was a MacGuffin to give narrative direction. I could have chosen different start and end points; and then I would have gained a walking-pace intimacy with other roads entirely, slept on different mountainsides and bogs. I'd have seen different hares tearing away across different fields, different lapwings, a different pine marten pottering across a different track. And I'd never have spoken to an Englishwoman selling ogham stones, two mountain bikers by the Royal Canal, three Traveller lads outside Newry. But that's the nature of any voluntary journey. And in any case, it doesn't end *here*. I've totted up 620 kilometres so far; there are another fifty-eight to go.

It has taken me longer than expected to get back to Newcastle. It's late September, and the beach is a very different place today. No warm breeze off the water, no happy holiday crowds. The lip of forestry at the foot of the Mournes has curled back, baring the white teeth of the town. Brittle sunlight slants low from the east; and all along the beach to the north stand the blackened uprights of old groynes, their horizontal planking long since rotted away. They look like an invading army, marching ashore through the shallows.

I drove up from Galway yesterday evening, skirted the western flanks of the mountains through villages and small towns, a quote from Bobby Sands on a gable-end mural here, a Union Jack snapping from a lamppost there. It was dusk when I knocked on the door of a B&B in Downpatrick. After a long delay a rosy-cheeked older man came to the door with a toddler in tow.

'Sorry, now, I was minding the grandson.' He shook my hand and said, 'My name's Cathal,' with deliberate force so that I could make my assumptions. He'd made his own already it seemed – was it the name and address on the online booking, or the number plate of the car? He showed me to the room in a hurry, talking all the time. He gave me so little chance to speak that I don't think he registered anything peculiar. 'You'll be looking for a pint of Guinness later,' he said as he handed me the key. Then he directed me to a particular sort of pub on the main street.

I was up before dawn, left the car on a side street, caught the first bus to Newcastle. And now I sit on the steps at the head of the beach, shivering over a pain au chocolate and a takeaway coffee from the Centra across from the bus station – the only place open at this early hour – and trying to close the two-month gap since I was here last. Perhaps I should take off my shoes, wade out into the shallows again. But it's too cold for that today. So instead I simply walk away northwards on the hard wet sand.

* * *

Paths through sand dunes, managed by the National Trust; marram grass and bracken, fox-coloured in the turning year. Caravan parks and traffic noise; wild geese in a stubble field and a dead rabbit in a gateway. I'd walked five kilometres before I reached the first tarmac – and that only a short stretch through a corridor of susurrating oaks to the edge of Dundrum. The cafés were open here, and I stopped for another coffee and a cinnamon bun on the main village street. The young woman behind the counter had spidery black eyelashes. She asked where I'd walked from, where I was going, and I did my best to explain.

'Are you doing it for charity?'

Another awkward attempt at justification: 'Just for the challenge, really.'

A friend came in from the street to chat to her, a tall blondish lad.

'Do you know what he's doing?' She nodded at me. 'Tell him what you're doing! He's walked all the way from Dingle!'

'Not *today*, though; not all in one go!' I said hastily through a mouthful of cinnamon bun. But the blond lad came across to look at the map I'd spread on the table.

'That's mad,' he said.

There was another path at the further edge of the village and a fingerpost with yellow arrows: the Lecale Way, the Ulster Way, the St Patrick's Way. The sense, again, that walkers were more welcome here than they had been south of the border. This was another old railway, running north towards Downpatrick. But there was no sterile tarmac surface, just a strip of well-trodden grass, beautifully soft underfoot. The tide was high, and the steely water of Dundrum's inner bay opened to the right, small waders picking among the stones of the foreshore. A few cheery morning walkers came past, older folks with labradors.

'It's a fine morning!'

'It is.'

After a couple of kilometres, the map showed the waymarked trail turning away towards the road. But the path ran on and, where it ended, instead of a barrier I found a neat wooden stile with the ivy cleared back on either side. It gave access to the salty meadows at the mouth of the Blackstaff River: an unmistakable signal, a friendly note in the countryside. It was a tiny thing, but a surge of gratitude rose from my chest with such force that my eyes prickled sharply for a moment. Then I stepped across and made my way through tussocky fields to a gate by a bridge. Two men were checking sheep in a pen nearby, but they paid me no heed.

Onwards along quiet lanes to Downpatrick. Flat grey light; a gentle roll to the land. Whenever I turned to look back the way I'd come, the Mournes caught me by surprise in their vastness, as if some exotic creature – a giraffe, perhaps, or an okapi – had materialised in a roadside field.

In crossing the Blackstaff I'd entered the peninsula known

as Lecale, the lower of the two jaws which bite together around Strangford Lough. The old name of this place is *Magh-Innis*, the 'Island Plain'. In the past, the estuaries of the Blackstaff and its northern counterpart, the Quoile, stretched much further inland. In the mid-sixteenth century, the Lord Chancellor of Ireland, Thomas Cusack, declared that 'The sea doth ebb and flow round that country so as in full water no man may enter therein upon dry land – but in one way which is less than two miles in length.' Cusack thought Lecale's almost-island a 'handsome, plain, and champion country', already long since stripped of its trees and 'as civil as few places in the English pale'.[1] It had been the core of the original Norman colony in Ulster, but there was no formal project to settle Scots and English colonists here during the wider Ulster Plantation of the seventeenth century. Strong and middling farmers of Old English and Irish ancestry held on to their lands here longer than elsewhere.[2] Even now, walking across Lecale, there is a certain palpable time-depth, a sense that this is *old* country, with the oldest stuff of all still pushing up through the modern field-scape: standing stones, stone circles, chambered graves. This was St Patrick's country too. The previous evening I'd walked up to his purported grave on the little hill at the heart of Downpatrick. The Anglican cathedral stood at the crown, a gothic stegosaur of a place with the grave beside it under a big grey boulder. Slieve Donard was in view beyond the low ridges to the southwest, a dull lavender pyramid set against a flaming sky. The sight of it brought one of those sudden and intense certainties: whether there really are saints' bones buried here, *this* place, this hilltop, has meant *something*, as long as there have been people in this landscape.

I came back into Downpatrick now past the racecourse and across the soccer pitch. It was midday. Two months earlier, the bulk of the day's walking would still have been ahead of me. But now the daylight felt finite, so I collected the car from its side street and drove twenty minutes east to a campsite just outside Strangford in the grounds of Castle Ward, the eighteenth-century seat of the viscounts Bangor. It was a beautiful site, a green oval with a hem of tall pines at the edge of the demesne – not a ruin or a working farm, this one, but a National Trust property. There were still a good few campers, happy to brave the chilly evenings. I parked and pitched the tent, then went into the little wooden office building to pay. A very merry woman called Kat was in charge. She gave me a leaflet, asked if I was planning to go for a walk.

'We've twenty-one miles of trails here,' she said.

Another woman who'd been cleaning the bins outside came into the office. 'Have you seen how small his tent is?' She pointed at me. 'You can't charge him full price for that – give him a discount!'

Afterwards, I went out to the road and flagged down the half past three bus back to Downpatrick to pick up where I'd left off.

The afternoon was already thinning towards evening. But with only a light daypack to carry I moved swiftly along the pavements, past red houses, pitches, a police station, out into the cool stillness of the countryside. A kilometre beyond the town a lane led to the wells at Struell. Chambers and bathing houses of grey stone roofed with crocodilian slabs stood around a walled dell where the heavy farmland seemed to have sagged below its natural baseline, one of those quiet spots where the weight of the landscape seems to accumulate, what some would call a 'thin place'.

The older maps named the wells for St Patrick, and his association with this place is an ancient one. A hymn, dating from the turn of the ninth century, describes Patrick praying, bathing and spending the night here – an effort, surely, to convert a place already storied in an older tradition:

> He slept on a bare flagstone then, and a wet quilt about him:
> his bolster was a pillar-stone; he left not his body in warmth.[3]

Struell remained a place of pilgrimage for many centuries. In 1515, Francesco Chieregati, a papal nuncio from Bologna, came here and reported that pilgrims would enter what is now known as the 'Women's Bathhouse' and kneel to pray in a cascade of cold water, channelled from a nearby stream: 'They remain there on their knees with the water falling all the time on top of them; and this, they say, was done by St Patrick.' Well into the nineteenth century, thousands gathered here each year in the week before midsummer's eve, some in search of cures and penance, others to roister in the temporary township of tents, 'where whiskey is sold, and entertainment of every kind is afforded'.[4] The pilgrimage only fizzled out in the second half of the century as Catholic officialdom turned sternly against the earthy popular faith of the wells and mountaintops and the local Protestant-owned newspapers fulminated about Struell's 'heathenism and debauchery' and 'pious orgies'.[5] The practice of nude communal bathing at the wells caused particular consternation.

There is only one way into Struell today: a lane from the road, ending in a small parking area. But imagine the countless people down the centuries who moved across the land towards it from all directions, following the streams and the field boundaries, crossing the long-forgotten stiles and cresting the final ridge to descend on a cluster of rough tents, a hubbub of voices, an aroma of spilt whiskey and grilled herrings.

The place was quiet on this late September afternoon. The old stonework and the sound of running water took me, again, briefly to bathing temples in Java and Bali. But there was no tropical heat here, no heaped petals and smouldering incense. Crisp sycamore leaves lay across the soft grass between the buildings.

There'd been a couple of women pottering about when I arrived, but they'd soon driven off. A few minutes later, a big red tractor rumbled out of the nearby fields and headed away to the road. An assumption that this was the farmer gone home for the day reignited that unexpected brazenness I'd experienced descending from the Cooley Mountains back in July. Instead of returning to the road I hopped across a gate into a long field behind the bathhouses, crossed a fence-line by a small pond and struck uphill along the edge of a maizefield, grown in thick with nettles, thistles and belladonna. The dark body of the Mournes reared into view once more. In the thinning light its vast form seemed part woman, part lion, and I felt again that forceful conviction: this place *meant* something.

Beyond a short stretch of road leading to a place marked as Ballyalton on the map, another path headed out onto the land, official this time, signposted as the 'Lecale Way'. It was a beautiful old foot-lane, too narrow ever to have taken wheeled traffic, too narrow ever to have counted as a *bóthar* under the Brehon Laws. It ran north between small, stone-walled meadows. A big fox with a full, white-tipped brush crossed a field beside the path at a slow run. I tried the old trick of sucking the back of my hand to mimic the squeal of a rabbit in distress. The fox stopped abruptly and made a fussy show of sitting neatly on its own curled brush. We eyed each other with an air of forced casualness for a long while. Then it rose, padded on across the field and disappeared into a bank of gorse without a backward glance.

Overripe blackberries; sloes the colour of the mountains at dusk; a small lake hemmed with short, steep hills. I passed a Neolithic dolmen in a field and a crusty menhir by the entrance to a farmyard, then came another path under a furzy slope. There hadn't been a day like this since Dingle, a day when so much of the walking had been off-road – not on mountain trails or canal banks or forestry tracks or bogs, but on *paths*, running out across the land, through the fields. This last path brought me out to a narrow lane between two hills. A sudden distance opened ahead. I could see the pale stripe of Strangford Lough and the low spine of the Ards Peninsula where I would walk tomorrow, then the sea with big hills rising beyond. It took me a moment to work it out: they had to be the hills of Galloway, eighty kilometres away across the water, hills on which you have a statutory right to walk wherever you please.

It was very nearly dark when I reached the southern gate of the Castle Ward demesne. As I passed into the gloom beneath the big trees, a figure appeared ahead, coming towards me along the avenue: blonde hair, a small dog on a lead; a woman. She was a hundred metres off, but I saw the sudden hesitancy in her stride, saw her tug the dog close then cross deliberately to the other side of the avenue. And then, abruptly, I saw myself: a big, shaven-headed and unmistakably male form, looming rapidly out of the gloaming with a stick in his hand. And all my anxieties camping out in bogs, walking through spruce plantations, ducking across fields were instantly absurd. I didn't know what to do other than to keep walking at an even pace, but to my relief I reached a side path branching away towards the campsite before she came level. I hurried along it in the darkness, fearful now only of frightening another lone walker in the woods.

* * *

Everything had changed in the night. Yesterday's brittle stillness had been swept away. A hard wind had risen from the southeast and all the trees were roaring. The final day; a final twenty kilometres from which to make a sense of an ending.

It was a Sunday, and the first ferry from Strangford to Portaferry didn't run until half past nine. I waited for it by the little harbour, stamping and shivering. The tide was flooding in through the narrows at astonishing speed. Strangford Lough is the largest enclosed inlet in Ireland, and with each tide all the water required to fill or drain 150 square kilometres must pass through a gap just 600 metres wide. Today's flood had such force that it seemed to have torn lumps of groundswell from the open sea, eight kilometres to the south, and carried them far inland: big bulges of ill-formed energy, jostling northwards like running bulls. The name here is a Viking one: Strangfjörthr, the 'fjord of the strong current'. But it made me think of strangulation: a place of strangled tides.

There were just a few cars aboard the ferry. I climbed to the upper deck and held fast to the rail as it yawed and slewed across the channel. On the far side I walked onwards through Portaferry without a pause, past houses with peeling paintwork and a red Methodist chapel with a lone old man shuffling up the steps. Twenty minutes out of town the map showed a track bending across the crown of a rise called Derry Hill. It turned out to be a narrow green lane with oaks and hawthorns and wizened ashes straining fiercely on either side in the hard wind. This was it: my requisite off-road quota, a mere kilometre, but enough to save the day and push me on along the quiet lanes across the middle of the Ards Peninsula. Rich farming country, this, with a strong smell of slurry and silage on the wind, big barns on the hilltops and dairy cows in the fields. These were not large agricultural businesses, just solid family farms, worked full-time like the places I knew in Cornwall. There were no footpaths across the fields here; but there were no 'no entry' signs in the gateways either.

The lanes brought me out to the other side of the peninsula at Cloughey. The air seemed to possess the same dark and unruly energy as the tide now. The wind came fierce and cold off the Irish Sea, driving ragged lines of surf ashore and carrying a stench of rotten seaweed. Gulls laboured against the gusts and oystercatchers piped with a tone of furious grievance. The air was gritty with windblown sand.

I followed the main coastal road north past low and weatherbeaten houses, scabby masonry, ragged cordyline palms swaying hysterically in the narrow gardens. There were Union Jacks and Ulster Banners on each lamppost here, reduced to knotted rags by the wind.

At Portavogie Harbour the wind came stronger still. A clatter of rigging, a clamour of gulls and a big bull seal hanging in the milky water. An empty Coke can rattled back and forth over the concrete. I sat to rest for a while on a bench here and looked out at the boats: rust-streaked stern trawlers, snub-nosed herring boats. And I thought, inevitably, of my father, Des.

After his flight to Cornwall from Dundee he'd become a deep-sea fisherman, spent fifteen years hunting mackerel, crawfish, turbot in the wild waters beyond Land's End. Even after nearly four decades ashore, he could never visit a working harbour without adopting a professionally appraising eye, without peering critically down from the quayside at winches and cables. And because I'd never shaken a youthful fascination with his maritime otherworld, I would always point and ask questions about the boats. That, in turn, would prompt a story of some long-ago incident at sea. I'd have heard it countless times before, but I relished the retelling in my forties as much as I had in childhood.

But now, hunched on a bench at Portavogie, a sudden strangulating sadness caught me, a long-deflected recognition that I'd never walk with him along another quay. His health had been failing for a few years now. But at home in Cornwall at the end of the summer, I'd driven with him to Newlyn, the fishing harbour from which he used to work. There'd been the usual critical appraisals, the usual stories. But we'd managed only a short distance along the line of boats, and suddenly I saw how small he'd become, how frail. I understood then that he would have to leave us, sometime in the coming winter. And then there would be no one left in the void between myself and M. T. Hannigan of the Dundee *Catholic Herald*, Bridget Halley from Roscommon and all the other people who had come up the Clyde from Ireland so that I could end up here, huddled on a bench by a harbour on the Ards Peninsula.

After he left the fishing industry, my father became a journalist on a local newspaper. And then, a few years later, he started working on guidebooks to Britain's long-distance walking trails: the Ridgeway, Peddars Way, Offa's Dyke and all the rest. In my early teens, our family holidays were often at campsites in Devon or Dorset or Somerset while my father walked the coast path or a moorland way with a little black notebook in his pocket. Sometimes I'd join him for part of the way and would have to wait impatiently when he stopped to scribble a description or make a note of a confusing path junction. That, I realise now, is how I came to learn of long-distance journeys on foot across unfamiliar landscapes – and to understand the possibility of writing about them afterwards. There was something else, too: the guidebook publishers that my father worked for insisted that the walks he wrote about were made up entirely of public rights of way, with no permissive paths that might one day be severed by a landowner. This was before the Countryside and Rights of Way Act 2000 opened up all the moors and mountains in Wales and England. I remember my father's wrangles over some of his routes, the difficulty in finding an officially designated footpath across certain stretches of open country. This was how I first learnt about countryside access legislation, and about the difference between a *right* to walk and a mere permission.

Throughout the earlier part of my journey, I'd been sending him little text messages: photographs and cheery greetings from the slopes of Moylussa, the heart of the Pollagh Bog, the summit of Pigeon Rock Mountain. I was never sure if they would hearten him or sadden him, now that he could no longer reach such places himself. But I sent them anyway because I wished he could be there too, a powerfully compact man with a precision of movement, a fine balance forged on the decks of fishing boats, moving lightly along the path ahead of me.

I drew a shaky breath, took out my phone, snapped the fishing boats and thumbed another message: 'At Portavogie and thinking of you. Some interesting boats here…' But I didn't know if he would see it. He was spending most of his days asleep now.

* * *

There was only a short distance remaining.

Burr Point came into view beyond a grey bay streaked with white foam at the northern edge of Portavogie: a low spit of land carrying a few bungalows on its back and straining towards an offshore outcrop marked on the map as 'Burial Island'.

I clambered down from the road to the foreshore. There were broken concrete slabs and rooftiles among the tidewrack, blades of vertical shale, a patchy pelt of yellow rockweed. I scrambled awkwardly across the rocks between the sea and the brambly scrub to landward. It was hard to work out where this low headland reached its terminus. But just as I was beginning to suspect that I'd already passed the easternmost point, a path materialised in the salt-stunted grass between the rocks at my feet. It was the thinnest of lines, and I wondered for a moment if it might be a smeuse, an animal track forged here by hares or otters. But no: other people had walked here on the same errand before me; people have *always* walked the land ahead of you.

The path led to a grey outcrop, crusted with turmeric-yellow lichen. This was it, then. A big freighter moved along the horizon, its deck stacked with containers. A pair of gannets skimmed the greenish waves and another bull seal rode upright in the swell. The Lake District and the Isle of Man showed as faint smudges beyond Burial Island. The wind came ever fiercer and a brief flash of lemony sunlight lit the whitecaps to the south. I sat for a minute, but it was too cold to linger, so I picked my way onwards, up to a stony track in front of a line of salt-faded bungalows and back around to a bus stop on the coast road.

Where does a journey end? Nowhere in particular, for you carry its residue with you until the very last – or at any arbitrary point that you choose. And so this one ends here, shivering on a weather-stained picnic bench across from a public toilet. I've walked 678 kilometres from Dunmore Head, and the bus back to Portaferry is running late.

In memory of Des Hannigan, who trained me up in the way
I should go. And for Róise and Merryn Hannigan:
may the paths rise up to meet you.

Notes

Introduction

1. Irish Legal Blog, 'Public Access', 2025. Available at: www.legalblog.ie/public-access/.
2. O'Toole, Fintan, 'Right of way: The great unmentionable of Ireland's outdoor recreation strategy', in *The Irish Times*, 22 July 2023.
3. Keep Ireland Open, 'Issues by County', 2023. Available at: www.keepirelandopen.org/issues-by-county/.
4. Carolan, Mary, 'Supreme court refuses to hear appeal in Glencree valley right of way dispute', *The Irish Times*, 4 March 2019. Available at: www.irishtimes.com/news/crime-and-law/courts/supreme-court/supreme-court-refuses-to-hear-appeal-in-glencree-valley-right-of-way-dispute-1.3813979.
5. Bouvier, Nicolas, *So It Goes: Travels in the Aran Islands, Xian and Places in Between* (London: Eland Books, 2019) p.45.
6. Burroughs, John, 'The Exhilarations of the Road', in *The Footpath Way: An Anthology for Walkers* (London: Sidgwick and Jackson, 1911), p.223.
7. Monbiot, George, 'The trespass trap: This new law could make us strangers in our own land', in *The Guardian*, 15 January 2020. Available at: www.theguardian.com/commentisfree/2020/jan/15/tresspass-trap-law-land-travelling-people-rights.
8. Moses, Jon, 'There's no right to roam over a staggering 92% of England. I've decided to take a stand', in *The Guardian*, 17 August 2022. Available at: www.theguardian.com/commentisfree/2022/aug/17/england-public-trespassing-reclaim-our-countryside.
9. 'Right-to-roam maps updated after 10 years', BBC, 11 August 2013. Available at: www.bbc.co.uk/news/uk-wales-23592620.
10. Norwegian Environment Agency, 'About the Right to Roam in

Norway'. Available at: www.environmentagency.no/areas-of-activity/right-to-roam/about-right-to-roam/.

11. Naturvardverket, 'Hiking in Nature', 2025. Available at: www.naturvardsverket.se/en/topics/the-right-of-public-access/activities-and-places/hiking-in-nature/.
12. Price, Linda and Simpson, Mark, 'The Trouble with Accessing the Countryside in Northern Ireland: A Comparison with Great Britain', in *Environmental Law Review*, Vol.19 No.3, 2017, pp.183–200.
13. Keep Ireland Open, 'Gallery', 2023. Available at: www.keepirelandopen.org/gallery/.
14. Taplin, Kim, *The English Path* (Woodbridge: The Boydell Press, 1979), p.3.
15. Ibid., p.13.
16. Somerville, Edith and Martin, Violet Florence, *The Real Charlotte*, Vol.1 (London: Ward and Downey Ltd, 1894), pp.197–198.
17. Owenson, Sydney, *The Wild Irish Girl, A National Tale* (Hartford: Silus Andrus and Son, 1855), p.32.
18. Le Fanu, J. Sheridan, *The House by the Church-Yard* (London: Richard Bentley and Son, 1886), p.211.
19. Kickham, Charles, *Knocknagow, or The Homes of Tipperary*, 13th edition (Dublin: James Duffy and Co., 1887) p.339.
20. Hillaby, John, *Journey Through Britain* (London: Constable, 1968), p.2.

Chapter 1 The Pack-Donkey's Way

1. Le Corbusier, *The City of To-Morrow and Its Planning*, trans. Frederick Etchells (London: John Rodker, 1929), p.5.
2. Ibid., p.6.
3. Ibid., p.xxi.
4. Grass, Michael, 'A Brief History of Donkeys', in *Science Direct*, Vol.32 No.19, pp.985–987. Available at: www.sciencedirect.com/science/article/pii/S0960982222014750.
5. Khadilkar, Dhananjay, 'How donkeys changed the course of human history', BBC, 2022. Available at: www.bbc.com/future/article/20230116-how-donkeys-changed-the-course-of-human-history.
6. Smyth, Jim, 'The strange history of the Irish donkey' (conference paper). Hydra Mule and Donkey Conference, 2014, p.1.
7. Cornish, Jack, *The Lost Paths: A History of How We Walk From Here to There* (London: Penguin Michael Joseph, 2024), p.8.

8. Asher Silberman, Neil, *The Oxford Companion to Archaeology*, Vol.1, 2nd edition (Oxford: Oxford University Press, 2012), p.205.
9. Sainsbury, Brendan, 'The Ridgeway: Hike the 5,000-year-old pathway that's Britain's oldest road', BBC, 2022. Available at: www.bbc.com/travel/article/20240723-the-ridgway-hike-the-5000-year-old-pathway-thats-britains-oldest-road.
10. Leary, Jim, *Footmarks: A Journey into Our Restless Past* (London: Icon Books, 2023), p.98.
11. Ibid.
12. Lee, Thomas, *Offaly Through Time & Its Townlands* (Sandycove: Ottait Publishing, 2009), p.61.
13. Raftery, Barry, *Pagan Celtic Ireland: The Enigma of the Irish Iron Age* (London: Thames and Hudson, 1994), pp.99–100.
14. Heaney, Seamus, 'In Gallarus Oratory', in *Door into the Dark* (London: Faber and Faber, 1969), p.22.
15. Harbison, Peter, *Pilgrimage in Ireland: The Monuments and the People* (London: Barrie and Jenkins, 1991), pp.77–82.
16. Woodman, Peter, *Ireland's First Settlers: Time and the Mesolithic* (Oxford: Oxbow, 2015), p.26.
17. Ibid., p.179.
18. Dowd, Marion and Carden, Ruth F., 'First Evidence of a Late Upper Palaeolithic Human Presence in Ireland', in *Quaternary Science Reviews*, Vol.139, 2016, pp.158–163.
19. McMahon, Paul, *Island of Woods: How Ireland Lost Its Forests and How to Get Them Back* (Dublin: New Island, 2023), p.15.
20. Harbison, *Pilgrimage in Ireland*, p.71.
21. Harbison, Peter, 'Early Irish Pilgrim Archaeology in the Dingle Peninsula', in *World Archaeology*, Vol.26 No.1, 1994, pp.90–103: 90.
22. Ibid., p.92.
23. Harbison, *Pilgrimage in Ireland*, p.73.
24. Ibid., pp.72–73.

Chapter 2 Forgive Us Our Trespasses

1. Sustrans, *The Great Southern Trail: A Report on a Railway Path from Tralee to Limerick* (Bristol: Sustrans, 1989), p.8.
2. McDonald, Frank, 'Come west along the railroad: Plans to turn disused railways into greenways – routes for cycling and walking – have proved contentious', in *The Irish Times*, 27 April 2013. Available

at: https://www.irishtimes.com/news/environment/come-west-along-the-railroad-1.1373757.

3. Keep Ireland Open, 'Who We Are' and 'Aims of KIO'. Available at: www.keepirelandopen.org.
4. O'Sullivan, Jennie, 'Section of new Kerry greenway blocked by locked gates', RTÉ, 1 November 2022. Available at: www.rte.ie/news/munster/2022/1101/1332582-kerry-greenway/.
5. Ray, Celeste, 'Beholding the Speckled Salmon: Folk Liturgies and Narratives of Ireland's Holy Wells', in *Landscapes Beyond Land: Routes, Aesthetics, Narratives*, Arnar Árnason, Nicolas Ellison, Jo Vergunst and Andrew Whitehouse (eds.) (New York: Berghahn, 2012), p.139.
6. Harbison, Peter, *Pilgrimage in Ireland: The Monuments and the People* (London: Barrie and Jenkins, 1991), p.229.
7. Carroll, Michael, *Irish Pilgrimage: Holy Wells and Popular Catholic Devotion* (Baltimore: The Johns Hopkins University Press, 1999), p.55.
8. Ibid., p.150.
9. Ibid., p.151.
10. O'Donovan, John et al., 'Ordnance Survey Letters: Westmeath Vol.1' (Dublin: Royal Irish Academy, 2008), pp.303–304.
11. Urban, Sylvanus, *The Gentleman's Magazine,* Vol.11 (London: William Pickering, 1839), p.312.
12. McAdam, Aine, 'From Wilderness to Wonderment: The Presentation of Irish Heritage, Durrow and Glendalough', Maynooth University (unpublished PhD thesis), 2021, p.286.
13. The Schools' Collection, Vol.0412, p.042. Available at: www.duchas.ie/en/cbes/4666596/4665370.
14. Solnit, Rebecca, *A Book of Migrations: Some Passages in Ireland* (London: Verso, 1997), p.59, p.82.
15. Waddell, John, *The Prehistoric Archaeology of Ireland*, 2nd edition (Bray: Wordwell, 2000), p.26.
16. Ó Corráin, Donnchadh, 'Prehistoric and Early Christian Ireland', in *The Oxford History of Ireland*, Roy Foster (ed.) (Oxford: Oxford University Press, 1989), p.18.
17. Dungan, Myles, *Land Is All That Matters: The Struggle That Shaped Irish History* (London: Head of Zeus, 2024), p.39.
18. Cited in Ó Cróinín, Dáibhí, *Early Medieval Ireland 400–1200*, 2nd edition (Abingdon: Routledge, 2017).

19. Ó Cróinín, *Early Medieval Ireland.*
20. *Ancient Laws of Ireland: Senchus Mor Part II* (Dublin: Alexander Thom, 1869), p.119.
21. *Ancient Laws of Ireland,* Vol. VI: Glossary to Vols I–V (Dublin: Alexander Thom, 1901), p.382.
22. Kelly, *Early Irish Farming*, p.31.
23. Ibid., p.432.
24. Ibid., p.431.
25. O'Loughlin, Ann, 'Woman injured in fox hunt loses action for damages', in *Irish Examiner*, 17 May 2019. Available at: www.irishexaminer.com/news/arid-30925077.html.
26. O'Faolain, Aodhan, 'Damages award to hillwalker who tripped on Wicklow Way is overturned', *The Irish Times*, 17 February 2017. Available at: www.irishtimes.com/news/crime-and-law/courts/high-court/damages-award-to-hillwalker-who-tripped-on-wicklow-way-is-overturned-1.2979242.
27. Government of Ireland, 'Recreation in Ireland's Outdoors: Property Rights, Access and People's Responsibilities: Information for Landowners and Recreational Users', 2025, pp.11–13.
28. Electronic Irish Statute Book, 'Housing (Miscellaneous Provisions) Act, 2002'. Available at www.irishstatutebook.ie/eli/2002/act/9/section/24.
29. Crowley, Una and Kitchin, Rob, 'Paradoxical Spaces of Traveller Citizenship in Contemporary Ireland,' in *Irish Geography*, Vol.40 No.2, 2007, pp.128–145.
30. *Update on the Economic Value of Recreational Trails in Ireland* (Fitzpatrick Associates, 2012), p.v.
31. Geissel, Hermann, *A Road on the Long Ridge: In Search of the Ancient Highway on the Esker Riada* (Newbridge: CRS Publications, 2006), p.13.
32. Kelly, *Early Irish Farming*, p.391.
33. Electronic Dictionary of the Irish Language, '1 casán'. Available online at: www.dil.ie/8304.
34. Doran, Linda, 'Medieval Communication Routes Through Longford and Roscommon and Their Associated Settlements', in *Proceedings of the Royal Irish Academy: Archaeology, Culture, History, Literature*, Vol.104C No.3, 2004, pp.57–80: 69.
35. Kelly, *Early Irish Farming*, p.391.
36. Doran, 'Medieval Communication Routes', p.57.

37. Ibid., p.378.
38. Ibid., p.236.
39. Ó Cróinín, *Early Medieval Ireland.*
40. Cornish, Jack, *The Lost Paths: A History of How We Walk From Here to There* (London: Penguin Michael Joseph, 2024), pp.149–155.
41. Beale, Charlotte, 'In Sweden you can roam anywhere you like, without the landowner's permission', World Economic Forum, 8 May 2019. Available at: www.weforum.org/stories/2019/05/sweden-roam-freely-law-Allemansr%C3%A4tt-access-nature/.
42. The National Trails Office, 'A Guide to Planning and Developing Recreational Trails in Ireland', 2012, p.9.
43. Carolan, Mary, 'Court rules in favour of Lissadell owners in right of way case', in *The Irish Times*, 11 November 2013. Available at: www.irishtimes.com/news/crime-and-law/courts/court-rules-in-favour-of-lissadell-owners-in-right-of-way-case-1.1590985; O'Loughlin, Ann, 'Hillwalkers fail to prove public "right of way" over Enniskerry route', in *Irish Examiner*, 15 May 2018. Available at: www.irishexaminer.com/news/arid-30843012.html.

Chapter 3 Between the Woods and the Water

1. Quoted online at: www.linkedin.com/posts/ecologicalconsultant_the-doonass-water-at-castleconnell-co-limerick-activity-7289279418177380352-CJ5j.
2. Connelly, Charlie, 'HV Morton: Terrific writer, terrible man', in *The New World*, 4 August 2022. Available at: www.theneweuropean.co.uk/hv-morton-terrific-writer-terrible-man/.
3. Morton, H. V., *In Search of Ireland* (London: Methuen, 1930) pp.179–80.
4. Ibid., p.176–77.
5. Ibid., p.178.
6. Ibid., p.175.
7. Clements, Paul, *Shannon Country: A River Journey Through Time* (Dublin: Lilliput, 2020), p.213.
8. Electronic Irish Statute Book, 'Shannon Electricity Act, 1925'. Available at www.irishstatutebook.ie/eli/1925/act/26/enacted/en/print#sec3.
9. Killeen, Richard, *A Brief History of Ireland: Land, People, History* (London: Robinson, 2012), p.36.
10. Dowd, Marion, 'Darkness and Light in the Archaeological Past:

Sensory Perspectives', in *The Routledge Handbook of Sensory Archaeology*, Robin Skeets and Jo Day (eds.) (London: Routledge, 2019), pp.193–210: 199.

11. Pellew, George, *In Castle and Cabin: Or, Talks in Ireland in 1887* (New York: G. P. Putnam's Sons, 1888), p.152.
12. Wilde, W. R., 'On the Unmanufactured Animal Remains Belonging to the Academy', in *Proceedings of the Royal Irish Academy*, Vol.7, 1857–1861, pp.181–212: 186.
13. O'Donovan, John, 'Ordnance Survey Letters of Galway'. Available at: www.galwaylibrary.org/letters/a18381101.html?p=20804.
14. Westropp, Thomas Johnson, 'Forests of the Counties of the Lower Shannon Valley', in *Proceedings of the Royal Irish Academy: Archaeology, Culture, History, Literature*, Vol.27, 1908–1909, pp.270–300: 278.
15. McMahon, Paul, *Island of Woods: How Ireland Lost Its Forests and How to Get Them Back* (Dublin: New Island, 2023), p.17.
16. Ibid., pp.70–71.
17. Ibid., pp.81–83.
18. Andrews, J. H., 'Notes on the Historical Geography of the Irish Iron Industry', in *Irish Geography*, Vol.3, 1956, pp.139–149.
19. Aalen, F. H. A., Whelan, Kevin and Stout, Matthew (eds.), *Atlas of the Irish Rural Landscape* (Cork: Cork University Press, 1997), p.85.
20. Costello, Eugene, 'Liminal Learning: Social Practice in Seasonal Settlements of Western Ireland', in *Journal of Social Archaeology*, Vol.17 No.2, 2017, pp.188-209.
21. McMahon, *Island of Woods*, p.100.
22. Ibid., p.115.
23. Ibid., p.123.
24. Electronic Irish Statute Book, 'Forestry Act, 1928'. Available at: www.irishstatutebook.ie/eli/1928/act/34/enacted/en/html.
25. Coillte, 'Explore'. Available at: www.coillte.ie/our-forests/explore/.
26. Ruddock, Marc et al., *The 2022 National Survey of Breeding Hen Harrier in Ireland* (Dublin: National Parks and Wildlife Service, 2022), p.24.

Chapter 4 River Ghosts

1. Spenser, Edmund, *A View of the Present State of Ireland* (Eugene: Renascence Editions, 1997), p.33.

2. Gibney, John, *A Short History of Ireland 1500–2000* (New Haven: Yale University Press, 2017), p.21.
3. Killeen, Richard, *A Brief History of Ireland: Land, People, History* (London: Robinson, 2012), p.77.
4. Sullivan, T. D., *Bantry, Berehaven and the O'Sullivan Sept* (Dublin: Sealy, Bryers and Walker, 1908), pp.18–19.
5. Ibid., p.22.
6. O'Sullivan Beare, Philip, *Ireland under Elizabeth: Chapters Towards a History of Ireland in the Reign of Elizabeth, Being a Portion of the History of Catholic Ireland by Don Philip O'Sullivan Bear*, trans. Matthew J. Byrne (Dublin: Sealy, Bryers and Walker, 1903), p.160.
7. E. W., 'The O'Sullivan Bear', in *The Dublin Penny Journal*, Vol.2 No.89, 1834, pp.294–95.
8. O'Sullivan Beare, *Ireland under Elizabeth*, p.163.
9. Ibid., p.164.
10. Ibid., p165.
11. Ibid., pp.165–166.
12. Mac Hale, Connor, *Annals of the Clan Egan* (Enniscrone: C Mac Hale, 1990), p.34.
13. O'Sullivan Beare, *Ireland under Elizabeth*, p.167.
14. Ibid.
15. McAuliffe, Mary, 'O'Connor Kerry of Carrigafoyle: History and Memory in Iraghticonor', in *Béaloideas*, Vol.82, 2014, pp.100–115: 108.
16. O'Sullivan Beare, *Ireland under Elizabeth*, p.173.
17. Kerney Walsh, Micheline, 'O Sullivan Beare in Spain: Some Unpublished Documents', in *Archivium Hibernicum*, Vol.45, 1990, pp.46–63: 46.
18. O'Scea, Ciaran, 'Documents Concerning Inter-Irish Political Rivalry at the Spanish Court and the Assassination of Domnall Cam O'Sullivan Beare, 1614–25', in *Archivium Hibernicum*, Vol.65, 2012, pp.7–75: 7.
19. Gibney, *A Short History of Ireland*, p.56.
20. Wheeler, Diarmuid, 'From Gaelic Lordships to English Counties: The Tudor Transition in Leix and Offaly, c. 1547–1603', National University of Ireland Galway (unpublished PhD thesis), 2018, p.13.
21. Ibid., p.136.
22. Gibney, *A Short History of Ireland*, p.30.
23. Spenser, *A View of the Present State of Ireland*, p.30.

24. Aalen, F. H. A., Whelan, Kevin and Stout, Matthew (eds.), *Atlas of the Irish Rural Landscape* (Cork: Cork University Press, 1997), p.23.
25. Atkinson, Ernest George (ed.), *Calendar of the State Papers Relating to Ireland, of the Reign of Elizabeth, 1599, February – 1600, February* (Liechtenstein: Kraus Reprint, 1974), p.138.
26. Never Felt Better, 'Ireland's Wars: Meelick Island', 2014. Available at: www.neverfeltbetter.wordpress.com/2014/06/04/irelands-wars-meelick-island/.
27. O'Keeffe, P., 'Ordnance Survey Letters of Galway', 1838. Available at: places.webworld.org/letters/a18381103.html.
28. *Indexes of Reports to Commissioners 1832 – 1847*, 1847 *(*Shannon Navigation), p.32.
29. Duffy, Aileen, 'Meelick Martello Tower', in *Banagher on the Shannon*, 2022. Available at: www.old.banagher.ie/2022/02/07/meelick-martello-tower/.

Chapter 5 The Wet Centre

1. Dungan, Myles, *Land Is All That Matters: The Struggle That Shaped Irish History* (London: Head of Zeus, 2024), p.53.
2. 'Act for the Settlement of Ireland', 1652. Available at: www.constitution.org/1-History/eng/conpur094.htm.
3. Killeen, Richard, *A Brief History of Ireland: Land, People, History* (London: Robinson, 2012), p.97.
4. Dungan, *Land Is All That Matters*, p.54.
5. Trinity College Dublin, 'The Down Survey of Ireland: Historical Context', 2013. Available online at: www. www.downsurvey.ie/about/.
6. Gibney, John, *A Short History of Ireland 1500–2000* (New Haven: Yale University Press, 2017), p.72.
7. Ibid.
8. The Schools' Collection, Vol.0816, p.005. Available at: www.duchas.ie/en/cbes/5044630/5027549.
9. Moloney, Michale F., *Irish Ethno-Botany and the Evolution of Medicine in Ireland* (Dublin: M. H. Gill & Son, 1919), p.59.
10. Montgomery Hitchcock, F. R., *The Midland Septs and the Pale* (Dublin: Sealy, Bryers and Walker, 1908), p.307.
11. Westropp, Michel Roberts and Edward Shirley Trevor, *Irish Chancery Reports Vol.III* (Dublin: Hodges and Smith, 1855), pp.152–153.

12. The Schools' Collection, Vol.0816, p.001A. Available at: www.duchas.ie/en/cbes/5044630/5027554/5142975.
13. Electronic Dictionary of the Irish Language, '1 Ríad'. Available at: www.dil.ie/35194.
14. Atkins, William, 'Bogland', in *Harper's Magazine*, 2020. Available at: www.harpers.org/archive/2020/07/bogland-bog-of-allen-ireland-peat-bog-bord-na-mona/.
15. McMahon, Paul, *Island of Woods: How Ireland Lost Its Forests and How to Get Them Back* (Dublin: New Island, 2023), p.21.
16. Heaney, Seamus, 'Bogland', in *Door into the Dark* (London: Faber and Faber, 1969), pp.55–56.
17. Atkins, 'Bogland'.
18. Aalen, F. H. A., Whelan, Kevin and Stout, Matthew (eds.), *Atlas of the Irish Rural Landscape* (Cork: Cork University Press, 1997), p.119.
19. Reid, Neil, 'The Irish Hare: From the Ice Age to the Present', in *British Wildlife*, Vol.29 No.4, 2018, pp.238–243: 38.
20. NAI Lodge/5/421, 'Grant to Sir JASPER HERBERT of land in King's County'. Available at: virtualtreasury.ie/item/NAI-Lodge-5-421.
21. Stokes, Canon, 'Descriptive Sketch of Places Visited During Excursion to King's County on 3rd August', in *The Journal of the Royal Society of Antiquaries of Ireland*, Vol.6 No.3, 1896, pp.264–324: 321.
22. The Schools' Collection, Vol.0807, p.109. Available at: www.duchas.ie/en/cbes/5044599/5024896/5139649.
23. McCullough, Joseph, *A Pocket History of Ireland* (Dublin: Gill & Macmillan, 2010), p.97.
24. Ibid.
25. Prendergast, John P., *Ireland from the Restoration to the Revolution 1660 to 1690* (London: Longmans, Green and Co., 1887), p.72.
26. Killeen, *A Brief History of Ireland*, p.105.
27. Dungan, *Land Is All That Matters*, p.54.

Chapter 6 Translations

1. Anon., 'Some Memoirs of Richard Twiss, Esq., F.R.S.', in *The Hibernian Magazine*, August 1776, p.550.
2. Finnegan, Rachel, 'Introduction', in Twiss, Richard, *A Tour in Ireland in 1775*, Rachel Finnegan (ed.) (Dublin: University College Dublin Press, 2008), p.xviii.
3. Ibid., p.xix.

4. Twiss, Richard, *A Tour in Ireland in 1775* (Dublin: University College Dublin Press, 2008), p.5.
5. Ibid., p.38.
6. Ibid., p.48.
7. Ibid., p.16.
8. Kennedy, Máire, 'The Readership of Books in Ireland, 1700-1800', in *Revue Lisa*, Vol.3 No.1, 2005. Available at: journals.openedition.org /lisa/2509.
9. Twiss, *A Tour in Ireland*, p.71.
10. Aalen, F. H. A., Whelan, Kevin and Stout, Matthew (eds.), *Atlas of the Irish Rural Landscape* (Cork: Cork University Press, 1997), p.75.
11. Dungan, *Land Is All That Matters*, p.96.
12. Gibney, John, *A Short History of Ireland 1500–2000* (New Haven: Yale University Press, 2017), p.103.
13. Dungan, *Land Is All That Matters*, p.80.
14. Ibid., p.81.
15. Twiss, *A Tour in Ireland*, p.72.
16. Ibid., p.20.
17. Ibid., p.77.
18. Ibid., p.69.
19. Ibid., p.137.
20. Anon., 'Some Memoirs of Richard Twiss', p.552.
21. Ibid., p.550.
22. Powell, Martyn J., *Piss-pots, Printers and Public Opinion in Eighteenth-Century Dublin: Richard Twiss's Tour in Ireland* (Dublin: Four Courts Press, 2009), p.26.
23. Ibid., p.28.
24. Ibid., p54.
25. Finnegan, Rachel, 'Introduction', p.xxix.
26. Ibid., p.xxiv.
27. Hyland, Cal and Kelly, James, 'Richard Twiss's *A Tour of Ireland in 1775* (London, 1776): The Missing Pages and Some Other Notes', in *Eighteenth-Century Ireland/Iris an Dá Chultúr*, Vol.13, 1998, pp.52–64: 52.
28. Giraldus Cambrensis, *The Topography of Ireland*, translated by Thomas Forester, Thomas Wright (ed.) (Cambridge, Ontario: In Parenthesis, 2000), p.48
29. Ibid., p.70.
30. Lithgow, William, *Lithgow's Nineteen Years Travels Through the Most*

Eminent Places in the Habitable World (London: John Wright, 1682), pp.408–409.

31. O'Donovan, John (trans.), *Annals of the Four Masters*, CELT: The Corpus of Electronic Texts. Available at: celt.ucc.ie/published/T100005A/.
32. O'Sullivan, Muiris and Downey, Liam, 'Early Historic Routeways', in *Archaeology Ireland*, Vol.29 No.3, 2015, pp.14–17.
33. Geissel, Hermann, *A Road on the Long Ridge: In Search of the Ancient Highway on the Esker Riada* (Newbridge: CRS Publications, 2006).
34. Doran, Linda, 'Medieval Communication Routes Through Longford and Roscommon and Their Associated Settlements', in *Proceedings of the Royal Irish Academy: Archaeology, Culture, History, Literature*, Vol.104C No.3, 2004, pp.57–80: 69.
35. Geissel, *A Road on the Long Ridge*, p.59.
36. Whitaker, Jane, '2014:291 - PALLASBOY, Toar Bog, Westmeath', *Database of Irish Excavation Reports*, 2014. Available at excavations.ie/report/2014/Westmeath/0024423/.
37. Dungan, *Land Is All That Matters*, p.220.
38. Kirwan, Richard, *If Maps Could Speak* (Dublin: Londubh Books, 2010), p.22.
39. Dungan, *Land Is All That Matters*, p.228.
40. Kirwan, *If Maps Could Speak*, p.29.
41. Colby, Thomas, *Ordnance Survey of the County of Londonderry* (Dublin: Hodges and Smith, 1837), p.7.
42. Porter, Catherine and Lilley, Keith, 'The story of the first all-Ireland mapping survey 200 years ago', RTÉ, 2025. Available at: www.rte.ie/brainstorm/2025/0613/1455340-first-ordnance-survey-maps-ireland-geography-townlands-place-names/.
43. Kirwan, *If Maps Could Speak*, p.27.
44. Smith, Gillian, 'An Eye on the Survey', *History Ireland*, n.d. Available at: www.historyireland.com/an-eye-on-the-survey/.
45. Friel, Brian, *Translations* (London: Faber and Faber, 1981), p.40.
46. Dungan, *Land Is All That Matters*, p.226.
47. Andrews, J. H., *A Paper Landscape: The Ordnance Survey in Nineteenth-Century Ireland*, 2nd edition (Dublin: Four Courts Press, 2001), p.119.
48. Dungan, *Land Is All That Matters*, p.224.
49. Andrews, *A Paper Landscape*, p.122.

50. Colby, Thomas, *Ordnance Survey of the County of Londonderry* (Dublin: Hodges and Smith, 1837), p.8.
51. O'Donovan, John, 'Ordnance Survey Letters of Galway'. Available at: www.places.webworld.org/letters/a18381003.html.
52. de Valéra, Ruaidhrí, 'Seán Ó Donnabháin Agus a Lucht Cúnta', in *The Journal of the Royal Society of Antiquaries of Ireland*, Vol.79 No.1/2, 1949, pp.146–159: 156.
53. Geissel, *A Road on the Long Ridge*, p.vi.
54. O'Flanaghan, Michael (ed.), *Letters Containing Information Relative to the Antiquities of the Counties of Armagh and Monaghan. Collected During the Progress of the Ordnance Survey in 1835* (Bray: 1927), p.50.
55. McWilliams, Patrick S., 'Reactions to the Ordnance Survey: A Window on Prefamine Ireland', in *New Hibernia Review/Iris Éireannach Nua*, Vol.13 No.1, 2009, pp.51–72: 59.
56. Robinson, Tim, *Setting Foot on the Shores of Connemara* (Dublin: Lilliput, 1996) p.160.
57. O'Donovan, John, 'Ordnance Survey Letter/s for County Offaly (King's County), Vol.1 No.12' (Dublin: Royal Irish Academy, 2024). Available at: https://doi.org/10.7486/DRI.n2979t384.
58. O'Donovan, John et al., 'Ordnance Survey Letters: Westmeath Vol.1' (Dublin: Royal Irish Academy, 2008), pp.370–371.
59. Ibid., p.425.
60. Borges, Jorge Luis, 'On Exactitude in Science', in *Collected Fictions*, translated by Andrew Hurley (London: Penguin, 1999).

Chapter 7 Exodus

1. Douglass, Frederick, 'Frederick Douglass to William Lloyd Garrison, February 26, 1846', The Frederick Douglass Papers Project. Available at: www.frederickdouglasspapersproject.com/item/4670.
2. Ó Gráda, Cormac, 'The Population of Ireland 1700–1900: A Survey', in *Annales de Démographie Historique*, 1979, pp.281–99: 283.
3. Miller, Kirby A., *Emigrants and Exiles: Ireland and the Irish Exodus to North America* (New York: Oxford University Press, 1985), p.14.
4. McMahon, Cian T., *The Coffin Ship: Life and Death at Sea during the Great Irish Famine* (New York: New York University Press, 2021), p.3.
5. Aalen, F. H. A., Whelan, Kevin and Stout, Matthew (eds.), *Atlas of the Irish Rural Landscape* (Cork: Cork University Press, 1997), p.87.
6. Ibid., p.81–83.
7. Ibid., p.88.

8. Woodham-Smith, Cecil, *The Great Hunger: Ireland 1845–1849* (London: Penguin, 1992), p.40.
9. Ibid., p.185.
10. Ibid., p.171.
11. Kelly, John, *The Graves Are Walking: The History of the Great Irish Famine* (London: Faber and Faber, 2012), p.210.
12. Woodham-Smith, *The Great Hunger*, p.165.
13. Lindsay, Claire, *Contemporary Travel Writing of Latin America* (Abingdon: Routledge, 2010), p.99.
14. 'Eviction of the Tenants in Ireland', in *The Illustrated London News*, 16 December 1848, p.380.
15. Aalen et al., *Atlas of the Irish Rural Landscape*, p.90.
16. *The Census of Ireland for the Year 1851 Part 1* (Dublin: Alexander Thom, 1852), p.275, p.285.
17. McMahon, *The Coffin Ship*, p.4.
18. O'Riordan, Ann, *East Galway Agrarian Agitation and the Burning of Ballydugan House, 1922* (Dublin: Four Courts Press, 2015), p.21.
19. McMahon, *The Coffin Ship*, p.285.
20. Ibid., p.30.
21. Woodham-Smith, *The Great Famine*, p.325.
22. Ibid., p.270.
23. Kelly, *The Graves Are Walking*, p.256.
24. Woodham-Smith, *The Great Famine*, p.271.
25. McMahon, *The Coffin Ship*, p.69.
26. MKO, 'Lisclogher West Bog, Co. Westmeath, Decommissioning and Rehabilitation Plan 2023' (Galway: MKO, 2023).
27. Dungan, Myles, *Land Is All That Matters: The Struggle That Shaped Irish History* (London: Head of Zeus, 2024), p.269.
28. Ibid., p.280.
29. Ritchie, Gayle, '"This city will kill me": Churchill, the maggot saga, and how the cigar-puffing statesman came to despise Dundee', in *The Courier*, 11 May 2020. Available at: www.thecourier.co.uk/fp/past-times/1315993/this-city-will-kill-me-churchill-the-maggot-saga-and-how-the-cigar-puffing-statesman-came-to-despise-dundee/.

Chapter 8 Road Frontage

1. Cited in O'Toole, Fintan, *We Don't Know Ourselves: A Personal History of Ireland Since 1958* (London: Head of Zeus, 2021), p.262.

2. Evers, Liz, 'Fitzsimons, Jack', *Dictionary of Irish Biography*, 2022. Available at: www.dib.ie/biography/fitzsimons-jack-a10217.
3. O'Toole, *We Don't Know Ourselves*, p.263.
4. Evers, 'Fitzsimons, Jack'.
5. Cited in Robinson, Tim, *Connemara: A Little Gaelic Kingdom* (Dublin: Penguin Ireland, 2011), p.311.
6. O'Riordan, Ann, *East Galway Agrarian Agitation and the Burning of Ballydugan House, 1922* (Dublin: Four Courts Press, 2015), p.21.
7. Dungan, Myles, *Land Is All That Matters: The Struggle That Shaped Irish History* (London: Head of Zeus, 2024), p.330.
8. Aalen, F. H. A., Whelan, Kevin and Stout, Matthew (eds.), *Atlas of the Irish Rural Landscape* (Cork: Cork University Press, 1997), p.91.
9. Dungan, *Land Is All That Matters*, p.441.
10. Gibney, John, *A Short History of Ireland 1500–2000* (New Haven: Yale University Press, 2017), p.162.
11. Moore, George, *Parnell and His Island* (London: Swan Sonnenschein, Lowry & Co., 1887), pp.230–231.
12. Pellew, George, *In Castle and Cabin: Or, Talks in Ireland in 1887* (New York: The Knickerbocker Press, 1888), pp.80–89.
13. Aalen et al., *Atlas of the Irish Rural Landscape*, p.95.
14. Ibid., pp.92–94.
15. Dungan, *Land Is All That Matters*, p.439.
16. Aalen et al., *Atlas of the Irish Rural Landscape*, p.95.
17. Miller, Kirby A., *Emigrants and Exiles: Ireland and the Irish Exodus to North America* (New York: Oxford University Press, 1985), p.435.
18. Hurlbert, William Henry, *Ireland under Coercion: The Diary of an American*, Vol.2 (Edinburgh: David Douglass, 1888), p.257.
19. McCullough, Joseph, *A Pocket History of Ireland* (Dublin: Gill & Macmillan, 2010), p.171.
20. Electronic Irish Statute Book, 'Irish Land Act, 1903'. Available at www.irishstatutebook.ie/eli/1903/act/37/enacted/en/print.html.
21. O'Riordan, *East Galway Agrarian Agitation and the Burning of Ballydugan House*, p.9.
22. Dooley, Terence, *Burning the Big House: The Story of the Irish Country House in a Time of War and Revolution* (New Haven: Yale University Press, 2022).
23. O'Riordan, *East Galway Agrarian Agitation and the Burning of Ballydugan House*, p.51.

24. Curtis, L. Perry Jr, *The Depiction of Eviction in Ireland 1845–1910* (Dublin: University College Dublin Press, 2011), pp.207–215.
25. *The Freeman's Journal*, 'An Extraordinary Eviction in County Louth', 7 August 1881, pp.7–8.
26. Dillon, Paul and McDonnell, Ciara, 'Collection List No.90: Louth Papers', National Library of Ireland, p.7.
27. Robinson, *Connemara: A Little Gaelic Kingdom*, p.311.
28. Cited in O'Toole, *We Don't Know Ourselves*, p.265.
29. Dooley, Terence, 'Land and Politics in Independent Ireland, 1923-48: The Case for Reappraisal', *Irish Historical Studies*, Vol.34 No.134, 2004, pp.175–97: 183.
30. Ibid., p.183.
31. Dungan, *Land Is All That Matters*, p.542.
32. Ibid., p.545.
33. Evers, 'Fitzsimons, Jack'.
34. Dooley, 'Land and Politics in Independent Ireland', p.184.
35. Reilly, Ciaran, 'Unveiling the Land Commission: A rare glimpse into the work of an inspector and the demise of an institution', *Irish Independent*, 8 August 2023. Available at: www.independent.ie/farming/rural-life/unveiling-the-land-commission-a-rare-glimpse-into-the-work-of-an-inspector-and-the-demise-of-an-institution/a1110060957.html.
36. Dungan, *Land Is All That Matters*, p.539.
37. Ibid., p.537.
38. Evers, 'Fitzsimons, Jack'.
39. Bishop, Hilary and Hurley, Michael, 'Mapping Through Memory: The Location and Nature of Mass Paths in Ireland', in *Irish Geography*, Vol.55 No.1, 2022, pp.:21–43.
40. Ibid.
41. Stearn, Jonathan, 'A Right of Way', in *History Ireland*, Vol.22 No.5. Available at: www.historyireland.com/a-right-of-way/.

Chapter 9 Partitions

1. Kinsella, Thomas (trans.), *The Táin: From the Irish Epic Táin Bó Cuailnge* (Oxford: Oxford University Press, 1970), p.282.
2. Ibid., p. 63–65.
3. Gosling, Paul, 'The Route of *Táin Bó Cúailnge* in Counties Westmeath and Meath', in *Archaeology Ireland: Heritage Guide No.86*, 2019, p.1.
4. Kinsella, *The Táin*, p.69.

5. Ibid., p.71.
6. Ibid., p.102.
7. Gosling, Paul, 'The Route of *Táin Bó Cúailnge* in County Louth', in *Archaeology Ireland: Heritage Guide No.69*, 2015, p.3.
8. Pratt, Mary Louise, *Imperial Eyes: Travel Writing and Transculturation*, 2nd edition (Abingdon: Routledge, 2008), pp. 197–198.
9. Ibid., p.213.
10. Price, Linda and Simpson, Mark, 'The Trouble with Accessing the Countryside in Northern Ireland: A Comparison with Great Britain', in *Environmental Law Review*, Vol.19 No.3, 2017, pp.183–200. https://doi.org/10.1177/1461452917720632.
11. 'Where you can walk in England and Wales', The Ramblers Association, 2015. Available at: www.ramblers.org.uk/go-walking-hub/where-you-can-walk-england-and-wales.
12. Price and Simpson, 'The Trouble with Accessing the Countryside in Northern Ireland'.
13. Macauley, Conor, 'Mourne Mountains: Who owns the County Down mountains?', BBC, 26 August 2019. Available at: www.bbc.co.uk/news/uk-northern-ireland-49437479.

Chapter 10 The Bull and the Field

1. Access to the Countryside Bill 2013: Explanatory Memorandum, p1.
2. Access to the Countryside Bill 2013, p.5.
3. Robinson, Tim, *Connemara: The Last Pool of Darkness* (Dublin: Penguin Ireland, 2008), p.290.
4. Cullen, Róisín, 'Greenway plans will make land unviable, farmers warn', RTÉ, 12 November 2025. Available at: www.rte.ie/news/regional/2025/1112/1543547-greenways-protest/.
5. Neilan, Paul, 'Galway farmer granted permission to challenge Greenway purchase decision "splitting" his farm', in *The Irish Times*, 23 July 2025. Available at: www.irishtimes.com/crime-law/courts/2025/07/23/galway-farmer-granted-permission-to-challenge-greenway-purchase-decision-splitting-his-farm/
6. Houses of the Oireachtas, 'Joint Committee on Transport debate – Wednesday, 12 Nov 2025'. Available online at: www.oireachtas.ie/en/debates/debate/joint_committee_on_transport/2025-11-12/3/.
7. Houses of the Oireachtas, 'Dáil Éireann debate - Friday, 14 Jun 2013'. Available at: www.oireachtas.ie/en/debates/debate/dail/2013-06-14/2/.

8. McLachlan, Noel, 'Michael Davitt', *Dictionary of Irish Biography*, 2009. Available at: www.dib.ie/biography/davitt-michael-a2437.

Chapter 11 A Sense of an Ending

1. Savage-Armstrong, G. F., *A Genealogical History of the Savage Family in Ulster* (London: The Chiswick Press, 1906), p.91.
2. Aalen, F. H. A., Whelan, Kevin and Stout, Matthew (eds.), *Atlas of the Irish Rural Landscape* (Cork: Cork University Press, 1997), p.281.
3. McCormick, Finbar, 'Struell Wells: Pagan past and Christian present', in *The Journal of the Royal Society of Antiquaries in Ireland*, Vol.139, 2009, pp.54–62: 54.
4. Ibid., p.54.
5. Ibid., p.56.

Picture Credits

All images belong to the author unless listed below:

p.61 National Library of Ireland MS G 11 / Wikimedia Commons
p.99 A plate from *The Image of Irelande*, by John Derricke (1581) / Wikimedia Commons
p.131 A plate from *The Image of Irelande*, by John Derricke (1581) / Wikimedia Commons
p.144 CC0 1.0 Digital Repository of Ireland / Wikimedia Commons
p.188 Leventhal Maps / Wikimedia Commons
p.226 The Print Collector / Alamy
p.246 History Collection 2016 / Alamy

Acknowledgements

First thanks, as always, must go to Robert Dudley for his efforts and advocacy with this and other books over the years. I am very lucky to have, in Richard Milbank at Head of Zeus, an editor who is himself an enthusiastic follower of footpaths. His encouraging response to the very first mention of the idea gave me the essential impetus to make a start, and our various energetic conversations about countryside access have kept me moving along. Also at Head of Zeus, thanks to Iain MacGregor for stepping into the breach, and to Megan Harris for all the practical help. And very special thanks to Matt Johnson for reading the manuscript with an artist's eye and bringing fine details from the text into another beautiful cover design.

I am very grateful for the existence of Keep Ireland Open – knowing that I'm not the only person concerned about these issues is always a relief! Thanks to Robert Dowds and the rest of the committee for their input and support, and, much more importantly, for all their work on access issues over the years. Anyone interested in protecting and improving public access to the Irish landscape should join the organisation: www.keepirelandopen.org. Thanks, too, to Micheal Guerin and Liam O'Mahony for sharing their stories from the long battle for the Great Southern Trail. They were working on this before anyone knew what a 'greenway' was, and without the dedication of the original volunteers there'd be no greenway in Limerick and north Kerry today.

Many thanks to my colleagues on the Writing and Literature programme and the MA in Creative Practice at ATU Sligo. I'm hugely grateful to be part of such a dedicated team of creative people and to know of all the other writing and creating that goes on. Thanks, too, to my students for reassuring me that the human-written word has a future. Our in-class debates around the ethics of nonfiction and the writing of place, space and culture have helped me figure out a few conundrums of my own. Also at ATU Sligo, I'm very grateful to Marion Dowd for giving me an invaluable reading list, and for gently nudging me onto the right track where I've trespassed on archaeological territory.

Finally and most importantly, thank you always to Cara Glynn for bringing me to this land and for helping me to find the paths that run through it.

Index

A

A Portrait of the Artist as a Young Man (Joyce), 231
A Tour of Ireland (Twiss), 173
A View of the Present State of Ireland (Spenser), 133, 177
Abbeyfeale Station, 45–47, 69
access land in England and Wales, 9
Access to the Countryside (private members bill), 296–297, 304
Access to the Countryside (Northern Ireland) Order 1983, 285
Act for Kingly Title, 118
Act for the Settlement of Ireland 1652, 146
  Ballycowan, 161
Act of Union 1800, 185–186
Act to prevent the further Growth of Popery 1704, 164
adverse possession, 47
affective identification, 211
afforestation
  see also deforestation
  postglacial, 99–100
  twentieth century, 101
Allemansrätten (Scandinavia), 10–11, 66
an Blascaod Mór (Great Blasket Island), 22
An Breisleach Mór (The Great Carnage), 272
an slíab coitchenn (the common mountain), 60
Andy (bicycle hire), 67, 68
Anglican Church of Ireland
  disestablishment, 240
  and tithes, 172
Anglicisation of Irish names, 192–193
Anglo-Irish Ascendency, 165
Ann, Caherhurly, 90
Annals of the Four Masters (Franciscan monks), 179
Annals of the Four Masters (Franciscan monks)
  translation, 191
annual closure of paths, 128
Archangel Michael statue, Ballinageragh, 53
Ardnacrusha, 82–83
arson, 248–252
ash dieback, 90, 128–129
Aston, Arthur, 137
Athenry to Tuam railway, 74
Athlone to Mullingar Cycleway, 67
Avondale House, 304
Axtell, Daniel, 138

B

B—family, 244–245
Back Lane Parliament, 49
Ballinageragh, 53
Ballycowan, 161–162
Ballysheil, 145, 148, 149
barmaid in hot-pink tee-shirt, 152
Barrahaurin, 243, 245–246
Bartinney, Cornwall, 10
Bath, John, 126
battle of Aughrim, 162, 256
battle of Boyne, 162, 256
Beara-Breifne Way, 127
bear's knee joint, 34–35, 93, 99
Beranger, Gabriel (Dutch artist), 144, 175–176
Bernas Bó Cuailnge, 275
Bishop of Kildare, 118
Black and Tans, 231
blanket bogs, 100
Blasket Archipelago, 23
bóaire (cowman), 62
boat building with horse skins, 123
bodach, 194–195
Bodyke eviction, 254
bogs, 154–158
bóithrín (little cow track), 70
Bonnell, Captain Samuel, 161–162
Book of Leinster, 272
Book of the O'Sheils, 149
booley hut as shelter, 121
booleying, 100–101
Boote, Rosie, 223
boots from horse hides, 124–125
Bord na Móna, 156
border between the Republic of Ireland and the United Kingdom, 278–279
boreen (narrow rural road), 70
Borge, Jorge Luis, 194
Boston Journal, 240
bóthar (cow track), 70
Bouvier, Nicolas, on footpaths, 7–8
boycotting, 242–245
Boyne Greenway, 67
Bran (Mount Brandon), 37
Brehon Laws, 62–64
  roadway categories, 70–71
  trespass by animals, 63–64
breitheamh (brehons), 62, 69
Brian Boru, 85–86
bride to be, 283
bronze shoes, 199, 211, 212
Bryan, on bike, 152
bull fight, 272–274
Bull McCabe, 299–300, 305
bulls and public footpaths, 59
Bungalow Bliss (Fitzsimons), 236–238
bungalows, 257–258
Burke, Michael Henry, 251–252
Burke, Ulick, 138, 139
Burr Point, 16
Burren, the, private land, 1–3, 7
Burroughs, John
  on footpaths, 8, 11
Butler, Thomas, Earl of Omand, 122
Butler, William, 118

C

caithchi (trespass), 63
Callaghan family, 243
Camino de Santiago (Spain), 182, 302
cannibalism, stories of, 133–134
Cara (partner), 68, 78, 284
  about, 3
  Under the Hawthorn Tree, 211
  teaching, 4
Carden, Ruth, 33
Caribbean, Irish shipped to, 137–138, 146
Carraig na Sasanach (The English Rock), 22
Carranstown Bog, 215
Carroll, Margaret, 228

Carroll, Michael, 228
casán (footpath), 70
Casán na nAsal (the Donkey's Path), 30
Cassidy, Cross, 152
Castle Ward, 311–312
Castleconnell, 80
Catholic church and Penal Laws, 163
Catholic Herald, 230
Catholics excluded from land ownership, 54
cattle, 206–207
cattle ranches, 258
Celtic Rainforest, 99
charcoal, 100
Charles I, 136
Chieregati, Francesco, 312
Churchill, Winston, 231
churls, 195
*Cill Dalu*a (Dalua's Church), 85
cillíní, 92–94
Civil Survey 1654, 147
clachans, 226, 247
Clermont Cairn, 275–278
Clermont Park, 275
clientship as bond between classes, 62
climate change, 100
Clochafarmore menhir, 269, 273
Clonarf, Battle of, 86
Clonmacnoise, 94, 272
coffin ships, 210, 218, 219
Coillte (forestry enterprise), 101–107
Colby, Thomas Frederick, 186–187, 224
Collins, Michael, 152
Colmcille, 55
colonialism, 277
Commission for Bogs 1810, 155
common waste, 60
commoners, 62
compensation
  culture in first millennium CE, 63
  for sports injuries, 71
Confederate Association, 136
Congested Districts Board (CDB)
  formed 1891, 247
  dissolved 1923, 258
Congo, 204
Conlon-McKenna, Marita, 211
Conn of the Hundred Battles, 179–180
Connacht army, 273–275
Connacht as open air prison, 146–147
Connolly, Catherine, 229
Connolly, James, 229, 304–305
Coole House, 252
Coote, Charles, 162
Córas Iompair Éireann (CIÉ), 46
Corlea bog road, 28
Cornish, Jack, 28
Cosán na Naomh (the Saint's Road), 23, 36–37
cottiers, 62, 171
countryside access legislation
  England, 10
  Ireland, 10
  Wales, 10
Countryside and Rights of Way Act 2000 (England and Wales), 10, 285, 296, 317
COVID-19, 13, 96, 142
Crawley, Lawrence, 254–255, 257
Croagh Patrick, 6, 36
Cromwell, Oliver, 137–139
Cromwellian Settlement, 17, 148
  Ballycowan, 11–162
  Ballysheil, 145
  and Down Survey, 187–189
  plan to remove Catholic landowners, 146
  post-Cromwell years, 161
Cromwell's Island, 137, 138
cross-country routes, formation, 180
Crown estate, open access, 9

Cúchulainn, 272, 273
Cunningham's cafe, 203–204
Curraghmore plank causeway, 28
Currie, Emer, 298
Cusack, Thomas, 311

D

Daily Express, 255
Dáire, 273
Dál Cais *túath,* 85
Dalua, 85
Daly, Jack, 193
Davitt, Michael, 241, 304
dedication (legal term), 73–74
Definitive Map of England, 50, 73
deforestation, 99–100
 see also afforestation
demesnes
 Durrow, 55
 Grangemore, 213
 Lisrenny, 249
 lost, 249–257
Dempsey, Michael, 251
Derricke, John, 99
Derry (prefix), 98
Derryoober Bog, 104
designated access land (England, Wales), 9
desire lines, 27
Desmond Rebellion, 119, 132
Desmonds of Munster, 119
 territories confiscated, 134
Dingle Peninsula, 23
Dingle Town, 26
Dingle Way, 23
dírann úas cách (undivided land above all), 60
dispossessions
 and colonialism, 277
 Cromwell's plan, 146, 162
 plantation process, 136
 Protestant Anglo-Irish Ascendancy, 10
 Quarter- Acre Clause, 217
 and rising population, 171
distrainment, 63
doing the rounds, 53
donkeys, 24–25
Donkey's Path, 30
Donn Cuailnge, 272, 273
Donoughmore, 244, 245
Dooley, Terence, 251
Doran, Linda, 70, 180
Douglass, Frederick, 205, 217
Dowd, Marion, 33, 34, 93
Dowds, Robert, 49, 50, 295, 297, 302–306
Down Survey, 147, 187–189
Drewstown, 222
Drogheda massacre, 137–138
Dublin poverty, 206
*Dún Mór (*Dunmore Head), 16, 21
Dundee and District Catholic Yearbook, 230
Dungan, Myles, 260
Dunnet Head, 16
Durrow well, 55

E

Early Irish Farming (Kelly), 64–65
Echtge Uathach, 98
Edward VI, 132
Eighth Amendment, 75, 197
Eiscir Riada see Esker Riada
Electricity Supply Board, 83
Elizabeth I, 119
 death of, 125
Elstob, Mark, 175
emigration, 218–220
 landlord assisted, 219
enclosures, 172
Encumbered Estates Act 1849, 224, 240, 248, 286
English settlers, 130

Enniskerry and Bray, 50
entailment, 223, 224
Esker Riada, 154, 179–181
eskers, 154
European Union, 278
evictions, 17, 97, 209
  Encumbered Estates Act, 240
  Galway, 246
  granite plaque, 233–234
  Lawrence Crawley, 254–256
  by strong farmers, 207

F

fairy forts, 92
famine, 208–212, 215–217
Fergus Lusca Mac Ruidi, 98
feudalism, 60
Fiji man, 88–89
Filgate family, 249
fines
  payment in livestock, 63
  payment in silver, 63, 71
  for trespass by animals, 63–64
Finglas, Lady Jane, 161
Finnbennach, 273
fitness, 271
Fitzsimons, Annie, 236
Fitzsimons, Jack, 235–236, 258
Flight of the Earls, 125
flotsam and jetsam ownership, 59
Flynn, James Christopher, 244
fogail (trespass), 63
footpaths, 1–18
  see also Scotland; Sweden
  and case law, 73
  and colonialism, 278
  Cornwall, 72
  in England, 11–12
  Greystones to Bray, 72–73
  historic, 13–15
  and Keep Ireland Open, 295–300
  and legislation, 71
  in literature, 12
  lost, 263–266
  made and maintained by walking, 27–35, 70–71
  Northern Ireland, 286
  in Wales, 11–12
Forestry Act 1928, 102
Foster family, 253
Fox family, 149
fox hunting, 241–242
free market economy and cash, 209
Friel, Brian, 189
Friends of the Cliff Path, 72

G

Gallarus Oratory, 31–32
Garrison, William Lloyd, 205
gavelkind, 164, 223
GeoHive website, 13–14
German man, 106–107
German Town, 82
German woman, 95
glaciers, 153–155
Glencree Valley, track blocked, 6
Glyde Court, 252–253
Gobnait, saint of the bees, 122
Golden Vale, Tipperary, 122
Grand Canal, 143–144
  around bogs, 155
Grangemore, 212–214, 215–216
Granny Catherine, 231
Gravelstown, 236
The Great Carnage, 272
Great Southern Trail, 45–48
Great Southern Trail Action Group, 46–48
Great Trigonometrical Survey of India, 187
Great Western Greenway, 67
greenways, 67–69, 202–203
  Dublin to Galway, 130, 144
  Galway to Clifden, 301–302

land grabbing, 242
Newry Ship Canal, 279
proposals, 301–302
Rathkeale–Listowel, 51
Gregory, Lady Augusta, 217
Gregory, William, 216–217
Greystones to Bray footpath, 72
Griffith, Richard, 189
Grosse Survey 1653, 147
Guerin, Michael, 48, 71–72

H

Halley, Bridget, 229, 232, 317
Halley, Catherine McGhee, 229
Halley, James, 229, 232
Halley, Mary, 229, 232
Hannigan, Des (father), 316–318, 321
Hannigan, M.T., 231, 317
Hannigan, Tim (author)
about, 3, 352
ancestry, 227–232, 281–284
walking when young, 5
hares, 158–160
Harris, Simon, 72
Headfort, 222
Heaney, Seamus, 31, 156, 157–158, 272
hedge schools, 189, 190
Heeley, family, 229
Heeley, Pauline, 230
hen harriers, 105
Henry II, 116
Henry VIII, 117
Herbert, Edward, 162
Herbert, Sir Jasper, 161
High Court
see also Supreme Court
woman fell from own horse, 65
woman grazed her knee on a boardwalk, 65
Hillaby, John, 15–16
Home Rule, 240, 245
kill with kindness, 246, 248, 304
horse, execution of by Whiteboys, 172
Housing (Miscellaneous Provisions) Act, 66
human presence in Ireland, 32–35
Hurlbert, William Henry, 248
hurling, 117, 204, 214, 283
Hymany Way, 127, 129

I

idiots, 272
In Castle and Cabin: Or, Talks in Ireland in 1887 (Pellew), 243
In Search of England (Morton), 80
incest, stories of, 134
Indonesia flashback, 51
Inishnabro, 22
Inishvickillane, 22
innmark (Norway), 10–11
IRA, 213
Ireton, Henry, 138
Irish Farmers' Association (IFA), 296, 297
Irish Literary Revival, 217
Irish Poor Law Extension Act 1847, 216
Irish Times, 237
Irish Town, 82
Irish War of Independence, 251
iron-smelting, 100

J

James I, 125
James II, 162, 256
Java flashback, 43
Jeanneret, Charles-Édouard (Le Corbusier), 25, 26
Jersey, 67
John Lackland, 116
John O'Groats, 16
Johnston, Eileen, 230

Journey Through Britain (Hillaby), 15–16
Judge family, 149
Judge, Martha, 149
Judge, Samuel, 149
Judy (campaigner), 50, 73

K

Kat, 312
Keane, John B., 68, 299
Keep Ireland Open, 11, 48–49, 71–72, 79, 295–300
  Coillte, 103–104
Kelly, Fergus, 64
Kerry, Bishop of, 37
Kickham, Charles, 13
Kilucan, 204
King Ailill, 273–275
King's County, 132, 161
kings, lords, and commoners, 62
Knocknagow, or The Homes of Tipperary (Kickham), 13

L

labourers
  and boycotts, 244
  Caribbean, 146
  and cattle, 206
  damming the Shannon, 82
  English Parliamentary rule, 147
  during famine, 209–210
  and Land Wars, 248
  landless, 136
  love of Ireland, 248
  and peasantry, 171
  spailpíni, 220
  and wealthy owners, 241
lámraite (byroad), 70
land
  allocations by Land Commission, 258–261
  control of
    England, 9
    Ireland, 10
  ownership, 241
Land Commission, 258–260
Land Law Act 1881, 242
Land League, 241, 245
  British response, 246
  tactic during evictions, 254
land reform
  dispossessions, 10
  footpaths, 266
  granite plaque, 233–234
  Land War, 241
  Lawrence Crawley, 254
Land Reform Act (Scotland), 66
land reforms
  Ireland, 10
Land Wars against high rents, 241–257
landowner liability limit, 65
landowner resistance, 47–48, 51
Land's End, 16
Larcom, Thomas, 187, 190
  reprimands O'Donovan, 191
Last Glacial Period, 32–34
Lateevemore, 26
Lateevemore ridge, 36
Lawler, Tom, 55
Le Corbusier, 24, 25, 110
Le Fanu, Sheriden, 12–13
Lebor na hUidre (Book of the Dun Cow), 271–272
Leeson, Liam, 152
legal manuscripts, 62–63
Lilliput, 184
Limerick, 78–79
  railway footbridge no right of way, 79
Limerick County Council, 46
Lisclogher, 221
Lisrenny demesne, 249
Lithgow, William, 177

litigation
  countryside access, 66
  trips and slips, 65
litigious society in first millennium CE, 63
the Lizard, 16
Londonderry, 135
longdogs, 215
Longfield, Mrs, 243
Lord of Laois, 99
Lord's Prayer, 58
Lordship of Ireland, 117
Lough Derg Way, 83–84
Louth, Lord, 254
Lughaidh, 85
Lughnasa pagan festival, 37

M

MacCarthy clan, 122
MacCoghlan clan, 148
MacEgan, Cairbre, 124
MacEgan clan, 123–124
MacEgan, Donnchadh, 124
Machado, Antonio, 29
MacNeill, Máire, 37
Magan, Manchán, 300–301
Mahon, Denis, 218–219
  assassination, 219, 224
Mahon, John, 219
maintenance
  client farmer obligations, 70
  of footpaths, 70
Malby, Henry, 124
man with blue tee-shirt and headphones, 212–213, 281
man with cycle and fishing rod, 130
man with Massey Ferguson, 96
maps of Ireland, 14
Martin, Violet Florence, 12
mass rocks on private land, 163–164
Matthews, Steven, 79
McBride, Ann, 227
McBride, Margaret, 228
McCarthy, John, 243, 244–245
McCarthy, Thomas, 56
McDonald, Frank, 237
McGilligan, Patrick, 83
McLaughlin, Thomas, 81–82
McMahon, Cian T., 211
McVeagh family, 223
menhir, 269
meracht a nuídlechais (madness of her newly-calved state), 64
merlins, 105
Merryn (daughter), 263
migration
  English and Scots to Ireland, 135–136
  Spanish to South America, 135
Mike, 87
Molua, 85
monarch-of-all-I-survey scene, 276
Monivea, 7
Morton, H.V., 80–82, 84, 160, 177
Mount Brandon, 26, 36–37
Mount Sandel, 33
mountain bikers, 200–203, 265, 302
Mourne Wall, 292, 293
Mournes, 289, 292
Mug Nuadat, 180
Mullinger, 218
  workhouse, 218
murder
  and land, 300
  of primary school teacher, 178
  by UDR and Red Hand Commando, 270
Murreagh, 26
Murtagh, Peter, 72

N

na gCath, Seán, 125
naked corn grinders, 174, 176

Narrative of the Life of Frederick Douglass, an American Slave (Douglass), 205
National Famine Way, 199 pic, 205, 211
National Greenway Action Association, 302
National Parks and Access to the Countryside Act 1949 (England), 10, 71, 266, 285
National Trust, 289
nationalisation of land, 305
Nazism, 80–81
Northern Ireland water board, 289
nude bathing, 313

O

Ó Dálaigh, Domhnall, 126
Ó Maolmhuaidh clan, 161
Occupiers' Liability Act 1995, 65–66, 111
O'Conor, Thomas, 191–192
O'Donovan, John, 190–192
ogham, 23
O'Mahony, Liam, 47
*On Exactitude in Science (*Borge), 194
one-room cabin, 240
O'Neill, Hugh, 119, 121
  lands siezed, 135
  submits to English crown, 125
Ordnance Survey
  benchmarks, 204
  Dingle map, 37
  Durrow visit, 55
  mapping of Ireland, 186–194
Ordnance Survey Ireland, 13
O'Riordan, Ann, 252
O'Rourke, Brian Oge, 125
O'Sheil family, 148–149
O'Sullivan Beare, Dermot, 121
O'Sullivan Beare, Donal Cam, 149
  Beara-Breifne Way, 127
  Count of Berehaven, 126
  description of portrait, 126
  escape to spain, 125–126
  murder, 126
  primogeniture in aristocratic title, 120
  resistance and flight, 116, 120–121, 125
O'Sullivan Beare, Philip, 121, 124
O'Sullivan, Eoin, 120
O'Toole, Fintan, 6
Otway, Randal Percy, 257
Oxford Companion to Archaeology, 28

P

Pack-Donkey's Way, 25, 110
Paddy Irishman jokes, 177
pain of road walking, 41, 44, 56–57
the Pale, 117
paludification, 154–155
Paris, human settlement, 25
Parnell, Charles Stewart, 241, 304
Parteen Dam, 85
partition, 250–251, 278
paths *see* footpaths
pattern day at Lixnaw, 55–56
peat extraction, 150, 153
pedestrians killed on roads, 303
Pellew, George, 239–240, 242–246
  death, 246
Penal Laws, 163, 240
permissive access, 103–104
Petty, William, 147, 187
pharmacy student, 143
Philip III, 126
Phoenix Park, 303
Phytophthora infestans (potato blight), 208
pine marten, 221
Plague of Justinian, 92

plank walkways, 28
plantations, 17, 131–139
Plunkett
  family, 256–257
  Oliver, 257
population
  1851 census, 217–218
  growth, 206–209
post-chaise, 170
potato ridges, 211–212
potatoes, 207–212
  blight, 208–212
Pratt, Mary Louise, 276
Price, Linda, 286
private dwellings and access rights, 66
Proleek Dolmen, 270
Property Defence Association, 254
Protestant elite, 174–175
Protestant Reformation, 118
  hostility to, 118–119
  Irish as barbarous and lazy, 131
Proverbs 22:6, 254
public footpath sign, 287
public footpaths
  England and Wales, 9
Punch, 177

Q

Quarter Acre Clause, 17, 217, 261
Queen Medb, 273–275
Queen Sadhbh, 172
Queen's County, 132
Quinn, Ruairi, 295

R

Raharney, 204
Rahinnane, 26
rail network in 1920s, 67
Raleigh, Walter, 134
Rathkeale, 69, 74, 75–76
Rathkeale–Listowel Greenway, 51, 67, 69, 70
Ray, Celeste, 54
Red Hand Commando, 270
red squirrel with baby, 179
rent strikes, 241
resistance against English, 115–139
Ridgeway (England), 28
right to roam in England, 10, 50, 59–60
rights of way in history, 59
rights of way in Ireland, 4–6
  Northern Ireland, 285
ringforts, 62, 91–92, 194–195, 264
River of Two Milk Cows, 98
road types, 70–71
Robinson, Tim, 192, 257, 300, 305
Róise Senara (daughter), 4, 68, 78, 284, 305
Roman Catholic Relief Act 1829, 163–164
Rotherham family, 223
rout (road), 70
Royal Canal, 200
Ruaidhrí Óg Ó Mórdha, 99
rundale system, 207
Rutherglen (Scotland), 228

S

Saints' Way, Cornwall, 36
Samuel Beckett lookalike, 88–89
Sands, Bobby, 308
Scotland, access to countryside, 11
Second Vatican Council, 93
Senchas Már, 61
serfs, 62
Settlement of Laois and Offaly Act 1556, 132
sex with goat, story of, 176
Shannon, 17, 74, 79–80
Shannon Development, 46
Shannon Electricity Act (1925), 82, 83
  and footpaths, 127

Shannon Hydroelectric Scheme, 82
Shirley, 141–142, 143–144
Shropshire, 50
Siemens-Schuckert, 82
sika deer, 105, 106
Silent Valley Reservoir, 292
Simpson, Mark, 286
Skellig Michael, 26
Slechta, the Hewn Place, 275
Sliabh Eachtaí, 96–100
Slieve Aughty, 96–100
Slieve League, 36
slige, 70
Slighe Asail, 180
Slighe Cualann, 180
Slighe Dala, 180
Slighe Mhór, 180
Slighe Midhluachra, 180
smallholders, 62
society strata in seventh century, 62
soldiers of Cromwellian army, 161
Solnit, Rebecca, 56
Somerville, Edith, 12
Soyer, Alexis, 209
spailpíni (itinerant labourers), 220
Spanish Armada, massacre of survivors, 119
Spanish fleet, 1601, 119–120
Spenser, Edmund, 117
  on Desmond Rebellion, 132–133
  on famished peasants in Munster, 210
Sport Ireland, 127
sporting rights, 250
Spruce plantations, 102
St Brendan the Navigator, 37
St Columbkille's (Rutherglen, Scotland), 228
St Cronan's Church, Tuamgraney, 94
St Flannan Cathedral, 85
St Leger, Sir Anthony, 118
St Malkedar church, 36
St Patrick, 311–312
Stacey, Robin Chapman, 63
Statutes of Kilkenny, 117
Stepney, Herbert Rawson, 55
Stewart and Kincaid agency, 256
stiles, 71, 265–266
stopping the hunt, 241
strata of society, 62
strong farmers, 207, 224, 259
Struell, 312–313
struggle against the foreigners, 115–127
suckling of babies over their shoulders, 174, 177
Supreme Court
  see also High Court
  Glencree Valley, 6
surrender and regrant, 118, 119
Sweden, cultivated land, 11
Sweet Track (Somerset Levels), 28
Swift, Jonathan, 184

T

Tailors' Hall, 49
Tailte Éireann, 13–14
*Táin Bó Cuailnge (*The Cattle Raid of Cooley), 271–275
Tanner, Charles Kearns Deane, 244
Taplin, Kim, 12
Tara, 180
Tawin, 7
Taylour, Lord Geoffrey, 223
Taylour marquesses, 223
Teamhair, five roads leading to, 180–181
tenants
  and Anglo-Irish landlords, 215
  boycotts, 245
  Catholic landowners become, 148
  Church of Ireland disestablishment, 240
  commercial agriculture, 206
  and emigration, 218–219

Encumbered Estates Act, 240
English, 134
and home rule, 304
labourers, 171
landlord class rights, 266
Louth Hall Estate, 255–256
1901 census, 225
redistribution of land to, 10
and rent, 216
Six Counties, 286
tenants (*cont'd*)
strong farmers, 207
Wyndham Land Purchase Act 1903, 246–247
The Coffin Ship (McMahon), 211
The English Path (Taplin), 12
The Fairie Queene (Spenser), 133
The Field (Keane), 299
The Great Hunger (Woodham-Smith), 218
The Hibernian Magazine on Twiss, 174
The House by the Church-Yard (Le Fanu), 12
The Image of Irelande, with a Discoverie of Woodkarne (Derricke), 99
The New York Sun, 240
The Outlaw (Heaney), 272
The Real Charlotte (Somerville), 12
The Schools' Collection of folklore, 195
The Wild Irish Girl (Owenson), 12
Thomas, Des, 230
Thomas, Desmond (Uncle Elephant), 230
Thomas, Michael, 228, 229
Thomas, William, 132
Tighe, Daniel, 211
time immemorial (legal term), 73
Tipperary Vindicator, 217
tithes, 172
Toar Bog, 181
tógraite (curved road), 70
toilet matters, 195–196
Toler, Hector (Earl of Newbury), 55
Tone, Wolf, 49
Topographia Hibernica (Gerald of Wales), 176–177
towerhouses, 148, 165
townlands as basis for taxation, 185–186
Tralee and Dingle Light Railway, 43
Translations (Friel), 189–190
travel writing in Ireland, 167–178
traveller community, 66, 280–281
Travels Through Portugal and Spain in 1772 and 1773 (Twiss), 169
Treaty of Limerick, 162–163
trespass
civil offence, 66
meaning, 58, 63
Trevelyan, Charles Edward, 209–210, 224
Triermore Stud Farm, 222
túatha (petty kingdoms), 62
Tuatha Dé Danann, 98
Turf Development Board, 156
Twiss, Richard, 168–176, 205
chamber pot, 176
criticism of the Irish and the response, 173–175
Tyndale, William, 58

U

UDR, 270
Uí Néill dynasty, 85
unbaptised children, 92–93
unconference, 109–111, 178
Under the Hawthorn Tree (Conlon-McKenna), 211
undertakers, of Desmond territories, 134–135
United Irishmen, 49, 186

V

Valentia Island, 26
Vesalius, Andreas, 149

W

Wales, rights of access, 11–12
walk across Ireland
  Planning, 17–18, 26
  bus journeys, 22
  desire line, 142
  Dunmore Head, 22
  Coumeenoole, 22–23
  Mount Eagle, 24, 29, 30–31
  Ventry–Dunquin road, 29
  Casán na nAsal, 30
  Gallarus, 31
  Kilmalkedar, 36, 37
  Cosán na Naomh, 36–38
  Mullach Bhéal, 39, 41
  snacking, 39
  Slí an Éisc (Fish Way), 39
  Cloghane, 39
  Castlegregory, 41–42
  Aughacasla, 42
  Dingle Way, 42
  Camp, 42
  Tralee and Dingle Light Railway, 43
  Killelton, 43
  Blennerville, 43
  Fenit - NO ENTRY, 51–52
  Abbeydorney, 52–53
  Lixnaw, 53, 55–56
  Ballinageragh, 53
  River Feale bridge - track vanishes, 57–58
  Listowel, 67–68
    bicycle hire, 68
    private property signs, 58
  Abbeyfeale, 68
  Rathkeale-Listowel Greenway, 68
  Rathkeale, 69, 74, 75–76
  Limerick to Foynes railway - no entry signs, 74
  River Maigue, 75
  Cloonaduff, 75
  Limerick, 78–79
  Cloonlara, 84
  Lough Derg Way, 84
  Parteen, 84
  Killaloe, 84
  Moylussa, 86–88
  Caherhurly, 90–91
  Tuamgraney, 94
  Scarriff, 94
  Slieve Aughty range, 96–103
  Mountshannon Road, 104
  Derrylahan, 105
  Rostura, 105
  on hands and knees, 106
  Portumna, 107, 127
  O'Sullivan's crossing, 126–127
  Meelick, 129–130, 137
    NO CYCLEWAY, 130
  Shannon Harbour, 142–143
  Grand Canal, 143–144
  Belmont, 145
  Ballysheil, 145–150
  Derries Bog, 150
  Offaly, 151
  Pollagh, 151–153
  bogs, 158
  Cornalaur, 160
  Offaly, 160
  Ballycowan, 161–165
  Ballycowan Castle - TRESPASSERS WILL BE PROSECUTED, 165
  Tullamore, 166, 178
  Mullingar, 167, 199
  Kilbeggan line, 178–181
    off limits, 181
  Kilbeggan Distillery, 181
  Westmeath Way, 182–183, 196
  bog with no name, 185

Dysart, 197
Riverstown, 204
Thomastown, 212
Raharney, 212
Carranstown Bog, 215
Girley Bog, 222
Kells, 222
  no trespassing, 234
  tarmac to Cooley Mountains, 233
  walked 40 km, 30 on tarmac, 223
Lobinstown, 238–239
Tallanstown, 252
Knockbridge, 257, 269
Dundalk, 269–270
Proleek Dolmen, 270
open land, 271
Clermont Cairn, 275–278
Newry Ship Canal towpath, 280
Newry, 280–284
Warrenpoint, 287
Rostrevor, 287–288
Mournes, 288–292
Slieve Muck, 292
Slieve Bearnagh, 293
Newcastle, 294, 308
Dundrum, 309
Downpatrick, 310, 311
Lecale, 311
Struell, 312–314
Castle Ward demesne, 312–314
Portaferry, 315
Strangford, 315
  Cloughey, 316
  Portavogie Harbour, 316–317
  end, 318–319
walking in Ireland, 3–4
walking on water, 151
Walks Scheme, 201–202
water rail, 105
Waterford Greenway, 67
wells
  holy, 53–56
  paths to, 56
  Struell, 312–313
Westmeath, 218
Westmeath Way, 182–183
Westropp, Thomas Johnson, 98–99
Wexford massacre, 138
White-boys, 171–172
White House, 210
Wicklow Head, 50
wild camping on common land, 60
William of Orange, 162
woman with four boys, 96
women in skimpy sports gear, 87
Women's Bathhouse, 312–313
Woodlawn, 7
Wyndham Land Purchase Act 1903, 246–247, 250

Y

yams, 209
Yellow Book of Lecan, 272
Yolland, George, 189
  Younger Dryas, 35